SCALING UP SUCCESS

SCALING UP SUCCESS

Lessons Learned from Technology-Based Educational Improvement

Chris Dede

James P. Honan

Laurence C. Peters

Editors

Foreword by

Ellen Condliffe Lagemann

THIS BOOK IS THE RESULT OF PAPERS COMMISSIONED AS PART OF A CONFERENCE COSPONSORED BY THE HARVARD GRADUATE SCHOOL OF EDUCATION AND THE MID-ATLANTIC REGIONAL TECHNOLOGY IN EDUCATION CONSORTIUM LOCATED AT TEMPLE UNIVERSITY'S CENTER FOR RESEARCH IN HUMAN DEVELOPMENT AND EDUCATION

JOSSEY-BASS
A Wiley Imprint
www.josseybass.com

Copyright © 2005 by John Wiley & Sons, Inc. All rights reserved.

Published by Jossey-Bass
A Wiley Imprint
989 Market Street, San Francisco, CA 94103-1741   www.josseybass.com

No part of this publication may be reproduced, stored in a retrieval system, or transmitted
in any form or by any means, electronic, mechanical, photocopying, recording, scanning,
or otherwise, except as permitted under Section 107 or 108 of the 1976 United States
Copyright Act, without either the prior written permission of the Publisher, or authorization through payment of the appropriate per-copy fee to the Copyright Clearance Center,
Inc., 222 Rosewood Drive, Danvers, MA 01923, 978-750-8600, fax 978-750-4470, or on
the Web at www.copyright.com. Requests to the Publisher for permission should be
addressed to the Permissions Department, John Wiley & Sons, Inc., 111 River Street,
Hoboken, NJ 07030, 201-748-6011, fax 201-748-6008, e-mail:
permcoordinator@wiley.com.

Jossey-Bass books and products are available through most bookstores. To contact Jossey-
Bass directly call our Customer Care Department within the U.S. at 800-956-7739, outside the U.S. at 317-572-3986 or fax 317-572-4002.

Jossey-Bass also publishes its books in a variety of electronic formats. Some content that
appears in print may not be available in electronic books.

Readers should be aware that Internet Web sites listed in this work may have changed or
disappeared between when this work was written and when it is read.

Library of Congress Cataloging-in-Publication Data
Scaling up success : lessons learned from technology-based educational improvement /
Chris Dede, James P. Honan, Laurence Peters, editors ; foreword by Ellen Condliffe Lage-
mann ; sponsoring association, Harvard Graduate School of Education.— 1st ed.
     p. cm. — (The Jossey-Bass education series)
  Includes papers from a conference held March 2003 in Cambridge, Mass.
  Includes bibliographical references and index.
  ISBN 0-7879-7659-8 (alk. paper)
  1. Educational innovations—Congresses. 2. Educational technology—Congresses. 3.
Technology transfer—Congresses. I. Dede, Christopher. II. Honan, James P. III. Peters,
Laurence, 1952- IV. Harvard University. Graduate School of Education. V. Series.

  LB1027.S2893 2005
  371.33—dc22

                                              2004019590

Printed in the United States of America
FIRST EDITION
HB Printing   10 9 8 7 6 5 4 3 2 1

The Jossey-Bass Educations Series

CONTENTS

FOREWORD

WHY ARE PROBLEMS OF SCALE so difficult in the field of education? The simple answer is that education is an enormously complicated activity, with many parts that must be aligned if learning is to take place. Consider, as an example, the situation of a particular learner—say, a young Hispanic boy in the first grade who is trying to learn to read in English. Whether he succeeds will depend on variables such as the development of his brain, the language skills of his family, the skill and caring of his teacher, the adequacy of learning materials, and much else, such as whether he is homeless, in need of glasses, or distracted by attention deficit disorder.

Given the complexity of each and every instructional interchange, it is inordinately difficult to diagnose what goes on in any individual learning moment. It is often impossible to discern which factor or combination of factors helped or impeded a child's progress. Add to this the recent enactment of the No Child Left Behind legislation, with its mandate for accountability and broad improvement in education, and the immediacy of the problem of scale comes into focus. How can a technique or curriculum or technological innovation that appears to be successful in one setting be transferred to another, so that more students can benefit from it?

This question branches into several streams of inquiry that are now being taken up by researchers, practitioners, and policymakers. Issues under examination include curriculum design; the consideration of geographical, cultural, and socioeconomic contexts in fostering educational reform; the great promise and considerable challenges of employing technology to enhance instruction in the classroom and improve data analysis, planning, and decision making in the district office, the school board meeting room, the individual school, and the classroom; and the question of sustainability as to the cost of these improvements and their potential flexibility in serving a wide range of educational settings. In addition, educating the public about best practices and the need for innovation is essential in garnering political support for meaningful reform in education.

To explore these concerns, the Harvard Graduate School of Education partnered with the Mid-Atlantic Regional Technology in Education Consortium, a state assistance, technical assistance, and professional development organization funded by the U.S. Department of Education, to present a conference addressing a variety of topics associated with the scaling up of educational innovations. A group of educators, researchers, and policymakers met for this conference—Scaling Up Success: Lessons Learned from Technology-Based Educational Improvement—in Cambridge, Massachusetts, in March 2003. This book, with the same title, presents most of the papers that were delivered at that time. Contributors from various fields shared knowledge gained through research and their own practical experience, citing both progress made and avenues requiring further research. Indeed, this linking of theory to practice informs the whole book, just as it must inform educational reform. Innovation in technology is another central concern of the authors, so case studies based in big-city school districts, where the challenges of scale are particularly pronounced, are featured in several chapters on that theme.

Undoubtedly a wide range of readers will find the contents of *Scaling Up Success* both timely and engaging. Teachers, school administrators, researchers, technology developers, government officials, and many others will find much that relates to their own concerns about strengthening American education. This book also underscores the need for usable knowledge (knowledge from research immediately applicable to practice), a type of scholarly product that we are only beginning to appreciate and generate. This book represents cutting-edge work that will benefit present and future efforts in scaling up educational innovations.

November 2004   ELLEN CONDLIFFE LAGEMANN
                                   Warren Professor and Dean
                                   Harvard Graduate School of Education

PREFACE

MANY PEOPLE BELIEVE that someone, somewhere has solved locally any particular educational problem one can identify. The documentation of "best practices" in schooling is prevalent, in the hope that somehow these successful innovations can be widely adopted and interrelated with each other, resulting in substantial improvements in educational effectiveness. Technology is often seen as an important aspect of this vision, because technology allows educators to reach a broad audience with rich depictions of and information about an innovative practice or policy.

Although these approaches to educational improvement are worthwhile, they have not led to the promised outcome of widespread effectiveness in teaching, learning, and schooling. A primary reason for this disappointing result and one of the greatest challenges in educational improvement is the immense difficulty of "scaling up": adapting a locally successful innovation to a wide variety of settings while retaining its effectiveness. In contrast to experiences in other sectors of society, scaling up successful programs has proved very difficult in education. Insights from changing operations at one fast-food location may easily transfer to every store in that franchise and perhaps to any comparable type of restaurant. However, a new type of teaching strategy that is successful with one practitioner often is difficult to generalize even to other instructors in the same school, let alone to a broad range of practitioners.

Educational innovations that rely in part on technology for their power face particular challenges in scaling up. Beyond the requisites for implementing any other form of innovation in schooling, the conditions for success in using educational technologies can include access to sufficient computers, telecommunications, and applications infrastructure; technological fluency on the part of teachers and students; and reliable maintenance and support. Moreover, technology keeps evolving to encompass new forms and expanded capabilities, potentially enhancing the power of already developed innovations at the cost of reconceptualizing their structure and process.

This book addresses a central question for those of us concerned with the wider challenge of integrating technology as part of school improvement efforts: To what extent is it possible to successfully scale up technology-based educational innovations? We decided to collaborate on this book because only a few syntheses of insights on scaling up have emerged in the past few years, even though much work has centered on ways to use technology to foster widespread educational improvement. We also felt that insights about scaling up technology-based educational innovations might generalize to heuristics for scaling up any form of improved education practice or policy.

The idea for a book-length treatment of this topic emerged in a dialogue between Chris Dede, professor at the Harvard Graduate School of Education (HGSE), and Laurence Peters, director of the Mid-Atlantic Regional Technology in Education Consortium (MAR*TEC) at Temple University, about hosting a conference dedicated to lessons learned from scaling up technology-based educational innovations. Technology-enhanced approaches are under increased scrutiny by policymakers and administrators, who find few fully articulated programs that have successfully "gone to scale" (been broadly implemented in contexts different from the site at which the innovation was developed). In several meetings with MAR*TEC staff and advisory board members, Chris had seeded the idea that to bring technology-based innovations to scale, their originators needed to specify conditions for success, which, if implemented with the innovation, would ensure its successful adaptation. The idea of devoting a conference to this issue occurred as a natural outgrowth of these discussions.

All parties agreed that the conference would not succeed if a parade of researchers talked about theories of scaling up and ignored the real struggles that practitioners experience in attempting to adapt innovations. Therefore we structured the conference to include researchers, policymakers, and practitioners with considerable on-the-ground experience in scaling up innovations. Each team of scholars, practitioners, and policymakers presented a case study of ongoing efforts to bring promising technology-embedded projects to scale. The learning we wanted to share at the conference was how particular contingencies related to implementation at individual sites affected the ability of others to replicate and sustain the projects.

When Chris took this concept to Ellen Condliffe Lagemann, dean of Harvard's Graduate School of Education, her long-held belief that educational theory should be married far more often to practice led her to express strong interest in HGSE's cosponsoring the conference with

MAR*TEC. Chris was also very fortunate in recruiting his colleague at HGSE, Jim Honan, to collaborate in the design and implementation of this initiative. Through the generosity of HGSE and Katharine E. and Albert W. Merck, the resources available for the conference were greatly expanded, including funding for commissioning a set of preconference papers to seed discussions at the meeting.

The papers were revised after the conference, which was held March 20–22, 2003, at HGSE; this volume presents those revised versions. The final chapter of the book includes insights synthesized from the papers and from discussions at the conference. Further information about the conference is available on its Web site (http://www.gse.harvard.edu/scalingup/). We hope that the ideas in this volume will inspire further work on the vital topic of generalizing and transferring local insights about educational effectiveness to aid practitioners and policymakers everywhere.

CHRIS DEDE
Harvard Graduate School of Education

JAMES P. HONAN
Harvard Graduate School of Education

LAURENCE C. PETERS
Temple University

Scaling Up Success

MOVING FROM SUCCESSFUL LOCAL PRACTICE TO EFFECTIVE STATE POLICY

LESSONS FROM UNION CITY

Fred Carrigg, Margaret Honey, Ron Thorpe

Successful reforms at the district level are being scaled up for statewide implementation in New Jersey.

GIVEN THE IMPORTANCE of local context, relevance, and ownership in achieving success in education initiatives, how do lessons from a local success get translated into policy that spreads the success to schools in more widespread jurisdictions? How can that policy be implemented so that fidelity of outcome is not sacrificed to fidelity of program? This chapter looks at two levels of scaling up—within a district and within a state—to examine emerging practices and strategies aimed at maintaining the integrity of an initiative as it expands to meet statewide objectives and outcomes. Our analysis is grounded in three broad assumptions:

- There is limited understanding of how to take a successful local education model and convert it into state-level policy that achieves similar results throughout the state.

- Coherence and support across state, district, and school levels are essential to an effective scaling-up process.

- Ultimate success is anchored in the opportunity schools and districts have to localize practices while maintaining high levels of coherence and consistency concerning the goals and principles of a given policy.

This chapter grows out of more than a decade of successful school reform work in Union City, New Jersey. Because of school reform efforts in this Latino, urban district—which in 1989 ranked second lowest in the state—more than 80 percent of Union City students meet state standards, the number of students attending first-tier and second-tier colleges and universities has increased dramatically, and the number of students opting out of school has seen a remarkable decline. Much of the district's reform efforts can be credited to the leadership of Fred Carrigg, Union City's executive director of academic programs for more than twelve years. In 2002, Carrigg accepted a new position in the New Jersey Department of Education. As special assistant to the commissioner for urban literacy, he is entrusted with finding ways to replicate Union City's accomplishments in the poorest districts in the state. Using Carrigg's own reflections and the observations of the researchers who worked with him, this chapter follows his efforts from program development and implementation at the district level through the translation into state policy and the first steps toward statewide implementation.

Getting Beyond Idiosyncrasy

The world of public schools seems to foster a deep-seated belief in idiosyncrasy, the notion that every classroom, school, or district is unique. In our view, this way of thinking reflects a belief in local control and autonomy rather than a devotion to quirkiness. On the good side, this belief allows everyone to feel special and each organization to make decisions based on local preferences; on the bad side, the belief stands as a barrier to the replication of good ideas and practices. It is all too common to hear educators at all levels speak admiringly of a program that is successful somewhere else but cannot possibly work in their local situation. This culture of idiosyncrasy presents an obstacle to efforts to take good programs to scale. It also reveals a much deeper challenge: the basic nature of the educational infrastructure in what we call a system of public schools is so powerfully lacking in alignment that it is difficult for improvement efforts to move in any direction.

These realities are especially confounding to policymakers at the state level, where ultimate responsibility for school quality resides, and at the local level, where teaching and learning take place. Not only do state administrators have trouble getting all their districts to adopt promising models or implement policy in a consistent and coherent way, but district superintendents also have trouble scaling up good practice among their schools. Even a principal may run into resistance when trying, for example, to get a good model into all third-grade classrooms or across all sections of ninth-grade English in her school. The challenge increases exponentially when a goal requires full-school integration among all teachers in a school, district, or state.

Another internal barrier to scaling up is resistance. Public school teachers, if they have been in the system for any time at all, are well accustomed to wave after wave of new ideas being thrown in their path. Whether the ideas come from a principal or a superintendent or from the chief state school officer via the state legislature or federal government, most teachers have learned that if they avoid the idea long enough, it will be replaced by the next equally ephemeral one. Such avoidance is especially easy to pull off in high-need and urban districts where leadership turnover is rapid and the interests of many different external forces tend to ebb and flow. Understanding the nature of the system is critical; simply having a good model to replicate—either by volition or compulsion—is not enough. The task must be imagined in the fullest possible context, including incentives, time lines, feedback loops, potential areas of compromise, deployment of personnel and resources, and changes to the environment; dedicated effort is needed to ensure that avoidance or turning back is not possible.

Policy Can Prime the Pump for Scaling Up

Scale is a relative term. A teacher might pilot some new approach in one class and then, based on its success, implement the same approach in all her classes. A principal might support introducing a program into the early grades of an elementary school and later try to spread it to all grades in that school. A district might introduce a science program in all of its schools, while a state might target all of its districts or a cluster of districts facing a similar need with a comprehensive literacy initiative. All of these efforts involve scaling up, and with each move to a level that encompasses more people, institutions, and physical facilities, the complexities increase by a quantum leap. This chapter describes a case of scaling up within the schools of Union City, New Jersey, and efforts to achieve similar results statewide through policy derived from this experience. We start with a close look at a districtwide reform effort and the implementation strategies and policies that appear to be associated with its success.

Later, we will look at a bold effort to translate the specific policies that worked in Union City into state policies targeted at twenty-nine disadvantaged districts and all Title I schools in New Jersey.

A Research Context

One of the most comprehensive studies concerning the impact of state policy on local instruction and learning practices is described in *Learning Policy: When State Education Reform Works,* by David Cohen and Heather Hill (2001). Their research presents findings from a decade-long study of a large-scale reform effort in California that was designed to improve the teaching of mathematics. The authors explore that reform effort in order to understand (1) the relationship between policy and practice, (2) the transferability of those lessons to other similar initiatives, and (3) how the resulting evidence can be used to improve policy and the nature of educational reform. The findings are based on research into the professional development available to California teachers and on surveys of nearly six hundred teachers who were involved.

Since the policy was successful for some teachers and students but not for others, as measured by performance improvement on the California Learning Assessment System tests, the authors analyzed the data further to shed light on possible explanations. Cohen and Hill conclude that the policy established by the California Department of Education improved the teaching and learning of mathematics only when teachers had sustained and significant opportunities to make sense of the reform initiative in their local context. While this finding strongly suggests that professional development was the key to success, by looking more deeply at the data, the authors further establish that it was among "teachers whose learning was focused around study of students' work on the new state assessments" that the greatest gains were found (Cohen and Hill, 2001, p. 3). In other words, it is not enough for policy to promote a particular curriculum by exposing teachers to it; effective professional development helps teachers gain a deep understanding of that curriculum as it appears in student work.

Policies that aim to improve teaching and learning depend on complex chains of causation. Making the policies work depends on defining and connecting the links in those chains. One crucial element in many of those links is instructional content: policies that offer professionals suitable chances to learn and coherent guidance for teaching and learning increase the opportunities to connect policy and practice (Cohen and Hill, 2001, p. 8).

Also linked to successful outcomes is the degree of coherence in both curriculum and the accompanying professional development. Cohen and Hill's study identifies the three key areas in which coherence is needed among as well as within the elements: (1) the primary elements of the curriculum, (2) assessment, and (3) learning opportunities for teachers. The rarity of such coherence and the difficulty of achieving it can be seen in the fact that only 10 percent of teachers in California elementary schools reported that they were experiencing it.

Cohen and Hill posit that this lack of cohesion at least in part reflects the many layers of governance and responsibility that exist within education and how poorly they are connected. As policy travels from a state department of education across these layers, en route to the teachers who have ultimate responsibility for its implementation, its integrity is threatened. Cohen and Hill report, "For most California teachers, reform was substantially less coherent in their school than it was in Sacramento" (2001, p. 9).

How professional development is delivered to teachers also affects implementation, because current practice both localizes the delivery (thereby increasing the variation in how curricular content is delivered and received) and often assigns the work to contract providers who have less of a stake in the outcomes than professionals within the schools and districts. Cohen and Hill, as well as other researchers, have found that most professional development providers deliver programs that are grounded in training paradigms, focus on teachers as individuals, and tend to be short-term, with little follow-up (Little, 1981, 1993; Miller, Lord, and Dorney, 1994; Spillane, 2002).

In addition, a lack of quality curricular resources proved problematic in the California initiative (Cohen and Hill, 2001, p. 23). Although the state offered replacement units as transitional instructional tools until more effective curricular materials were developed, most districts purchased curricula from a handful of large, well-established commercial publishing firms. Other research confirms that textbooks structure approximately 75 to 90 percent of classroom instruction (Grouws and Cebulla, 2000; Woodward and Elliot, 1990). Traditional commercial textbooks dominate the instructional landscape; two-thirds of teachers report that they use them every day (Clements, 2002; Grouws and Cebulla, 2000). The large publishing companies, concerned with meeting state adoption requirements, often attempt to meet every objective of every state, resulting in an incoherent mix of instructional strategies that do little more than give the appearance of meeting state and national standards (Clements, 2002; Ginsburg, Klein, and Starkey, 1998).

A final factor that emerged as a powerful determinant of failed state policy in Cohen and Hill's study is the culture of professional individualism that governs the instructional work of the majority of teachers in most schools. On measures of instructional practice, teachers working in the same schools were only slightly more likely to resemble colleagues in their own buildings than they were to resemble teachers they did not know working in buildings hundreds of miles away (p. 176). In striking contrast, Cohen and Hill found that this individualism did not pervade all aspects of teachers' professional life. When asked about school conditions such as the state of parent involvement or student attrition, teachers were much more likely to agree with their building colleagues than with teachers they did not know. On technical and affective points, then, teachers had much more of a shared understanding. Still, Cohen and Hill suggest that for teachers in the United States, professionalism is synonymous with instructional individualism.

Cohen and Hill conclude by suggesting that policy is most likely to succeed in producing the desired outcomes under the following conditions:

- Policy is understood as separate from the instruments used in deploying the policy (curriculum, assessment, and learning opportunities for teachers).
- Teachers' knowledge goes beyond the framework of the reform effort.
- Teachers and students have access to curricular materials.
- Assessments enable students to demonstrate their learning.
- Teachers have access to professional development that is grounded in student work.
- Policy instruments are marked by consistency and coherence.
- Safeguards ensure the integrity of the policy and its implementation as it moves from its source to those who must use it in the service of student achievement.

These recommendations are consistent with the findings of other policy researchers, as well as those who have studied large-scale education reform efforts (Bryk, Sebring, Kerbow, Rollow, and Easton, 1998; Elmore, 1995; Fullan and Pomfret, 1977; Fullan, 1991, 1994; 1999; McLaughlin, 1987, 1990; Pogrow, 2001). They provide a compelling context in which to discuss the policies of Union City and the proposed state policies derived from them.

Going to Scale at the District Level: Union City

In 1989, the Union City school district was the second worst performing district in New Jersey. It had failed forty-four of fifty-two indicators that the state uses to determine the efficacy of school systems; in fact, the state had threatened to take over governance unless radical and successful restructuring was implemented within five years. Such poor performance results are not surprising for a school district located in arguably the most densely populated U.S. city, which the Brookings Institute classifies among the ninety-two most impoverished communities in the nation. The student population, numbering approximately 11,600, has the following demographic profile:

- 93 percent Latino
- 75 percent living in homes where English is not spoken
- 86 percent receiving free or reduced-price lunches
- Nearly 30 percent living below the poverty line
- 14 percent have been residents of the United States for less than three years

Thus, the transformation in academic achievement that the district experienced during the 1990s and has sustained into the current decade constitutes a surprising success story. By 1995, Union City's average scores on the state's eighth-grade readiness test surpassed those of its urban counterparts by as much as 20 percentage points. In one seven-year period, the percentage of students who received passing eighth-grade test scores jumped from 33 percent to 83 percent in reading, from 42 percent to 65 percent in writing, and from 50 percent to 84 percent in mathematics. By 2000, 80 percent of the high school students passed New Jersey's High School Proficiency Test. By 2002, Union City's test scores ranked highest among New Jersey cities with populations of 50,000 or more.

The high schools also substantially increased the number of students enrolled in advanced placement (AP) courses. In 1994, 25 students were enrolled in AP classes and 20 percent passed. In 2000, the number increased to 146, with 38 percent passing. In addition, from 1996 to 2002, the district witnessed a fivefold increase in the number of students gaining acceptance to first-tier and second-tier colleges and universities. Of the 1,613 Union City public high school students who graduated in the years 1999–2001, 763 (47 percent) went on to four-year institutions, and another 283 (18 percent) to two-year institutions. Data on college major choices for 110 of the top-ranked graduates across those years reveal substantial inroads into areas in which Latinos are particularly underrepresented (Georges, 1996). Sixty students (55 percent) were pursuing a science, math, or technology major, and twenty-eight students (25 percent) elected to attend an engineering school. Female students are strongly represented in these numbers; sixty-three women (57 percent) went on to college, and of that group, twenty-nine (46 percent) pursued a science, math, technology, or engineering major (Union City Board of Education, 2001).

How did this remarkable transformation take place? Faced with the possibility of a state takeover, the school board authorized district leadership to revamp the entire educational system. It turned to supervisors whose departments had not been cited for violations: Tom Highton, principal of the Gifted and Talented School, and Fred Carrigg, supervisor of bilingual and English as a second language (ESL) education. They were promoted, respectively, to superintendent and executive director for academic programs. Before accepting the new positions, however, Highton and Carrigg negotiated unprecedented power over budget lines, appointments, curriculum, schedules, and more. A native English speaker who speaks Spanish fluently, Carrigg brought much-needed strengths to the challenges that lay before Union City. Prior to assuming oversight for academic programs, he had been the supervisor of bilingual and ESL education for twelve years. In addition, Carrigg could build on a substantial base of teacher support; a third of the city's teachers had previously worked under his direction.

The district decided that the first focus of the reform efforts should be literacy. All areas of the curriculum were initially viewed as an opportunity to teach language and reading. Working within the five-year time frame imposed by the state, leaders of the initiative developed a long-range strategy that phased in the reforms gradually. During the first year, they conducted research and made plans for implementation. In year two, they focused on new curriculum for grades K–3; in year three, for grades 4–6; in year four, for grades 7–8. In the fifth year, they began planning for change at the high school level. It took ten years to implement the plans that would transform the district. The phase-in strategy meant that no student schooled with the new methods would enter a new grade only to face old-style instruction. Further, lessons learned from each successive implementation could ease the transition in subsequent years. Although Union City's reforms have been extended successfully to all grade levels and subject areas, in this chapter we describe only the policies effecting literacy in prekindergarten through third grade, because these accomplishments are the ones being considered in creating state policy for the same grades and content area.

Carrigg, the leader of the reform effort, understood that true learning takes place between the teacher and the student. To be successful, reform ideas would have to originate with teachers and be supported by a broad consensus. Carrigg also believed that nothing new needed to be invented in Union City; enough was already known about effective education. Rather, all stakeholders needed to build on both the district's prior success (particularly in bilingual and ESL education) and what could be gleaned from the research literature about effective early literacy instruction. In general, five principles guided the district's work:

- There must be broad consensus that all students can learn.
- The design of successful programs should be tailored to local conditions.
- Reform requires a long-term process with commitment to annual review and revision.
- Continual communication between policymakers and implementers is essential.
- Effective implementation requires ongoing support for teachers.

Carrigg's first step was to convene an elementary literacy committee heavily weighted with teachers. The committee began its work by examining the specific circumstances of Union City. Besides the previously mentioned demographic composition, the district had aging buildings and no extra space for new facilities, and the student mobility rate was 44 percent, meaning that only about half the students attending a class in June had been there the previous September.

Union City's curriculum, built around a basal reader series published by a major textbook company, had been developed for students with stable places of residence, family support, and consistent attendance at the same neighborhood school year after year. This traditional model of cumulative subskill acquisition assumes that students have mastered the material in the previous year's reader, so it need not be reintroduced in the subsequent year—an assumption clearly not valid in the case of Union City students.

Moreover, general academic, special education, bilingual/ESL, and Title I students had separate curricula with different guides for the scope and sequence of skills and assessment; this often worked against students. For example, when a student went from a bilingual to a monolingual program, the levels test in the new class focused on specific, prescribed vocabulary words, not the skill of reading; consequently, many bilingual students were held back when in fact they could read at a more advanced level. In response, the committee decided to produce one inclusive guide that represented real diversity and did not single out any group.

The reform leaders went on to examine the way that American schools are traditionally organized around literacy instruction and found that education is based on the following general concepts:

- K–2 students work on decoding (literacy skills).
- Middle elementary students learn to read for meaning (for example, main idea, inferences, and author's intent).
- Upper elementary students (grades 6–8) learn to read for content (information).
- High school students read for new information and usable knowledge and to develop their own creativity and writing skills.

While the committee felt that this approach was sound, they decided to dig further by looking at the state-mandated lists of skills and achievement levels and surveying the Union City teachers on what they considered necessary skills for students and when to teach them. The committee then combined these two lists and opened up ways of achieving the desired results. Traditional literacy instruction stipulated mastering initial consonants, then final consonants, and then medial vowels in first grade. Instead of working from the phonetic sound system built for students with an English language background and covering the alphabet by starting with "A" and ending with "Z," the committee suggested that elementary-level teachers work from authentic stories that featured particular initial consonants. For example, they selected Eric Carle's *Very Hungry Caterpillar* to teach the initial *h* sound, which in Spanish is silent and therefore particularly difficult for Spanish speakers to master. Similarly, *The Three Little Pigs* can be used to teach the initial *p* sound through its repetition of words. By reading these stories, children practice listening and speaking, repeat phrases, see how letters are used, and enjoy a story that captures their imagination.

In addition, the committee suggested using a personal alphabet (same letters but in a different order and with different examples). Teachers were asked to keep records to ensure that they eventually worked through the entire alphabet in a way that built on students' familiarity with various sounds. These activities build knowledge of core English phonemes through repetition of key vocabulary and transmittal of Anglo-American cultural values that native English speakers usually bring to school. Thus, the committee localized the curriculum to fit its population, basing the transition to English proficiency on a process more likely to achieve success than the sequence of sounds most easily learned by native English speakers. In essence, the committee's focus on comparative linguistics helped them view Spanish-speaking students as advantaged rather than deficient.

Next, the committee conducted an in-depth examination of all the textbooks and materials available that claimed to teach state-mandated skills. They asked publishers to deliver K–3 materials, spent three months analyzing the content and methods, and discovered little congruency between the desired skill outcomes and the actual materials. A similar inventory of textbooks already in use in Union City led to the decision that existing texts should be demoted from core materials to supplemental ones. Furthermore, the committee noted a dearth of children of color in the illustrations, making the textbooks poorly suited to a district with 95 percent minority children.

The committee also decided to abandon rote learning, whole-group lecture teaching, and basal readers, moving to a balanced approach to early literacy instruction modeled on the already successful bilingual and ESL curriculum that had been used since the mid-1980s. The new curriculum immersed students in print-rich environments with literature-based instruction taught through thematic units that connected subject areas, freeing teachers from the problematic cumulative subskills model and allowing them to address individual students in their individual areas of need. To address the problem of mobility, the committee instituted the reforms districtwide. They also recognized that teachers needed training to successfully negotiate the transition from basal readers to literature-based instruction.

Based on their research and the experience of the bilingual and ESL teachers, the committee conducted pilot tests involving 20 percent of a grade level, providing an opportunity for teachers and administrators to experiment and refine their strategies. Average test scores doubled within a year in kindergarten and first grade, and the population that piloted the reform accounted for virtually all of the improvement.

Thus, the district moved from a formalized rote learning of English to a natural approach, building up oral language by reading good stories to students and starting English conversation slowly, using topics close to students' lives. This change in philosophy opened the door to a wave of other changes, ranging from selection of materials to block scheduling to teacher mentoring.

The focus on literacy led to the recognition that multiple simultaneous changes were needed in time management and structure, learning methodology, use of pull-out programs, assessment, professional development, physical environment, and instructional technology. More details can be found at the Union City Web site: http://www.union-city.k12.nj.us/curr/k12curr/escurr/1-4humanities/index.html.

Time Management and Structure

The first major change was in the use of time. Since literacy skills would be taught through a variety of activities, it was evident that that the old bell schedule would be inadequate; reading, writing, and communicating needed to be pulled together to reinforce learning from different perspectives. The restructuring produced a 111-minute block of time known as the communications period. Within this block, teachers were told what to accomplish but not how to do it. The single guideline stated that instruction should take place in small, goal-centered groups, avoiding whole-group instruction except when clearly appropriate for organizational and management activities. Teachers were to organize the time as they saw fit. For the first time, they were asked to provide instruction in accord with individual student needs.

Learning Methodology

Every year, 20 percent or more of Union City students are new entrants into the school system. Since acquiring skills in a linear format is virtually impossible under such conditions, the committee decided that it made more sense to help students learn how to learn rather than focus on skill acquisition. Such a shift meant that students would learn to understand, comprehend, apply, analyze, synthesize, and evaluate. (This approach is known as Bloom's taxonomy.) These skills were taught within the context of thematic units. Themes were broad enough to allow variation, but all teachers at a particular grade level were teaching the same themes at the same time.

Within a given theme, teachers could identify materials to provide multiple points of entry for students with varying levels of skill and background knowledge. In early elementary classrooms, for example, this meant creating classroom libraries with materials that supported themes through pictures, words, and multimedia resources. An additional benefit of the thematic approach is that students go home with broad ideas to talk about with their parents (for example, "I learned about animals today"), inviting parents into children's school life in a way that subskill strategies in basal readers never do.

The End of Pull-Out Programs

Prior to the reforms, approximately 80 percent of first-grade students in Union City participated in pull-out programs. It was not unusual to find classrooms populated by only five students at a time, making it difficult to keep track of students' progress in learning. In addition, the committee believed that children need to feel accepted as part of the group, and pull-out programs lead them to believe that something is wrong with them and must be fixed, an attitude that impedes their progress. The committee eliminated all pull-out programs, eliminated the word *remedial* from district vocabulary, and instituted coteaching (team teaching), whereby resource and support teachers went to the K–3 classrooms to provide the classroom teacher and the students with extra help.

Implementing this philosophy was a major struggle because both specialists and traditional classroom teachers had to learn new skills in working together to determine which instructional practices would best meet the needs of individual students. On the other hand, the ESL and bilingual teachers had cotaught for years and knew that the approach would work.

Assessment

Union City tested various methods of assessment, ultimately choosing to employ a variety of formal and informal methods that monitor students' growth and achievement over a period of time. The goal was to enable teachers to focus on students as individuals and to assess students based on their abilities and learning styles. The district uses a mix of diagnostic, formative, and summative assessments. In the early years of reform, teachers were not to be penalized if their students' test scores declined while they worked out new practices. This strategy encouraged experimentation, freeing teachers to try out new methods and materials, and in fact produced good results. Test scores did not decline; rather, they improved markedly.

Professional Development

The committee understood that professional development is a process and not an event. Professional development opportunities increased from fewer than eight hours a year to a high of forty hours a year, with many more offerings available for voluntary staff development (twenty-four hours were mandatory). The training included counseling on differences in teaching styles, so that teachers would understand and respect what others were doing with the new curriculum. The district used a five-stage model to support teachers as they worked toward proficiency in the new educational paradigms: awareness, practice, sharing, peer coaching, and mentoring.

AWARENESS. In this stage, broad or new core concepts are introduced to large groups of faculty. Orientations on balanced literacy (an approach that combines whole language and phonics methodologies) and cooperative learning (techniques in which students work in groups that are expected to assume responsibility for what the group produces, as opposed to working individually) are presented through awareness workshops, and hundreds of teachers attend training sessions sponsored by professional groups outside of the district and at state and national conferences.

PRACTICE. During the second stage, specific basic strategies and techniques are introduced and practiced. One technique is Wall Story, a single story made up by an entire class over time. The completed result is produced by the entire class; each student feels a part of it; and the lesson communicates that many small contributions can add up to one unified whole.

SHARING. In workshops, practitioners of new approaches discuss their experiences, both successful and not so successful. At least two half-day sessions are conducted every year, run by local school improvement teams, which include a principal, teachers, parents, and, at the high school level, students. Periodically the district gathers team members from several schools to participate in more advanced workshops.

PEER COACHING. In response to the need for extensive training for the new system of teaching, Union City developed peer coaching for new teachers. A new teacher is paired with an experienced colleague who teaches the same grade. They spend two to five days going over the curriculum guide and meet periodically for consultations during the school year. At the beginning of the year, the pair team-teaches in class. The peer coach observes and provides suggestions and ideas on successful practices. This system of one-on-one individualized support proved so effective that Union City now has five full-time coaches.

MENTORING. As an extension of peer coaching and as required by the state, Union City has a system of mentors, with at least one mentor per building. New teachers can consult these mentors on a one-to-one basis about any bureaucratic issue on the classroom, school, or district level. Each mentor is assigned no more than three protégés for a marking period or a full school year.

Physical Environment

The district insisted that every classroom in grades K–3 should have a reading center. Rather than mandate that teachers redesign their entire classroom, the district awarded new furniture to those who were willing to embrace the new curriculum. Teachers who agreed to try the reform approach were allowed to purchase cooperative-learning tables, classroom libraries, and often computers. They also got furniture for a second center for listening (to tapes), computers, science, math, or art. Over the years, these classrooms slowly added one center at a time, and now most elementary and middle school classrooms have five to seven centers. Classroom centers are also becoming increasingly common in the high schools.

Instructional Technology

Beginning in 1992, the district made a concerted effort to integrate computers into classroom instruction. The reforms had reached a plateau, and teachers were complaining about massive paperwork and record keeping. Process writing—a key element of the district's balanced literacy approach—was faltering. In response, the district decided to provide computers for all classroom teachers. In addition, the district wanted the educational experience of Union City students to be competitive with that of their suburban counterparts, and technology seemed to promise comparable advantages, providing access to information generally denied to the inner-city poor and developing skills that would help students study and find jobs.

Union City invested substantially in technology resources, which was possible because of the redistribution of state funds. Local administrators had had some limited experience with computers and knew enough to recognize the power of technology and to ask for help. The district also benefited from a variety of partners who provided assistance. New Jersey's Quality in Education Act made possible significant investment in new technology, Bell Atlantic and the National Science Foundation provided funding and expertise, and Education Development Center's Center for Children and Technology helped design technology to achieve the district's goals. The partners arrived at a sophisticated, multipurpose objective for technology in the Union City schools. The most important basic decision was to network the multiple groups that constitute the school system—students, teachers, school and district administrators, and parents. Nearly all of the four thousand instructional computers became part of a districtwide network connecting eleven schools, two public libraries, city hall, and the local day care center through T-1 lines linked to the central office servers. With a ratio of four students per computer, Union City is one of the most wired urban school districts in the United States.

Going to Scale at the State Level: District Policy Informs State Policy

Bringing a single school district to a level of measurable, sizable, and unquestionable success is an accomplishment that has been elusive on the American landscape, especially in urban areas where the majority of children are poor and do not speak English. Taking such a successful model to scale statewide, with special focus on districts with similar demographics, may be a rational dream of educators and policymakers, but no one would ever underestimate the challenge. The fact that there is virtually no precedent for such scaling speaks of the difficulty. Yet that is the effort that educators launched in the fall of 2002 in New Jersey, using Union City as the model.

State policy is established according to rules and practices that vary in detail from state to state but follow largely similar paths. Given the complexity of state laws and regulations, it is not unusual for several policies targeted at the same challenge to compete, create redundancies, and even contradict one another. These policies come from different federal and state agencies; administrations and personnel frequently change; and communication among those in charge is not always effective. The system, for all its good intentions, often leaves schools and districts overwhelmed with the task of following policies.

Is policy derived from models of good practice, or does policy create them? Typically, people think that policy drives practice: policymakers know or determine what needs to be done and how to do it; teachers and building-level and district-level administrators receive that knowledge and implement it; and improvement occurs. That pattern can work under some circumstances, but it is not the only pattern. Writing in the early 1980s, Gene Hall and Susan Loucks suggested that effective policy should "emanate from the realities of life in schools" (1982, p. 135) but that "there is a fundamental gap between policy initiatives and the realities of life in schools. Neither policy makers nor practitioners have sufficient cognizance of the other's . . . worlds" (p. 134). A dynamic relationship should exist between practitioners and policymakers in an environment that encourages and supports local innovation so that it might become a model for best practice that then gets fed back into the larger system.

The context for scaling up presented here includes all of these factors. The work exists at the confluence of Reading First, a federal literacy program administered through the states, and the Abbott Implementation Regulations for Improving Standards-Driven Instruction and Literacy (Intensive Early Literacy), a state program designed to govern the way economically disadvantaged districts administer early literacy programs in prekindergarten through third grade. New Jersey thereby must attend to early literacy challenges on two separate fronts: first, the state, court-ordered mandate that governs the thirty Abbott districts (New Jersey Department of Education, 2003), which have a special relationship to the state department of education and function according to the Abbott rules and regulations, and second, the federal requirements associated with Reading First and the federally approved administration of that program at the state level through New Jersey Reading First (K–3). That program is voluntary, but for the schools applying for and receiving funds to support it, the requirements are prescriptive. Because a strong overlap exists between the goals of the New Jersey Reading First program and the goals of Intensive Early Literacy, the program being designed for the Abbott districts, the policies governing both also have a strong overlap. The Abbott policies must be cognizant of the standards of New Jersey Reading First, but it is possible for the state to create Abbott policies that are both more prescriptive and more far-ranging than the Reading First regulations. Also, the Intensive Early Literacy policies are being phased in over a period of several years.

Knowing that New Jersey would be facing a complex challenge in implementing statewide early literacy reform and knowing of Union City's success, Assistant Commissioner for Education Gordon MacInnes recruited Fred Carrigg as director of New Jersey Reading First and special assistant to the commissioner for urban literacy. His assignment is to establish and manage both literacy programs. In other words, he is to take the successful Union City model to scale statewide. The decision to recruit Carrigg was driven by measurable gains in Union City's student achievement data and sets the stage for achieving the kind of coherence within and across policies that is a key to success. (Such intentional actions are not always associated with state bureaucracies.) It models the kind of behavior that should be much more central to the way education, especially at the state level, operates, and the way policy is imagined, written, and implemented.

The policies being designed for both of these programs are only in their beginning stages. No claims are being made about their current or eventual effectiveness. What makes this particular moment interesting, however, is the process for scaling up that is being tested. Given how little is known about successful scaling efforts in education, especially in matters of such consequence, we believe that the more that people can study and share their observations about the work, even work in progress, the greater the potential benefit will be.

Charting the Transfer of Successful Policy from District to State

At the time this chapter was being written, the statewide reform effort was focused solely on Intensive Early Literacy (prekindergarten through third grade) rather than the full K–12 program currently in place in Union City. This effort is being mounted, however, with the expectation that, if successful, the reform will be expanded to all grades. In this section, we describe the connections between the salient parts of the Union City early literacy model and the process used to transfer those local policies into state policies in the hope of eventually achieving similar results in Title I schools funded through the New Jersey Reading First program and in the thirty Abbott districts through the Intensive Early Literacy program (IEL).

Policy 1: Philosophy and Principles

The Union City reform effort began with an exploration of literacy as the foundation of all academic achievement. Decisions were based on research in the areas of language acquisition, development of English proficiency among Spanish speakers, cooperative learning, and the use of learning centers. Both New Jersey Reading First and IEL adhere to standards of scientifically based research on reading and the U.S. Department of Education's list of five literacy essentials: phonemic awareness, phonics, fluency, vocabulary, and comprehension. New Jersey has added a sixth essential, motivation and background knowledge—defined as an understanding that children read for meaning, message, and communication—which was a central part of the Union City literacy initiative and led to a focus on authentic literature. Background knowledge consists of oral, topical, and personal knowledge of phonemes and vocabulary essential for success in reading in English. This change to the federal mandate—allowable because it adds to rather than supplants federal expectations—is an excellent example of how experience from a successful local model can improve state policy.

Policy 2: Structure of Time and Space

Union City began with a block of 111 minutes of uninterrupted time for reading every day. The federal requirement for Reading First is 90 minutes. IEL also stipulates 90 minutes, but another feature of the program (addressed later under compensatory and supplemental services) allows for an additional 30 minutes to be appended to either end of the 90-minute block for students needing more work, resulting in a 120-minute block.

A central feature of the Union City reform was the physical restructuring of classrooms to include a library, a technology center, a writing center, and other centers for science, math, art, and so on. Although the physical structure of a classroom may be less important than teacher knowledge and skill and the quality of curriculum, the designers of the Union City reform found that this change of physical structure actually facilitated the new pedagogies. Primarily, it helped differentiate instruction, encouraged children to be more responsible for their own learning, helped achieve the goals of pull-out programs while keeping students in the same classroom, created a climate in which educators could work as partners, and helped everyone become more grounded in students' work. Though early adopters who piloted the reform measures got new classroom furnishings and equipment, eventually, of course, the district made similar resources available to all classrooms. In fact, New Jersey Reading First requires a classroom library and recommends literacy centers, while IEL requires classroom libraries and reading, technology, and writing centers.

In Union City, Fred Carrigg had visited all K–3 classrooms regularly to monitor how teachers were deploying these classroom resources and to use natural rewards or lack of rewards as additional incentives. He will attempt to replicate that level of presence in classrooms through a team of twelve people from the New Jersey Department of Education; they will conduct random site visits to make sure these structures exist and are being used appropriately. For such monitoring to be effective, of course, district-level people must share the responsibility and establish the same type of learning culture that Carrigg fostered in Union City.

Union City, because of crowded conditions and lack of funds, was not able to mandate maximum class sizes, but it compensated by structuring learning centers in classrooms and using small-group instruction. IEL mandates that prekindergarten classes not exceed fifteen students and K–3 classes not exceed twenty-one students. Both programs require small–group instruction. Union City also actively supported teachers in adopting cooperative-learning models, which are not currently part of New Jersey Reading First or IEL but could be introduced in the future.

Policy 3: Curriculum

The Union City model supports a strong and continual effort to align curriculum, materials, supplies, goals, strategies, and assessments. A similar expectation exists in New Jersey Reading First and IEL.

The Union City literacy curriculum used basal readers only as supplemental materials. Classrooms were required to have libraries with at least two hundred books that were selected to meet the diverse needs of early learners, and a strategic effort was made to teach all skills through core books and novels. The New Jersey Reading First and IEL policies also go beyond commercial curriculum. The New Jersey Reading First regulations state that in order to receive funding, the local education agency "must also incorporate a sufficient quantity of leveled books at all grades, including Big Books and decodable books [that incorporate the phonics elements being learned] for grades K–1, to be fully integrated into their overall, comprehensive and core reading program. These books can be used effectively to comply with the five essentials of reading and the requirements of Reading First." That language, which also appears in similar form in the proposed Abbott regulations, is close to Union City's policy on early literacy curriculum.

Key to Union City's success was a dramatic shift in philosophy toward requiring differentiated materials that provide multiple entry points for different populations, including native language and ESL reading. These materials align closely with the center-oriented structure of classrooms and promote the kind of teaching and learning that was the primary goal of the program. The same policy now exists for New Jersey Reading First and IEL.

The successful and ubiquitous integration of technology was another key component of Union City's success, even in the early grades; WiggleWorks was chosen as the core software used to support the acquisition of early literacy skills. In the New Jersey Reading First regulations, it is clear that successful applicants must describe how students will use "technology-assisted resources to enhance their reading experiences," and WiggleWorks is listed among the state's approved reading programs. Abbott classrooms are required to have a technology center with appropriate district-approved supplemental computer software.

Preschool was always a part of the districtwide curriculum planning in Union City. Although there is no mention of preschool in New Jersey Reading First, IEL requires that Abbott districts demonstrate a seamless transition from preschool to kindergarten. And since New Jersey's preschool curriculum is defined entirely by early literacy skills, that piece of the alignment is solidly in place.

Union City teachers and administrators spent considerable time identifying and learning specific strategies, techniques, and activities for advancing their curricular goals. What once was a list of thirty agreed-on items has since grown to fifty. Both New Jersey Reading First and IEL name specific strategies, and while the list has fewer items than Union City's, there is complete overlap.

Policy 4: Assessment and Testing

Both New Jersey Reading First and IEL have similar levels of assessment, including screening, benchmarks, diagnostics, and annual testing using norm-referenced tests. Union City's assessment strategies also included Running Records, a recording procedure that helps assess students' reading behaviors quickly as students engage in the reading process, and an extensive use of portfolios. Portfolio work is introduced in New Jersey Reading First and IEL, but only as a part of benchmarking. The proposed Abbott regulations indicate that the "Chief School Administrator shall implement a clear assessment plan that includes: (1) home language screening and English language proficiency assessment; (2) screening in reading in grades K–3; (3) diagnostic assessment of students below reading level; (4) annual spring-to-spring assessment with a state-approved norm-referenced instrument in grades K–2 and NJASK 3 and 4, state-devised criterion-referenced instruments; (5) a locally devised system of assessment based on six- to ten-week thematic units to evaluate students' progress." This last item, which comes directly from Union City policy (along with aspects of the first four), ensures the district's commitment to thematic curriculum and aligns assessment with that curriculum.

Policy 5: Compensatory and Supplemental Services

Union City was adamant that pull-out programs not be permitted. The small-group, center-oriented structure in Union City classrooms supported differentiated instruction to meet the individual needs of children, and review of the research and their own experience convinced Union City teachers and administrators that the harm done to students by pulling them out of class exceeded the benefits. Therefore, special services were delivered to children within the classroom. Compensatory and supplemental services are required in the regulations for both New Jersey Reading First and IEL, and in accordance with federal policy, traditional pull-out programs are permitted. Because of the structure of classrooms in both New Jersey Reading First and IEL, districts are strongly encouraged to provide these services without pulling children out of class.

Policy 6: Professional Development

Of all the components of the reform effort in Union City, none is more important than the way the district imagined, designed, and delivered professional development for teachers and aligned it with specific strategies and goals. As described earlier, Union City made a comprehensive commitment to professional development in order to strengthen content knowledge, philosophy of education, strategies, and techniques. Of particular note was the requirement that all nontenured teachers pursue six credits of college-accredited courses in ESL or bilingual education. Later, a similar commitment was made in regard to special needs and computer education.

Union City, where well over 90 percent of the students were Latino, needed a critical mass of teachers with great facility in Spanish and an understanding of the needs of learners who lived in Spanish-speaking homes and whose education by definition included transferring skills from another native language in order to achieve English proficiency. Similarly, the district's commitment to technology required that all teachers have a certain level of proficiency in using technology and integrating it into instruction. It is not surprising, then, that both New Jersey Reading First and IEL have specific requirements for professional development, which are guided by similar principles. The New Jersey Reading First regulations state: "All professional development activities must specifically address teachers' needs as they relate to the five essentials of data-driven early reading instruction as well as student motivation. . . . Professional development should be planned to include both initial preparation and ongoing support for teachers who are implementing new strategies and programs." The regulations identify particular opportunities that should be provided for K–3 teachers, bilingual and ESL teachers, and K–12 special education teachers, stipulating that professional development be aligned with the state's plan as well as the expectations of those who provide the training. The proposed IEL regulations are similar, emphasizing the need to include early literacy, bilingual and ESL, and special education teachers and alignment with district strategies, curriculum, materials, and assessments.

Policy 7: Populations Served

In Union City, the districtwide reform effort began in the primary grades and extended to upper grades over a period of years. New Jersey Reading First and IEL are targeted at all K–3 students. (IEL includes prekindergarten.) Because New Jersey Reading First uses federal dollars, the program is now limited to K–3, with no particular expectation that it will be extended. There is active planning, however, in regard to how IEL can be extended to higher grades.

Policy 8: *Additional Personnel*

Union City established curriculum resource teachers to help implement their reform efforts, but those positions were phased out with the advent of whole school reform, which recognized that a school is a system made up of interlocking parts that affect each other and that understanding the parts and how they relate to one another is critical to achieving lasting change. New Jersey Reading First uses reading coordinators and literacy coaches to implement the program, and each school also is required to have a literacy team that includes the building principal as a working partner with the coordinator and coach and other identified school personnel (New Jersey Department of Education, 2002).

Conclusion

This chapter begins to tell a story that is not yet finished. Indeed, given that our topic is an exploration of how successful local programs are scaled up to reach a much larger audience and how that process is supported and encouraged through effective state-level policy, one could say that publication of this study is premature. We believe, however, that there is much to learn from the process itself. We also believe that there is much to suggest that the process being implemented in New Jersey can have a strong measure of success.

Improving schools by meeting the learning needs of all students is a complex goal. In the United States, we have spent decades of time and countless hundreds of billions of dollars trying to meet this goal. But despite this massive commitment of resources, success has been so elusive, especially for our poorest children, that the federal government recently enacted No Child Left Behind, legislation that is unprecedented in its scope, its demands, and the consequences for those who fail to meet its requirements. Those in the profession of education and in the policy arena must learn all they can about what it takes for all children to achieve at high levels. Educators and policymakers must also determine the most productive relationship between practice and policy, understand the reciprocal processes of transferring good practice into good policy and good policy into good practice, and ratchet up the reach of policies and practices to benefit equally the largest numbers of people—a tall order, to be sure.

We are encouraged, however, by the reform process that was put into place in Union City, a poor urban community. That process itself, although undertaken in a single district, was an important experience in successful scaling up. It possessed all of the characteristics that Cohen and Hill associate with successful reform.

Moreover, we want to add two points. The first concerns time line and time frame. The Union City results emerged over a period of many years, in conjunction with logical steps of implementation. A year of planning was followed by a year of implementation, during which only the early grades were involved. With each subsequent block of years, additional grades were added until eventually the reform effort arrived at the high school exactly when the children (and their parents) who had experienced it in the earlier grades were also arriving there. Willingness to allow change to occur over time not only fits well with what is known about effective and sustainable change processes in adults but also gives people time to make the continual adjustments that are inevitably needed in a task of this complexity. Indeed, one could argue that this strategy helped build a system wherein experimentation and modification are second nature. Early positive results and continuity of staffing throughout the reform process also encouraged people to be patient as changes unfolded.

The second point relates to the stability of the people involved but goes beyond that. Although many policymakers like to imagine that programs and policies are independent from the good luck of having the right mix of personalities, it is unlikely that such independence will ever accompany anything as intimate and personal as a child's process of learning and development. Union City had the advantage of stable leadership at a number of levels, including the effective personal and professional traits of Fred Carrigg. No program ever succeeds as the result of the contribution of one person, yet it is just as true that success seldom happens without that one person. This statement should not discourage policymakers but rather serve as a reminder of how important it is to hire the right people.

The New Jersey Department of Education is now in the process of determining how the different strands of the Union City model can be woven into state policy, which in turn can be used by other districts in achieving the same, if not better, results. The question is clear: how can something that worked for 11,600 students in one part of the state meet with similar success for perhaps fifty times that number in the twenty-nine other Abbott districts and an array of Title I schools? From our perspective, the first two steps are promising. First, by choosing Union City as its model, the state used compelling data to drive an important decision. This district has sustained and increased its record of student achievement over ten years, working with a population of students whose profile is considered by many as a key reason for failure in schools: large numbers of poor, diverse children, many of whom do not speak English as their first language. Second, the state recruited the person most responsible for designing and implementing the Union City model to take a leadership role in the statewide effort.

The policies established thus far for New Jersey Reading First and Intensive Early Literacy are encouraging. Putting in place the right people at the district and school levels and providing the support and the time to do what is needed will be crucial. Ultimately, these will be the safeguards that ensure the integrity of the policy and its implementation as it moves from the state department of education in Trenton to the districts.

REFERENCES

Bryk, A., Sebring, P., Kerbow, D., Rollow, S., & Easton, J. (1998). *Charting Chicago school reform*. Boulder, CO: Westview Press.

Clements, D. H. (2002). Linking research and curriculum development. In L. D. English (Ed.), *Handbook of international research in mathematics education* (pp. 599–636). Mahwah, NJ: Erlbaum.

Cohen, D. K., & Hill, H. C. (2001). *Learning policy: When state education reform works*. New Haven, CT: Yale University Press.

Elmore, R. (1995). Going to scale with good educational practice. *Harvard Education Review, 66*(1), 1–26.

Fullan, M. (1991). *The new meaning of educational change*. New York: Teachers College Press.

Fullan, M. (1994). *Coordinating top-down and bottom-up strategies for educational reform*. Retrieved from http://www.ed.gov/pubs/EdReformStudies/SysReforms/fullan1.html

Fullan, M. (1999). *Change forces: The sequel*. Philadelphia: Falmer Press.

Fullan, M., & Pomfret, A. (1977). Research on curriculum and instruction implementation. *Review of Educational Research, 47*(1), 335–397.

Georges, A. (1996). Keeping what we've got: The impact of financial aid on minority retention in engineering. *NACME Research Letter, 9*(1), 1–20.

Ginsburg, H. P., Klein, A., & Starkey, P. (1998). The development of children's mathematical thinking: Connecting research with practice. In W. Damon, I. E. Sigel, & K. A. Renninger (Eds.), *Handbook of child psychology: Vol. 4. Child psychology in practice* (pp. 401–476). New York: Wiley.

Grouws, D. A., & Cebulla, K. J. (2000). Elementary and middle school mathematics at the crossroads. In T. L. Good (Ed.), *American education, yesterday, today, and tomorrow* (Vol. 2, pp. 209–255). Chicago: University of Chicago Press.

Hall, G., & Loucks, S. (1982). Bridging the gap: Policy research rooted in practice. In A. Lieberman & M. W. McLaughlin (Eds.), *Policy making in education: Eighty-first yearbook of the National Society for the Study of Education* (pp. 133–158). Chicago: University of Chicago Press.

Little, J. W. (1981). *School successes and staff development: The role of staff development in urban segregated schools.* Paper presented at the annual meeting of the Southwest Educational Research Association, Dallas.

Little, J. W. (1993). Professional community in comprehensive high schools: The two worlds of academic and vocational teachers. In J. Little & M. McLaughlin (Eds.), *Teachers' work* (pp. 137–163). New York: Teachers College Press.

McLaughlin, M. (1987). Learning from experience: Lessons from policy implementation. *Educational Evaluation and Policy Analysis, 9*(22), 171–178.

McLaughlin, M. (1990). The Rand change agent study revisited: Macro perspectives and micro realities. *Educational Research, 19*(9), 11–16.

Miller, B., Lord, B., & Dorney, J. (1994). *Staff development for teachers: A study of configurations and costs in four districts.* Newton, MA: Education Development Center.

New Jersey Department of Education. (2002). *New Jersey Reading First Grant, Notice of Grant Opportunity.* Retrieved August 9, 2004, from http://www.state.nj.us/njded/readfirst/NGO/

New Jersey Department of Education. (2003). *Improving standards-driven instruction and literacy in Abbott districts.* New Jersey Administrative Code regulations proposed by New Jersey's Commissioner of Education. Retrieved March 2003 from http://www.nj.gov/njded/code/title6a/chap10a/

Pogrow, S. (2001). Avoiding comprehensive schoolwide reform models. *Educational Leadership, 5*(2), 82–83.

Spillane, J. P. (2002). Local theories of teacher change: The pedagogy of district policies and programs. *Teachers College Record, 104*(3), 377–420.

Union City [NJ] Board of Education. (2001). [High school AP classes, graduation and college placement totals]. Unpublished raw data.

Woodward, A., & Elliot, D. L. (1990). Textbook use and teacher professionalism. In D. L. Elliot & A. Woodward (Eds.), *Textbooks and schooling in the United States: Eighty-ninth yearbook of the National Society for the Study of Education* (Part 1, pp. 178–193). Chicago: University of Chicago Press.

DEWEY GOES DIGITAL

SCALING UP CONSTRUCTIVIST PEDAGOGIES AND THE PROMISE OF NEW TECHNOLOGIES

Martha Stone Wiske, David Perkins

Harvard's WIDE World initiative has enhanced the craft of teaching through Internet-based professional development.

THE RECENT HISTORY OF EDUCATIONAL CHANGE contains a central irony. Journals and books addressing educational practice offer a cornucopia of strategies to enhance student learning. By and large, these have a constructivist cast: engaging learners actively in the learning process, recognizing the hazards of prior conceptions, and respecting the multiperspectival nature of knowledge. Many of the strategies have a substantial research basis. Their wide-scale use, with some craft and consistency, would almost certainly help students from kindergarten through college to learn with more breadth and depth. Yet for the most part, their serious pursuit on a schoolwide basis remains limited to the occasional educational oasis.

While this is a stubborn fact of educational history, it does not have to remain so. Besides a store of research-based pedagogical practices, educational research and development over the past three decades have produced new and deeper views of teacher learning and school development, including better understandings of the dynamics of change, especially in public-sector contexts with their complex political dimensions, and new technologies that might break down some of the barriers to change, such as cost and distance.

The challenges of change are certainly complex, and no single project is likely to address them all. In this chapter, we examine one particular intervention—the WIDE World initiative of the Harvard Graduate School of Education—as a case in point.

Operating through the Internet, WIDE (Wide-scale Interactive Development of Educators) World is one effort to help Dewey go digital. It focuses on professional development of constructivist teaching practices for schools and other settings. Participants include practicing teachers, professors, teacher developers, administrators, and others who are engaged actively in education. WIDE World courses emphasize active experimentation in one's professional context, using various constructivist pedagogical frameworks. The program aims not only to help educators but also to investigate scaling up educational improvement via the World Wide Web.

This chapter describes WIDE World, analyzes the challenges related to scalable designs for educational change, and makes the claim that any initiative with aspirations to scale should articulate a scaling model, a causal theory of how the initiative deals with the inherent problems of scale. Finally, we examine WIDE World's scaling model, how WIDE World uses Internet technology to address certain challenges of scaling, and how the project might deal with some remaining challenges.

The Challenge of Change at Scale

To frame the description of WIDE World, we present a perspective on the conditions fostering widespread educational improvement and the shortcomings of traditional attempts to meet these conditions. This analysis outlines the challenges that a scaling model must address.

Local Change and the Knowledge-Action Gap

Local change is a natural starting point for considering change at scale. Just as there is little point in building a chemical plant before one can get the desired reaction in a test tube, so there is little point in trying to spread a pedagogical practice far and wide before one can cultivate it and assess its impact in a particular educational setting, classroom, or school.

The key to improving education in any particular setting is changing teaching practice so that students learn better. This is not simply a matter of transmitting propositional knowledge about effective pedagogical principles. The challenge lies in helping educators to understand such knowledge relative to their contexts and needs, to see its power, to make it their own, and to put it into practice in a sustained way. The *knowledge-action gap* is the gulf between current understandings of best practice and actual practice (see Perkins, 2003; Pfeffer and Sutton, 2000).

Decades of research on educational change show that actual implementation of innovations requires attention to multiple dimensions of educational settings. Elmore, Peterson, and McCarthey (1996) analyze the process of trying to shift toward ambitious teaching for understanding in schools. Their focus is the relationship between changing teachers and changing schools, which they call the "puzzle of organization and practice." They conclude that "the transformation of teaching practice is fundamentally a problem of enhancing individual knowledge and skill" but that "structural problems arise as teachers become aware of the demands that accompany new ways of teaching" (p. 241). Thus, they recommend concentrating first on creating good teaching on a large scale and then attempting to foster the contextual conditions necessary to support such teaching practice.

Judith Warren Little (2001, pp. 41–42), in an analysis of the relationship between professional development and school reform, advocates coordinated attention to "individual, collective, and organizational capacity for reform," including development of a pervasive "culture of inquiry." Bolman and Deal (1997) present a useful taxonomy of four dimensions that need attention and coordination when fostering change in organizations: *human resources* (knowledge, skills, and beliefs of people), *structural* (roles, relationships, schedules, and other forms of organizational structures), *cultural-symbolic* (norms, values, symbols, rituals, and rewards that affect perceptions of meaning and well-being), and *political* (the allocation of authority and responsibility, and commitment from stakeholders). To this helpful list, we would add a fifth dimension, *technical* (tools, technologies, materials, and other tangible resources), because the nature and availability of texts, tests, computers, and other equipment are so influential in shaping what teachers and their students are able and inclined to do.

For educational settings, it's useful to cluster these dimensions into two categories: *craft* variables, which principally concern Bolman and Deal's first dimension of human resources, and *context* variables, which concern the rest. Although this may seem to be a lopsided partition, like Elmore, Peterson, and McCarthey (1996), we argue that it makes a great deal of sense when pondering educational change. In educational systems, helping people understand how to change their craft is especially important.

Teachers ply their craft primarily in isolation and must embody their expertise personally in order to have a positive impact on their learners. Although much is known about principles of effective pedagogy, which constitute a fund of what Lagemann has termed "usable knowledge," the state of this knowledge is still "elusive" (Lagemann, 2002a, 2002b) in comparison with that in more scientific fields; most educators experience their work as an "uncertain" profession (McDonald, 1992). Consequently, the improvement of teaching practices cannot be accomplished simply by disseminating information about a new technique. Instead, teachers must be helped, one by one, to integrate effective approaches into their professional repertoire.

Changing the craft of teaching is itself an extended educational process. Research on effective approaches to fostering teachers' learning includes features such as these:

- Focusing on principles and practices that relate to the teacher's particular priorities, concerns, and circumstances, such as subject matter, students, and setting
- Providing explicit guidelines for improved practice, coupled with opportunities to hear about and see models of these new principles enacted in practice
- Active learning through experiences that model the target practices, including opportunities to try out the new practice early and often, in an exploratory spirit, without feeling pressure to succeed instantly or to decide right away whether the practice should be adopted
- Ongoing guidance from coaches about the new practice (Coaches may be more experienced colleagues in the same school or experts from outside, but they need to appear with some regularity and to provide specific, constructive suggestions about revisions toward improved practice.)
- Time to reflect with colleagues about how well the new practice works, what needs it addresses, and the nuances of its craft (Collegial exchange promotes sharing of professional expertise, providing an opportunity to learn from the tips and trials of like-minded peers.)

The other dimensions of change that Bolman and Deal describe are concerned with creating a conducive context that increases teachers' inclination and capacity to enact constructivist practices. Returning to Bolman and Deal's dimensions, plus our added technical dimension, contextual factors include the following: *structural* (time enough built into school schedules and in-service opportunities for serious learning on the part of teachers); *cultural-symbolic* (incentives for taking the risk to make changes that may not demonstrate immediate positive impacts; acceptance of the change by teacher colleagues, in contrast with a negative stance toward innovation, based, for instance, on a union's aggressive work-for-pay stance); *political* (compatible policy mandates regarding curriculum standards and assessment procedures; community buy-in represented by school board, parents, and students, which, if not marked by enthusiasm and advocacy, at least reflects openness and tolerance for a period of trial; and support from school leaders); and *technical* (access to the necessary educational resources and technologies).

An important cultural attitude that must permeate both the craft and the context factors is commitment to inquiry, reciprocity, and respect, so that everyone—administrators, teachers, students, and parents—participates in learning and teaching. When these conditions are met, teachers have good prospects for gaining skill and confidence with constructivist practice and making it a stable part of their repertoire. However, when either the conditions in support of learning new craft or the contextual conditions are not met, new practices generally do not take hold. To mention a well-known case, the one-time workshop rarely budges established patterns of practice out of their rut. Even though teachers may greatly enjoy the experience and emerge from it with an enlarged sense of what they could do, as they return to the familiar environs of their classrooms, old habits, pressures, and other realities quickly reassert themselves.

Moving to Scale and the Replica Trap

It is heartening to realize that we understand broad principles about how to cultivate innovative teaching practices and conducive contexts in particular settings. They provide enormous help both in informing initiatives and warning us away from what almost certainly will not work—the one-time workshop and its kin. However, these principles have usually been put to work in selected settings, under favorable circumstances. Such cases pose a hazard one might call the *replica trap*. They suggest that we can accomplish the same result widely simply by doing the same thing all over the place.

Regrettably, it is not that easy. On a small scale, one can achieve many conditions by choosing reasonably conducive sites—for instance, schools with visionary principals and preexisting cultures of innovation, schools where a high proportion of teachers are willing to learn and try fresh practices, and schools that can secure extra resources through affluent communities or special funding. One can achieve other conditions by deploying local talent—for instance, using graduate students who are also experienced teachers as coaches. Indeed, during the pilot stage of an innovation, these are reasonable tactics, unless they result in circumstances that are so luxurious as to be deeply misleading about the innovation's broader applicability.

However, as one turns to the challenge of wide-scale change, one must confront two core problems: *magnitude* and *variation*. In regard to magnitude, a scalable design for educational improvement must foster the necessary conditions for change in large numbers of settings with average resources at considerable distances from one another. The following teeth of the replica trap specifically concern magnitude:

• *The temptations of materialism.* One natural seduction of scaling is to substitute prepared materials—texts, videotapes, CD-ROMs, and the like—for personal contact. Such materials can certainly be powerful supplements and supports, but they do not provide the human interaction and sustained follow-up needed for sustained shifts of practice.

• *The scarcity of coaches.* We noted earlier that cultivating new practices depends on expert coaches. Initially, these are not likely to exist on site, although local coaches may be developed over time. The best coaches are often experienced teachers, but they already have jobs. In some cases, students pursuing advanced degrees might become full-time coaches, but the economics and uncertainties of educational change do not make this terribly attractive. Finding enough able coaches is a major challenge.

• *The cost of travel.* Suppose the needed coaches are available. The natural way to spread their influence is for them to travel. But travel is expensive and burdensome, particularly because coaches need to show up frequently for brief periods rather than occasionally for longer periods, which greatly increases travel costs.

• *The "telephone effect."* Telephone is the game in which people form a row, someone starts a message at one end, and each whispers it to the next in line. The message usually becomes wildly distorted in the process. Many scaling-up efforts involve a cascade model of "training the trainers," which relays the target practice through multiple layers of interpreters, just like the game. How the practice emerges in a particular classroom can be very different—and often much less powerful—than the initial conception.

These and other problems of magnitude plague the scaling of educational change. In addition, problems of variation from setting to setting add more teeth to the replica trap. A scalable design for educational improvement must accommodate diverse and unfavorable conditions across settings.

• *Variable capacity to meet costs.* Innovations inevitably incur costs: fees for consultants, release time for teachers, support for people from within or outside the institution who function as coaches, and, possibly, travel costs. For many reasons, some school systems are in a much better position to meet such costs than others.

• *The culture of isolation and norms of privacy.* Typical building layouts and schedules for schools keep teachers isolated in their own classrooms, too busy and separated to observe one another's practices. Compounding these barriers to peer learning are norms of privacy (Little and McLaughlin, 1993) that discourage teachers from engaging in detailed conversations about their craft—for instance, how they promote and assess their students' learning. Under these circumstances, teachers often do not even share a common vocabulary for participating in reflective, collaborative dialogues about improving their practice (Putnam and Borko, 2000) and are unable to engage in the process of reflective analysis (Schön, 1983) and the collaborative refinement of concepts and designs (Wenger, 1998) that promote improvement in professional practice. All of these conditions cause variation and impede the spread of effective practices even to near neighbors, let alone across school buildings and districts and beyond.

• *Diverse philosophies.* The educational landscape bristles with advocacy for many perspectives on what teaching should be like and what should be taught. Priorities are not the same in different settings, so one needs to mix persuasion with adaptation, showing how one's agenda can be tweaked to match local concerns.

• *Politicization of education.* Schools are public institutions buffeted by the shifting crosswinds of politics, which generate variation across settings and within settings over time.

• *Diverse leadership, school cultures, and established practices.* Philosophy and politics aside, attitudes and styles of leadership differ, school cultures differ, and established patterns of practice differ. Even if the situation tolerates the new practice, local adaptation will likely be needed to make it viable.

To generalize a bit further, if we go all the way back to the Rand change agent study (Berman, 1974–1978), we might say that the core problem is one of mutual adaptation, leading to an approach that both retains the elements that generate effectiveness and fits comfortably into the local context that has been shaped by the influences of the teacher, classroom, department, school, district, and community.

The Idea of a Scaling Model

How can one address such an array of challenges systematically and analytically? We recommend that any serious effort to take educational innovations to scale explicitly articulate a *scaling model* that would identify the particular challenges of scaling up a given initiative and how they would be addressed. A scaling model is basically a causal theory of how an intervention that is viable locally under reasonably conducive conditions might get to scale. In hindsight, we can say that many attempts at wide-scale change have depended on partly implicit and deeply flawed scaling models, ones that were too generous in their assumptions and too narrow in their scope to cope with the true problems of scale.

A scaling model might be articulated in many ways. That said, the two key contrasts foregrounded here—matters of craft versus context and challenges of magnitude versus variation—suggest one way of representing what a scaling model needs to deal with, as shown in Table 2.1.

Table 2.1. Challenges That a Scaling Model Needs to Address

	Magnitude	Variation
Craft	• Reliance on materials rather than human interaction • Limited population of coaches • Telephone effect: distortion in transmission of practices • Average rather than advantageous in-service resources such as budget and time	• Diverse philosophies • Range of established practices • Differences in individual attitudes toward change
Context	• Logistics and costs of physically or electronically connecting • Average rather than advantageous political support, community support, technical infrastructure, and so on	• Differences in capacity to meet costs • Culture of isolation • Differing community environment and educational politics • Differences in school leadership • Differences in technical capacity

The idea of a scaling model does not imply that every scaling initiative should address all of the many challenges related to scaling, although that would be ideal. It simply encourages developers to be up front about the scaling challenges that their program presents and addresses.

WIDE World: An Internet-Based Scaling Initiative for Constructivist Pedagogy

We will now describe WIDE World, outlining its history, discussing its pedagogy and curriculum, sketching one course by way of example, and reviewing some formative research findings. The concluding section examines WIDE World's scaling model and further challenges.

History and Goals of WIDE World

WIDE World began in 1999 as an effort to connect educational research on teaching and learning to the improvement of practice. We had long been involved in such endeavors and since the mid-1990s had explored the use of the Internet to fortify them. We initiated both ALPS (Active Learning Practices for Schools), directed by David Perkins, at http://learn web.harvard.edu/alps and ENT (Education with New Technologies), directed by Martha Stone Wiske, at http://learnweb.harvard.edu/ent as on-line learning environments to help educators apply research-based pedagogies. The two projects shared some infrastructure and staff. ALPS supports a range of pedagogies developed at Project Zero, a research and development center at the Harvard Graduate School of Education (HGSE), including the Teaching for Understanding framework, the use of multiple intelligences, and development of thinking skills. ENT builds on work conducted at the Graduate School of Education's Educational Technology Center and the Teaching for Understanding framework to support the use of new technologies to improve teaching and learning.

Experience with these Web sites demonstrated the potential of linking university-based and school-based educators in mutually beneficial dialogues via the Internet. But Web sites do not provide the kind of sustained guidance and support that most teachers need in order to make sustained significant changes in their ways of teaching and in their professional relationships. We developed WIDE World with this challenge in mind. WIDE World offers semester-long professional development courses in which participants learn about research-based pedagogies, apply these principles in designing and enacting new approaches with their own students, receive frequent support and feedback from a coach, and engage in regular reflective exchanges with fellow participants in the course. The courses are not like on-site or on-line university courses that foreground academic learning. Instead, WIDE World courses focus on development of new practices.

We pilot-tested three courses in the fall of 1999. Since then, we have built up an on-line learning platform and progressively evolved the course design through ongoing assessment. We have experimented with marketing strategies that have steadily expanded course enrollments, and the number of courses has increased. Some courses are also offered in Spanish. We have also developed on-line courses for both instructors and coaches, in order to ensure a steady stream of people to fill these essential roles in the program. In the fall of 2002, WIDE World courses involved 308 learners from the United States, Latin American countries, and twenty other countries, which brought the cumulative number of participants since WIDE World began to just over one thousand.

WIDE World addresses a quartet of goals: (1) *wide-scale impact* on the practice of teachers, administrators, and other educational professionals, (2) *research* on on-line learning, educator development, and the challenge of scale, (3) *serving the mission of HGSE and Harvard* by collaborating and sharing with other on-line learning initiatives at GSE and across Harvard, and (4) *economic viability* through achieving these goals in a way that is financially self-supporting. To elaborate on the first goal, WIDE World aims to reach a large number of educators with research-supported methods of professional development addressing a select set of research-supported pedagogies in a way that yields sustained wide-scale change in practice and consequent wide-scale improvement in students' learning.

Overall Approach of WIDE World

The design of WIDE World takes advantage of networked technologies to address some of the persistent challenges of bridging the knowledge-action gap at scale. WIDE World emphasizes these four features:

- *Modeling of desired practice.* Provide professional development that enacts the same constructivist principles that teachers are asked to enact and that gives participants ample opportunities, through case studies and collegial exchanges, to see the practice in action.

- *Human facilitation.* Develop an adequate supply of expert coaches and deploy them to provide tailored support and suggestions as teachers change their practice; rely on coaches to manage mutual adaptation and to augment the support provided by materials.

- *Sustained community of inquiry.* Cultivate new habits of mind about learning and teaching as a profession, based on continual inquiry and construction of new understandings rather than transmission of preset, inert knowledge.

- *Economic viability.* Devise effective marketing and sales strategies that reach large numbers of educators in a self-supporting financial model.

By and large, these components foster wide-scale change in the *craft* of teaching. WIDE World as now organized does not directly address most of the significant factors in scaling up change in the *context* of education, meaning organizational structure, political support, compatible mandates, access to resources, and so on. While context is important, our expertise lies in developing craft. Also, attention to contextual variables depends on local knowledge and relationships that are difficult to develop and affect from a distance. Thus, we are exploring synergistic alliances with organizations that are better positioned to influence contextual variables and thereby leverage WIDE World's contributions—a matter we will revisit toward the end of this chapter.

WIDE World Pedagogy and Curriculum

WIDE World (http://wideworld.pz.harvard.edu) courses take place entirely on-line, using a platform developed by the project's technology team in collaboration with other technology developers at Harvard and elsewhere. Instructors may designate times for synchronous interaction among participants by using the chat facility, but courses use asynchronous threaded discussion tools as the primary means of communication among participants.

Currently, most courses consist of six on-line sessions, occurring approximately every two weeks, for a total of six to twelve weeks. Each course has one or two instructors but may have large numbers of participants. Participants are clustered in groups of eight to twelve, each with a coach. The content of courses focuses on application of research-based pedagogical principles or frameworks, such as engaging multiple intelligences, teaching for understanding, and teaching to standards with new technologies. Learning is not focused on abstract theories but instead emphasizes applying principles to practice—for instance, drafting and revising curriculum designs, experimenting with new approaches in the classroom, reflecting on one's own and peers' practices in relation to criteria, and devising suggestions for improvement. Learning occurs through presentations of ideas by the instructor; short assignments of reading or examination of on-line models; activities in which participants try out new practices and post designs or reflections on-line; feedback from coach and peers; and participation in reflective on-line discussions. WIDE World courses guide participants in designing, applying, critiquing, and revising new practices, through multiple cycles of exchange with peers and coaches, with an emphasis on changing participants' practice as well as their minds.

An Illustrative Course: Teaching to Standards with New Technologies

The WIDE World course called Teaching to Standards with New Technologies (TSNT) helps participants learn how to design lessons that take advantage of new technologies to improve students' understanding in relation to key curriculum standards or goals. The course is structured by the Teaching for Understanding framework, an educational model developed through a multiyear collaborative research project based at the Harvard Graduate School of Education (Perkins and Unger, 1999; Wiske, 1998). Participants in this course make extensive use of the ENT Web site, which itself is structured by the same framework.

Like most WIDE World courses, TSNT explicitly models the same educational principles that it teaches. For example, the Teaching for Understanding (TfU) framework includes four elements: (1) *generative curriculum topics* that are central to the subject matter, relevant to the learners' experiences, approachable through multiple entry points, and rich enough to generate sustained inquiry; (2) explicit, public *understanding goals,* which focus on the active use of key concepts and methods in appropriate ways; (3) engaging learners in active *performances of understanding* that are centered on the target goals and that go beyond simply repeating facts or rehearsing routine skills; and (4) *ongoing assessment,* including constructive suggestions from self, peers, and coaches, based on public criteria linked to target goals.

The TSNT course explicitly enacts these elements. Each session begins with an on-line note that summarizes themes in the participants' responses to the prior session, introduces new ideas, and articulates the understanding goals, performances, and ongoing assessment activities for the current session. As the course unfolds, participants read about the TfU elements and how new technologies can enhance them. Participants investigate model curriculum units that integrate new technologies (such as calculators, computers, the Internet, video) and that use the elements of the TfU framework. They also study multimedia pictures of practice on the ENT

Web site, which show how teachers have carried out such curriculum designs in their own classrooms.

Over several sessions, participants develop their own curriculum unit, using an on-line workspace specifically programmed to support collaborative curriculum design incorporating TfU elements and new technologies. This Collaborative Curriculum Design Tool provides tailored scaffolding, links to curriculum standards and resources for identifying appropriate technologies, and a built-in message board for exchanging comments with peers and coaches. As participants progressively refine their own curriculum design, they receive ongoing assessments from their coach and fellow learners on each element, using a rubric explicitly related to the course goals.

Learning to participate in a collaborative reflective professional group is an explicit goal for participants in the TSNT course. In every session, participants are required to post a response to one or more reflective questions. As they become more familiar with the other participants in their study group, they also begin to respond to their fellow learners' posts and provide feedback on curriculum designs. The TSNT course also models its advocacy of using new technologies to enhance learners' understanding. Participants use threaded discussion conferences, the Collaborative Curriculum Design Tool, and a range of other on-line resources. This explicit "walking the talk" allows participants to learn from reflecting on their own experience, including their own qualms and satisfactions as learners. Some participants report that this direct and coherent experience is as valuable as any particular assignment in fostering their understanding and appreciation of teaching for understanding with new technologies.

Early Formative Evaluation of the WIDE World Architecture

WIDE World faced a host of early architectural decisions: How long should courses be? Should they be synchronous or asynchronous? How should a course be paced? During initial development, we addressed such questions by working with a range of early adopters: educators who were willing to give WIDE World a try. We devised and offered some pilot on-line professional development courses and asked the participants to offer suggestions for improving their content and design. Key findings from this period include the following:

• *Preference for a cohort model.* Fully automated courses with little interaction or dialogue allow for self-paced, start-anytime models. However, from the first, we believed that changing teachers' practice required interaction with coaches and peers toward the development of a reflective, professional community. This required that participants be in about the same place in their progress through a course, so that meaningful conversations could occur and coaches could provide support for participants. We learned early that participants viewed this as an extremely positive feature. The self-paced, start-anytime model was dropped in favor of a cohort progressing through a WIDE World course over a number of weeks.

• *Asynchronous communication, structured in sessions.* We found that even teachers in the same school found it difficult to get on-line simultaneously because of conflicting schedules. As WIDE World began to expand, teachers and administrators from many parts of the world and their associated time zones enrolled, making it impossible to schedule synchronous on-line meetings at times manageable for most participants.

• *Coached study groups.* We group participants who have shared or complementary interests with a coach of appropriate background and interests. We experimented with the number of participants per coach and have gradually increased the ratio of enrollees to coaches (currently 10:1). We will continue to assess this and other aspects of the coaching model as we work to improve the WIDE World model.

• *Semester-length courses, with sessions occurring every other week.* The pilot courses consisted of approximately eight weekly sessions. This rapid pace did not allow enough flexibility in the midst of teachers' busy lives and interfered with drawing participants into peer collaborations and assessment, so most sessions were extended to two weeks. The sixteen-week courses seemed too long, however, so we are experimenting with six sessions over periods of six to twelve weeks.

Gauging the Impact of WIDE World Courses on Participants and Practices

Measuring the impact of WIDE World is complicated, for several reasons. First, the goals are multiple. Most WIDE World instructors hope not only to promote specific pedagogical techniques but also to foster new habits of mind, so that participants develop a capacity and a commitment to engage in ongoing reflection, collaboration, and inquiry with other educators. Second, the kinds of results we seek—improvements in teaching practice and ultimately in student achievement—are not easily isolated from a myriad of intertwining influences. Conducting classic controlled experiments seems misguided and probably impossible. Third, results are difficult to study from a distance, and they may not be evident until some time after the course has ended or after a participant has taken two or three synergistic courses.

Despite these challenges, we are working to assess the impact of WIDE World courses. Researchers track participants' responses to courses through midcourse evaluations and end-of-course surveys. The midcourse evaluation focuses primarily on participants' satisfaction with the course content, activities, and support, so that coaches and instructors can make adjustments. Surveys at the end of each course assess a range of factors that inform the future design of WIDE World offerings and provide some information about impact. For example, on evaluations conducted at the end of fall 2002 courses, all respondents said their course provided a quality learning experience (for example, "ideas learned are valuable and important to my professional growth"). Ninety-eight percent of respondents said their practice improved as a result of taking the course (45 percent said "significantly"; 53 percent said "somewhat"). Of those who work directly with students, 81 percent felt "this course has enhanced student learning and understanding." Comments that participants added to their end-of-course evaluations included these: "It's focused me. I now realize that everything I do needs to be about education." "I now have a whole new orientation towards teaching for understanding. I plan in much more detail." "My lesson plans are now really aligned with standards and the kids are really benefiting." "I'm a lone ranger, so learning from my peers was a real breakthrough for me. I really learned from others' insights." "My head is just spinning with new ideas."

In addition, we undertook a study to clarify the goals of WIDE World courses (based on analysis of the course syllabi and interviews with instructors) and the impacts on learners in relation to these goals. Data to analyze impacts on learners were gathered from work that participants produced during the course—for instance, curriculum plans and rationales that reflect principles taught, reports about experiences in putting plans into practice, and descriptions of participants' beliefs about the impact of the course. We are still analyzing the results but believe they will contribute to clarifying the goals and design of WIDE World courses and will help to identify more systematic ways of measuring the courses' impact on participants and, in turn, on those they teach.

Internet Technology and the WIDE World Scaling Model

As summarized in Table 2.1, we have argued that improving education requires bridging the *knowledge-action gap* by cultivating research-based pedagogical *craft* while adapting to or adjusting the *context* to support wide-scale change. Scalable designs for educational transformation must avoid the *replica trap*—the erroneous strategy of trying to repeat everywhere what worked locally, without taking account of local variations in needs and environments—and solve the problems of *magnitude* and *variation*. Such designs should be based on explicit *scaling models*—causal theories about how the designs address some, if not all, aspects of craft and context as they are complicated at scale by problems of magnitude and variation.

The WIDE World Scaling Model

The four features of WIDE World mentioned earlier illuminate the WIDE World scaling model and the ways that Internet technology alleviates some dilemmas of scale.

- *Modeling desired practice.* The use of the Internet and the tiered structure of instructor, coaches, and enrollees in WIDE World courses permits large numbers of geographically dispersed participants to obtain a constructivist experience of learning with considerable individual attention while maintaining quality control in regard to course content and process. The on-line architecture allows participants to apply new learning to their own situation, post the results of this work, and receive personalized feedback from their coach. The on-line course materials easily accommodate variations from setting to setting. For instance, on-line archives present large numbers of examples so that participants can select material that matches their interests. Enrollees with common priorities, such as a particular subject matter or location or working with learners of a certain age group, can be grouped with a coach who tailors the course to their interests. Learners can thus collaborate with other participants facing similar situations. In these ways, the on-line course models constructivist pedagogy through active learning tailored to learners' interests.

- *Human facilitation.* The WIDE World architecture allows coaches to facilitate learning without physical proximity to course participants. Skilled teachers and graduate students can function as coaches on a part-time basis, fulfilling a professional role that does not demand travel or dependence on coaching as principal livelihood. Coaches are recruited from prior enrollees in WIDE World courses; they also take an on-line course for coaches. The telephone effect—loss of quality control due to chains of "training the trainer"—is minimized because the model uses a structure with only three tiers (instructor, coaches, and enrollees) and because the on-line nature of the interactions allows instructors and WIDE staff to track the coaching groups regularly to monitor and support their quality.

- *Sustained community of inquiry.* Teachers and other practitioners in educational settings lead very busy lives. The asynchronous design of WIDE

World makes it possible to maintain facilitated microcommunities—the coaching groups. Courses offer participants a shared language and set of concepts for discussing practice, and the written nature of on-line communication encourages more deliberate and reflective dialogue. Opportunities to learn new principles, apply them, reflect on the results, and revise them encourage inquiry. Networked communication technologies support collegial exchange of ideas, resources, and encouragement.

- *Economic viability.* The entirely on-line architecture of WIDE World eliminates most printing and travel costs. The part-time, relatively engaging nature of coaching helps keep personnel costs moderate. With very large courses (which we have not yet achieved), the relatively fixed costs of technology, course design, and instructors become secondary to the cost of coaches. To accommodate settings with thin resources, we have successfully tried a learning team system, in which up to four people from one setting enroll as a team, greatly reducing the cost per person. Members of a learning team collaborate off-line, but only one posts work on-line. The diminished opportunity to participate on-line is offset because the team itself becomes a learning group. We are also exploring ways to build expertise within school systems while reducing payments to WIDE World, such as developing local coaches and facilitators who could be compensated directly by the school system.

Lest this appear too positive an account, we do not claim that professional development through WIDE World serves as well as a skilled process of professional development conducted regularly on site by able coaches. The problem is that such a pattern of intervention is not easily scaled up, for reasons already discussed. WIDE World and similar models should be compared not with best-case versions of local professional development but with typical versions of local professional development, which tend to feature one-shot workshops with little staying power.

We further caution that WIDE World's scaling model does not simply fall into place as one switches on the computers. It requires strong technical and human infrastructure, careful interface design, sustained development of skillful coaching practices, regular monitoring of coaching groups to maintain quality, and attention to many other fronts, in ways that are constantly evolving as we conduct more formative evaluation, learn more, and strive to improve. WIDE World is a complex and often difficult enterprise, calling for the best the team can offer in pedagogical ideas and research practices and posing problems of finance, marketing, intellectual property, and more that lie outside the familiar realm of most academics.

How WIDE World Might Address Contextual Factors

WIDE World's current scaling model emphasizes helping teachers learn the craft of constructivist practices much more than promoting conducive contexts on a wide scale. The professional expertise of the project leadership lies more in teaching and learning than in educational administration and organizational change, and, as argued earlier, interactions at a distance are intrinsically more suited to cultivating craft. That said, addressing problems of context is not entirely beyond the scope of WIDE World. Early steps in that direction include trying to keep costs low, given the quality of service provided, and designing WIDE World courses that mesh well with school calendars and the many time demands that teachers face. But these efforts are only a beginning.

One promising way to develop contextual supports is through alliances with groups and institutions better positioned to deal with their own local and regional contexts than we, based in Cambridge, Massachusetts, could ever be. We see these relationships as valuable for at least two reasons. First, the partner organizations in large part create the contexts in question and thereby enable WIDE World to work with clusters of teachers who can support one another, surrounded by conditions that encourage them to enact what they learn in WIDE World courses. For example, by collaborating with school districts, states, or national ministries of education, we gain access to teachers whose leaders, mandates, technical resources, organizational structures, and cultures are reasonably supportive of the approaches advocated in WIDE World courses.

Second, these collaborations augment WIDE World's initial retail marketing strategy, which focused primarily on advertising to individual participants (although school systems often pay the bill), with a more wholesale approach focused on institutions. Marketing to institutions holds the promise of bringing large numbers of learners into WIDE World courses, which is necessary to achieve a scalable economic model.

The following are some examples of the kinds of activities that we are exploring in order to create institutional collaborations:

- Market to organizations that provide at least partial funding for participants.

- Create tailored study groups and coaching for participants from sponsoring organizations—for example, teacher educators sponsored by the Namibian National Institute for Educational Development who are interested in designing curriculum and instruction for preservice teachers, or educators from the Oklahoma VISION project who are interested in mathematics education. In collaboration with a local facilitator, the course instructor or coaches help learners develop connections between the WIDE World course and the particular priorities of their local context.

- Develop local coaches from participants in the early rounds of courses supported by sponsoring organizations, so that the organizations build capacity to provide both on-line coaches and on-site local facilitation of WIDE World courses. We are exploring this model in our work with Namibia and are developing similar proposals for some other institutions.

The same networked technologies that enable WIDE World to scale up support for constructivist craft provide promise as means to scale up support for conducive contexts. Local groups representing multiple constituencies that participate in a WIDE World course develop shared goals and shared understandings for how to achieve them. Such groups of teachers, administrators, curriculum designers, and professional developers can work together to develop local conditions that support successive cohorts in participating in similar courses. WIDE World's on-line courses for developing coaches can be used to cultivate local coaches from a distance. On-line examples of locally crafted curriculum designs, pictures of practice, and case studies of change initiatives may also promote the development of capacity and commitment within local educational contexts.

Conclusion

The Internet and associated technologies are neither necessary nor sufficient for scaling up educational change, but they are powerfully enabling. They provide means of communication and interaction to sustain dialogue, reflection, and collaboration from a distance among communities of educators attempting to improve practice. Turning again to the scaling model introduced earlier, one can see how WIDE World uses networked technologies to address some of the characteristic challenges of scale. Other on-line initiatives are devising their own scaling models and finding further ways to exercise the enabling power of the Internet.

At least in one respect, however, an Internet-based solution is inherently limited today: it does not serve settings where the needed technologies are lacking or overlooked, connectivity is erratic, or teachers are generally unfamiliar with and wary of computers. In these cases, creative solutions must be found to augment on-line professional development with hard-copy materials and face-to-face contact. Indeed, WIDE World is currently investigating ways of combining on-line and on-site strategies.

Meanwhile, networked technologies clearly offer significant promise as a means for overcoming persistent barriers to wide-scale educational improvement along constructivist lines. To realize this promise requires forms of invention and collaboration that take academics beyond their usual realms, that depend on support from donors and deans and innovative educators, and that are themselves mediated by new technologies. Yet Dewey can indeed go digital, and now is the time to get started.

REFERENCES

Berman, P. (1974–1978). *Federal programs supporting educational change*. Prepared for the Office of Education, U.S. Department of Health, Education, and Welfare. Santa Monica, CA: Rand.

Bolman, L. G., & Deal, T. E. (1997). *Reframing organizations: Artistry, choice, and leadership* (2nd ed.). San Francisco: Jossey-Bass.

Elmore, R. F., Peterson, P. L., & McCarthey, S. J. (1996). *Restructuring in the classroom: Teaching, learning, and school organization*. San Francisco: Jossey-Bass.

Lagemann, E. C. (2002a). *An elusive science: The troubling history of education research*. Chicago: University of Chicago Press.

Lagemann, E. C. (2002b). *Useable knowledge in education: A memorandum for the Spencer Foundation board of directors*. Unpublished paper.

Little, J. W. (2001). Professional development in pursuit of school reform. In A. Lieberman & L. Miller (Eds.), *Teachers caught in the action* (pp. 23–44). New York: Teachers College Press.

Little, J. W., & McLaughlin, M. W. (Eds.). (1993). *Teachers' work: Individuals, colleagues, and contexts*. New York: Teachers College Press.

McDonald, J. P. (1992). *Teaching: Making sense of an uncertain craft*. New York: Teachers College Press.

Perkins, D. N. (2003). *King Arthur's Round Table: How collaborative conversations create smart organizations*. Hoboken, NJ: Wiley.

Perkins, D. N., & Unger, C. (1999). Teaching and learning for understanding. In C. Reigeluth (Ed.), *Instructional design theories and model* (Vol. 2, pp. 91–114). Hillsdale, NJ: Erlbaum.

Pfeffer, J., & Sutton, R. (2000). *The knowing-doing gap*. Boston: Harvard Business School Press.

Putnam, R. T., & Borko, H. (2000). What do new views of knowledge and thinking have to say about research on teacher learning? *Educational Researcher, 29*(1), 4–15.

Schön, D. (1983). *The reflective practitioner.* New York: Basic Books.

Wenger, E. (1998). *Communities of practice: Learning, meaning and identity.* Cambridge, UK: Cambridge University Press.

Wiske, M. S. (Ed.). (1998). *Teaching for understanding: Linking research with practice.* San Francisco: Jossey-Bass.

ADAPTING INNOVATIONS TO PARTICULAR CONTEXTS OF USE

A COLLABORATIVE FRAMEWORK

Barry J. Fishman

The Detroit Public Schools and the University of Michigan together met the challenges of scaling up.

THE PROCESS OF SCALING UP an innovation is fundamentally about the adoption and diffusion of ideas across contexts. This process of moving between one context and the next raises critical problems. In the space between originating context and broader application, which has been referred to as a "chasm" (Moore, 1999), most innovations either disappear or become unrecognizable. Traversing this chasm is a central problem for research and development of technology innovations for schools. Most research projects fail to cross this chasm, and though they may yield valuable knowledge about the nature of cognition, teaching, and learning and therefore inform the research community, they do not have a broad or lasting impact on mainstream K–12 education.

This chapter describes a framework for assessing innovations and the contexts in which they might be adopted, in order to better understand the challenges that must be addressed if such adoptions are to be successful and sustainable, whether on the level of a single classroom, a whole school, or an entire district. The framework presented here calls for a fundamentally collaborative stance between the developers of innovations and their potential adopters in schools. Collaboration is necessary because, as I will argue, crossing the chasm is about working together to reduce its size, by tailoring a given innovation so that it becomes more usable in a specific context of use. I begin by defining the types of innovations in learning technology that this chapter is intended to address and by describing a collaboration between my research group, the Center for Highly Interactive Computing in Education (hi-ce), and the Detroit Public Schools on a systemic reform effort in science education. I also present the framework that my colleagues and I developed for examining potential challenges in the use of innovations in school contexts (Blumenfeld, Fishman, Krajcik, Marx, and Soloway, 2000), with two examples. The chapter concludes with a consideration of specific challenges and ways to address them.

Innovations in Learning Technology

This chapter discusses a type of learning technology that goes beyond what is typically found in K–12 classrooms. National surveys indicate that the primary uses of technology in schools remain drill and practice, word processing, and Web surfing (Anderson and Ronnkvist, 1999). These important initial steps for schools fall short of using the tremendous potential of technology to support the rich, inquiry-oriented learning called for in national standards documents and embodied in Learning Sciences research (Bransford, Brown, and Cocking, 1999).

The learning technology innovations described here include technology as a core component but are built around curriculum or have strong linkages to other teaching materials. Such innovations range from intelligent tutoring systems that help students learn mathematics (for example, Anderson, Corbett, Koedinger, and Pelletier, 1995) to environments that foster communal knowledge building and support for writing (for example, Scardamalia and Bereiter, 1991) and tools that scaffold rich explorations in science (for example, Linn and Hsi, 2000). These innovations are typically rooted in cognitive or constructivist learning theories (Bransford, Brown, and Cocking, 1999). Technology is not the object of learning in these innovations; rather, it supports teaching and learning. For example, instruction can be delivered via computer, or computers can function as resources in classrooms where much learning takes place away from them. With these innovations, technology scaffolds teaching and learning practices that would be difficult to achieve otherwise, thereby going beyond what could be achieved without technology.

Generally speaking, schools have found these kinds of inquiry-oriented technology innovations challenging to use without substantial technical and pedagogical support. One reason for this is that these innovations typically support reform-oriented learning, requiring that schools diverge from prior uses of technology or classroom organization. If an innovation deviates too widely from everyday school practice, teachers and administrators may react defensively by simply ignoring the innovation, hoping that it will go away before they are forced to change everyday methods they use out of habit. This reaction has been documented in studies of technologies that were not adopted (Cuban, 1986) as well as technologies that were adopted but then co-opted into existing everyday practice, making little contribution to teaching and learning (Cuban, Kirkpatrick, and Peck, 2001). This is why technologies such as drill-and-practice tools have been taken up so broadly in education; they can easily be integrated into existing practice. For example, students can be assigned to use drill-and-practice tools in a computer lab, requiring little intervention from a subject-area teacher (Hodas, 1993). However, such uses of technology have little effect on learning when compared with more challenging inquiry-oriented or project-based uses (Wenglinsky, 1998). The gap between current school practice and approaches that would maximize the learning benefits available through technology must be closed in order for an innovation to become usable.

Researchers who study innovative learning technologies have typically established "hothouse" environments wherein innovations can thrive for the purpose of the research. Much of this research has been conducted using design-based methods, in which researchers test theories by instantiating them in innovations and then studying the innovations intensively in the classroom (Cobb, Confrey, diSessa, Lehrer, and Schauble, 2003); classrooms are supported with infusions of hardware, technical support, and often teaching support from university personnel. This support is critical, because explorations into innovative teaching or learning require changes on multiple fronts simultaneously. In order to be effective, "technology needs to be part of a coordinated approach to improving curriculum, pedagogy, assessment, teacher development, and other aspects of school structure" (Roschelle, Pea, Hoadley, Gordin, and Means, 2000, p. 78). The most effective uses of technology are interwoven with the challenges and problems of school reform itself. While design experiment and test bed environments are helpful for establishing the potential value of technology, they are not designed to create useful knowledge about how such environments might be established or supported outside the research context, and that knowledge is essential if such efforts are to become scalable and sustainable.

LeTUS: An Example of Innovation in Learning Technology

The work of hi-ce in the Center for Learning Technologies in Urban Schools (LeTUS) exemplifies the type of learning technology innovation I mean to describe. LeTUS is a four-way partnership between the Detroit Public Schools, the University of Michigan, the Chicago Public Schools, and Northwestern University. Its goal is to develop inquiry-based science curricula with embedded technology that is also integrated with systemic reform efforts in the school districts. In Detroit, this work includes extensive curriculum development, design and integration of technologies to support student and teacher learning, broad-based professional development, and collaboration with teachers and school and district administrators (for details and papers related to this work, see http://www.hi-ce.org/). A key to the success of the program is the dedication of a high-level central administrator with responsibility for curriculum, who helped to shepherd LeTUS through various district policy shifts; this person formed a partnership with University of Michigan education faculty because of a shared belief in project-based and inquiry-oriented learning and the desire to support that belief by introducing technology into science classrooms.

To date, the Detroit Public Schools–University of Michigan collaboration has developed five science units for the sixth, seventh, and eighth grades, on the topics of air quality, water quality, communicable diseases, force and motion, and mechanical advantage. Each unit is based on the principles of project-based science (Blumenfeld and others, 1991), driven by a central question that is anchored in a real-world problem, such as "How is the quality of the air in my community?" Other features of these units are investigations and artifact development that provide opportunities for students to learn concepts, apply information, and represent knowledge; collaboration among students, teachers, and others in the community; and use of computational technological tools to promote inquiry. Each unit lasts for eight to twelve weeks, or roughly one marking period.

The range of technologies embedded in these curriculum units was developed with the goal of enabling sustained inquiry (Krajcik, Blumenfeld, Marx, and Soloway, 2000). These tools support data collection, visualization and analysis, dynamic modeling, planning, and information gathering from the Internet. Some software is designed for use at single computers that do not need to be networked. Other applications use Internet resources, such as Artemis, the user interface of a digital library tailored to young learners (Wallace, Kupperman, Krajcik, and Soloway, 2000). More recently, we have added handheld technology to our curriculum materials, enabling students to use Palm computers for data gathering, concept mapping, animation, and disease simulation (Soloway and others, 2001).

Another key product of the LeTUS collaboration is professional development for teachers, related to our materials and research on teacher learning and the design of professional development (Fishman, Marx, Best, and Tal, 2003). Our professional development venues and activities consist of extended summer workshops, monthly Saturday work sessions, in-classroom consultations, on-line professional development environments (Fishman, 2003), and the design of curriculum materials that are educative for teachers (Ball and Cohen, 1996).

Our work began in the fashion of most innovations in learning technology. We developed materials using focused design-based research methodologies (Krajcik, Blumenfeld, Marx, and Soloway, 1994). When we believed that our innovation was working well, we attempted to expand its use as part of Detroit's systemic reform initiative (that is, we tried to "scale it up"). But this process proved difficult, and challenges arose that limited the utility and use of the innovation. Grappling with these challenges led us to develop the framework presented here. But before presenting it, I wish to reconsider what is meant by the term *scale* and its use in the context of learning technology innovations.

Reconsidering Scale

What do we mean when we say that an innovation has been "scaled up"? Presumably, we mean that it has moved beyond early adopters and into mainstream use. Rogers (1995) depicts adoption as a bell curve, and in a model constructed from empirical observations, he labels the first 2.5 percent of all potential adopters as "innovators" (two standard deviations from the population mean) and the group between 2.5 percent and 16 percent as "early adopters" (one standard deviation). A marketing writer describes the break between that first 16 percent and the remaining potential users as a "chasm," "the most formidable and unforgiving transition in the Technology Adoption Life Cycle . . . all the more dangerous because it typically goes unrecognized" (Moore, 1999, p. 19). How is the field of learning technologies doing in this arena? There are approximately 3 million teachers in the United States. Rogers would predict that 2.5 percent of those, or 75,000, are likely to be innovators. Now let us consider research-derived innovations in learning technologies from the past twenty years. Has any one of them come to be used by as many as 75,000 teachers? What about the chasm that exists at 16 percent, or 480,000 teachers?

From my own exploration and conversations with members of the learning technologies community, it appears that the majority of work in innovative learning technologies has not yet crossed the chasm. Most projects work with a handful of teachers; many work with fewer than one hundred teachers; and only rarely do learning technology projects work with thousands of teachers. And when projects do engage thousands of teachers, the participants are often scattered across many different settings, with only a handful in any single district. Without crossing the 16 percent chasm, it is unlikely that an innovation will become integrated into everyday school practice nationally.

What is one to conclude from these hypothetical estimates? Is there no hope that innovative learning technologies will have a meaningful impact on education on a national scale? Schools are essentially local institutions, and therefore we might alternatively consider scale as a measure of the percentage of teachers within a local school, district, or state who are using an innovation. Numbers are harder to come by at these levels. A few examples do exist of entire school districts transforming teaching and learning through innovative uses of technology linked to standards-based curriculum— for example, in Union City, New Jersey (see Chapter One; see also Becker, Wong, and Ravitz, 1999). But in most cases, it is likely that teachers within a particular subject area or grade level within a school or district will adopt a reform program. That is what happened in the LeTUS collaboration with the Detroit Public Schools, which focuses on middle-grade science and to date has involved approximately 65 teachers, representing 26 percent of all middle-grade science teachers in Detroit. (Eighty-five teachers in Detroit have worked with LeTUS over the years, but due to promotion and attrition, roughly twenty no longer directly teach science; there are approximately 250 middle-grade science teachers in Detroit.) Thus, although no learning technology innovations seem to have crossed the chasm on a national scale, significant headway has been made on a local scale.

The concept of sustainability is an important complement to scale. Sustainability means that an effort can continue without special or external resources. In the aforementioned example of the design-based research on learning technology innovations, it means that the effort can continue without the involvement of the researchers and developers who were involved in the initial classroom implementation.

I would argue that anyone who is working to create lasting changes with technology that have a sustainable impact on teaching and learning is in fact concerned with creating innovations that function as part of systemic reforms. A fundamental goal of systemic reform is alignment across components of school systems (such as administration and management, curriculum and instruction, assessment, policy, and technology), both within a district and between districts, states, and the federal government (Smith and O'Day, 1991). If an innovation is aligned with stable structures, it has a better chance of being sustained and scaled. Systemic reform itself is a struggle between established and desired school practices; that is why, as discussed earlier, innovative learning technology projects are so challenging to implement in most classrooms and schools. If researchers and developers carefully design an innovation to fit a school organization's larger reform agenda, that innovation will almost certainly be more sustainable and therefore scalable.

A Framework for Implementing Innovations in School Systems

The work of LeTUS explicitly concerns the development of technology-infused science curricula in the context of our partner districts' systemic reform initiatives. This makes the LeTUS work different from our organization's previous research efforts, which were concerned with creating ideal local contexts for teaching and learning in order to understand the role of inquiry and technology. Although we began LeTUS work with the design-based approaches of earlier work, as the number of teachers involved grew larger, it became impossible to continue to support teachers in their classrooms at a high level or even to provide the necessary technology from grant funds. Overall, the effort has been successful; students participating in LeTUS have made steady gains in both science content knowledge and process skills. But working at scale has revealed that aspects of our innovation are not functioning in the way we had envisioned, for a variety of reasons. These include challenges related to technology use (discussed in depth later in the chapter), design of curriculum materials to educate teachers (Schneider and Krajcik, 2000), design of professional development for teachers with a broad range of experience, and development of innovations that are sensitive to community needs beyond the school curriculum (Moje, Collazo, Carrillo, and Marx, 2001). In fact, some of the most intriguing research opportunities to emerge from this collaboration come from the challenges of working in real-world as opposed to hothouse research settings and addressing what have been called "the dilemmas of practice" (Shepard, 2000). Experience in the LeTUS collaboration led us to reflect on the nature of our innovation and its relationship to the evolving reform context in Detroit. The result was the development of a framework (Blumenfeld and others, 2000) for evaluating the fit between innovations and intended contexts of use.

In developing this framework, we viewed the challenge of developing an innovation that was sustainable (well matched to the systemic reform goals of the district) and scalable (able to be used by a majority of teachers in the district) as a usability problem. We took the term *usability* from the study of human-computer interaction (Nielsen, 1993), where it denotes the extent to which people can employ tools to accomplish work. This struck us as a useful way to consider whether an innovation fit the reform context of a school. In reality, such good fits are rare, especially when innovations involve reform-oriented practices; in fact, all innovations probably need improved usability in one area or another. We considered usability along three dimensions: capability, policy and management, and school culture. These dimensions can be arrayed in the form of three axes originating from a common point (the origin, which represents the current capacity of the district to use the innovation) to form a three-dimensional space we call the "usability cube" (see Figure 3.1).

This cube represents a school organization's overall capacity for implementing an innovation. The innovation can be placed in the space created by the three axes; the distance between it and the origin represents a gap

Figure 3.1. Framework for Evaluating the Usability of Innovations

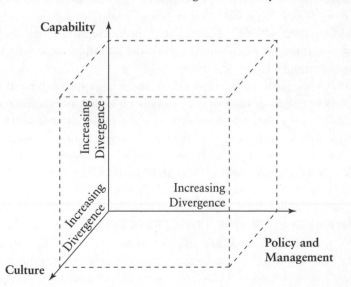

between the capacity required to successfully use the innovation and the current capacity of the district. Conceptualized in this manner, creating usable innovations is a process of working to close gaps that exist between the innovation's demands and the system's capacity. Changes to both the innovation and the school system are typically required in order to foster maximum usability.

The capability axis describes the extent to which intended users of an innovation have the conceptual and practical knowledge necessary to use it—for example, knowledge of teaching practices, knowledge of how technology works, and so on. A gap on this dimension may be reduced by providing high-quality professional development for teachers and others involved or by reducing the demand for knowledge, perhaps through modifying activities or redesigning technology.

The policy and management axis describes the extent to which policies of the district and the management systems that carry them out are favorable to the demands of the innovation. This dimension includes the rules and procedures that operate at different levels of the system and the degree of compatibility and coordination within and across levels. A gap on this dimension can be reduced either by changing policies and procedures or by changing the innovation to bring it in line with them.

The culture axis describes the extent to which an innovation adheres to or diverges from the existing norms, beliefs, values, and expectations for practice at different levels of the system. A gap on this dimension can be reduced by providing opportunities for teachers and administrators to gain new visions of practice that are congruent with the demands of the innovation. In our work, we have found the culture dimension hardest to change; therefore, it often requires the most attention, especially early in the development of an innovation.

Perhaps the most useful approach to reducing gaps is close collaboration between the school and the innovation's developers. Such collaboration helps the developers to better understand the status of the school along each dimension and helps the school organization to better appreciate the true demands of the innovation. Careful consideration needs to be given to how the components of an innovation can be revised or reinvented to reduce gaps. Research on the diffusion of innovations explicitly addresses reinvention, finding that it is positively related to successful adoption (Rice and Rogers, 1980). Often, however, potential adopters embark on reinvention without the involvement of the developer, and this can be problematic. Often reinvention leads to uses of the innovation that are vastly different from the designer's original intent, such as employing a tool intended to support inquiry for drill-and-practice activities (Cuban,

Kirkpatrick, and Peck, 2001). Collaboration effectively avoids reinvention that is adverse to the intended goals of the innovation. The following two examples reveal this process in action.

Scaffolded Internet Search Tools

Artemis is an Internet search tool specifically designed for middle school students as part of inquiry-based curricula to improve their ability to conduct Web-based research (Wallace and others, 1998). In its original implementation, Artemis was a Java applet designed to run within a Web browser, which accessed an age-appropriate library at the University of Michigan. Artemis also gives teachers access to tools for evaluating students' research; overall, Artemis makes such research more productive (Wallace, Kupperman, Krajcik, and Soloway, 2000). The initial development of Artemis was separate from LeTUS curriculum development, and we first introduced it to LeTUS teachers in 1997, the second year of our collaboration. The initial attempts to foster use of Artemis among teachers and students uncovered a range of usability gaps that created challenges for using it in the context of the in the Detroit Public Schools. These gaps are explored here in terms of the axes of the usability cube.

USABILITY GAPS RELATED TO CAPABILITY. Using Artemis requires a range of capabilities. First, a school must have computers that can run a Java-enabled Web browser, connected to and configured properly for the Internet. Teachers and students must have the technical knowledge to use a Web browser (not an assumed skill in 1997) and to use Artemis. Teachers must possess the pedagogical knowledge to conduct a computer lab for a classroom full of students or, in the context of smaller classroom-based clusters of computers, how to manage students either working in groups or engaged in different activities simultaneously. Finally, teachers have to know how and when to integrate Artemis activities with other aspects of the curriculum.

The first capability demand, access to Internet-connected computers, presented the largest gap that needed to be addressed before Artemis could be used in Detroit. Teacher and student abilities to use Web browsers and Artemis were addressed through professional development and training and did not prove difficult. Integrating Artemis into curriculum materials presented a larger usability problem for teachers. During regular professional development sessions, we initially suggested multiple ways in which teachers might integrate Artemis into extant LeTUS curriculum materials. However, given the limited time available for enacting the LeTUS curricula and a lack of specific guidance on how to integrate Artemis into the regular flow of a curriculum unit, few teachers employed this resource. On reflection, we see that we might have predicted this, given our own focus on the importance of educative curriculum materials (Ball and Cohen, 1996). Subsequently, we integrated Artemis directly into three of the five LeTUS units, which mitigated this barrier to its use.

USABILITY GAPS RELATED TO POLICY AND MANAGEMENT. One of the primary responsibilities of school district administration with respect to policy and management is the acquisition, distribution, and maintenance of technology (Blumenfeld and others, 2000; Fishman and Gomez, 2000). In the Detroit Public Schools, as in many large urban districts, access to the Internet is controlled by a central management and information services (MIS) division. This presented a problem because the MIS department saw management and security of information, not learning, as its highest priority. In order to use the Internet, classroom teachers must believe that it will be available when they need it. If it is viewed as unreliable or prone to failure, any prudent teacher would avoid it. Internet access, unfortunately, is prone to reliability problems in school settings, due to the complexity of establishing connectivity and the many different points at which it might fail (Fishman and Gomez, 2000). Teachers in Detroit quickly realized that they could not rely on access to Artemis when they needed it and that the central MIS office was not set up to support their classroom-level uses of the Internet.

Also, Artemis itself introduced a problem at the policy and management level. To allow a two-way connection between a Web browser and the digital library collection at the university, the Artemis Java applet required that a particular network port be opened, which was against MIS security protocols. Furthermore, because security arrangements included a centralized proxy server between the district and the outside world, a bottleneck was created that made use of Artemis unbearably slow during times of peak Internet usage.

Through the intervention of the central administrator who championed LeTUS, meetings were arranged with key personnel in the MIS department to raise the status of classroom uses of the Internet and to facilitate communication between the various LeTUS partners and district personnel. This meeting increased communication and helped decrease the policy and management gaps that made Artemis unusable. Another major shift occurred when it became apparent that district plans for improving classroom Internet service would not be completed rapidly enough to support LeTUS use of Artemis. As a result, schools working with LeTUS were permitted to contract with an outside Internet service provider for high-speed access in classrooms where Artemis was to be used. This arrangement became possible through the collaboration between the district and the university. Also, the university developers made a final change that greatly reduced the policy and management challenges of using Artemis. During negotiations concerning Internet access, university personnel rewrote Artemis as a regular Web-based application and not a Java applet. This removed the persistent firewall access problems, allowing Artemis to be used more easily within the district.

USABILITY GAPS RELATED TO CULTURE. Teaching with the Internet presented a tremendous challenge in terms of school culture. Whereas before teachers had been self-reliant when it came to classroom activities, Artemis required that teachers rely on a host of unseen and unknown outside personnel for success, presenting a tremendous challenge in an environment that lacked a well-established means of communication beyond the boundaries of the classroom. The case of Artemis illustrates the way that culture is embodied in policy and management and manifests itself in capability. With respect to management of Internet access, district policies had made it difficult to establish reliable classroom connectivity, and this (among other factors) restricted teachers' ability to use Artemis. The meeting between senior MIS administrators, senior curriculum administrators, and LeTUS staff that I described in the preceding section represented a major step toward changing the district culture of isolation. Changes in policies—for example, allowing externally provided Internet connectivity for LeTUS schools—led over time to changes in teachers' expectations for availability of the Internet. That was a critical precursor to the adoption of Artemis in LeTUS classrooms.

PROGRESS IN ENHANCING THE USABILITY OF ARTEMIS IN LETUS. During the first year that Artemis was introduced into the LeTUS partnership, four teachers attempted to use it but were unable to integrate this resource into their instruction because of problems it presented in terms of the district's technology infrastructure. Because the LeTUS partnership was able to negotiate changes in policy and management, as well as make changes to Artemis itself, the usability gaps closed, and use of Artemis has increased steadily. For example, among those who taught a seventh-grade unit on communicable diseases (the first unit to explicitly integrate Artemis), nearly 47 percent of teachers used Artemis with their students in the 2001–2002 academic year, and approximately 70 percent of them did so in the 2002–2003 academic year. Through the collaborative efforts of LeTUS, the usability gap for Artemis has been reduced, and the district's capacity is more closely aligned with the capacity demands of the Artemis component of our learning technology innovation.

Handheld Computers in the Science Classroom

Partly in response to ongoing challenges in regard to personal computer acquisition, distribution, and maintenance (Blumenfeld and others, 2000), LeTUS began developing Palm-based software that we believed would be easier to employ in inquiry-based science learning (Soloway and others, 2001). The software included a concept-mapping tool, a frame-based animation tool, and a disease simulation that was developed specifically for use in the communicable diseases unit. Although not problem-free, the introduction of handheld computers into the LeTUS curriculum was a good deal smoother than the introduction of Artemis. This is because handheld computers posed far fewer usability challenges than Artemis in the Detroit context, especially on the policy and management and culture dimensions.

USABILITY GAPS RELATED TO CAPABILITY. Most of the usability challenges related to handheld computers for use in LeTUS occurred on the capability axis. Because few teachers in LeTUS had any personal experience with handhelds, there was a need for training. To facilitate this, LeTUS gave Palm handheld computers to teachers so that they could play around with them at their own pace and become familiar with the features of this technology. Shortly thereafter, Palms were incorporated into LeTUS professional development activities, with a focus on their classroom uses.

The other major capability challenge was how to manage the use of Palms in instruction. At first, this was addressed in a manner akin to design experiments: graduate students were sent out to support teachers. From these early experiences, teachers built pedagogical knowledge with respect to using Palms in the classroom. Teachers who were early adopters of Palms developed a set of routines for making sure that Palms could be easily stored and retrieved by students, that batteries were properly charged, and so forth. The early adopters then became sources of knowledge in professional development for the broader group of teachers who next planned to use Palms. Teachers found that using Palms in the classroom was less challenging than using desktop or laptop computers; because Palms are inexpensive, each student can have one. It was not necessary to move science classes to computer labs or to create complex arrangements for small-group work. As with Artemis, teachers faced a capability challenge in integrating the Palms into their teaching. Because Palms were introduced to LeTUS teachers only recently, so far they have been written only into the communicable diseases unit.

USABILITY GAPS RELATED TO POLICY AND MANAGEMENT. Handheld computers presented relatively few problems in regard to policy and management. Because handheld computers are cheaper, issues of acquisition were less problematic than they would have been for desktop computers. Whereas a classroom set of fifteen desktop computers costs at least $15,000, a set of thirty Palm computers could be purchased for around $4,500. The price of Palms resembled that of basic classroom supplies rather than computer hardware, and therefore the district's curriculum division purchased classroom sets of Palms for LeTUS schools. No interaction was necessary with either the MIS department or the usual technology-purchasing channels within individual schools. Another benefit was that in most cases, there was no need for LeTUS teachers to negotiate for scarce time in computer labs.

USABILITY GAPS RELATED TO CULTURE. Palms as a technology innovation presented few challenges to extant school culture. Because they are small and easily stored in science classrooms, teachers do not have to interact with others in the school building to coordinate access or schedules. Because Palms do not (in most cases) require access to the Internet, they do not force teachers to rely on resources beyond their own classroom.

PROGRESS IN ENHANCING THE USABILITY OF HANDHELD COMPUTERS IN LETUS. Because the gap between the capacity demands of handheld computers and the capacity of the district was relatively small in comparison with those related to Artemis, the use of Palms was established much more rapidly. In the initial year of use (2000–2001), Palms were used only in a few well-supported classrooms. In the subsequent year, the communicable diseases unit was introduced to a broader group of teachers, and Palms were used in 87 percent of classrooms where it was taught. In the year 2002–2003, all teachers who taught the unit used Palm computers in their classrooms.

Challenges for School-University Collaboration

This chapter has argued that extended and deep collaboration between schools and universities (or other partners) is critical to reducing gaps in the usability of innovations; the broad range of knowledge required to successfully identify and resolve usability challenges is unlikely to exist within a single organization. Universities, for example, may have expertise on the design of technologies and the development of standards-based materials. School districts, on the other hand, have expertise on the pedagogical needs of their own students, the nature of the assessment systems and frameworks through which they are held accountable, and the cultural context in which the innovation is to be used. Collaboration is necessary because gap reduction is hard work, requiring a long-term commitment on the part of all parties. This goes beyond endorsement by the central office (although that is important), and requires true buy-in on the part of all who are involved. But many challenges complicate efforts at collaboration, including schedule conflicts and the different work cycles of schools and universities, issues of ownership, and the nature of the organizations.

Schedules are a major challenge to collaboration, in that the calendar and pace for work in schools tends to be very different from those of universities or research groups. For instance, in schools much of the planning for the coming academic year takes place during the summer. University developers need to be sensitive to this and provide materials in a timely manner so that schools can evaluate them and incorporate them into summer professional development. Funding cycles are also problematic, because many grants extend over relatively short periods of time (one to three years). The LeTUS collaboration with Detroit has been in progress for more than five years, and there is still a lot of work for us to do together. Short funding cycles may catalyze partnerships, but longer-term funding is needed to sustain them.

Issues of ownership are another area of potential stress. All participants in the collaboration should feel like equal owners of the innovation. But tensions may develop concerning modifications that are contrary to core principles that the university developer held at the outset of the collaboration. In the LeTUS collaboration, there is a constant effort to help teachers own the curriculum and feel free to modify it to suit their own needs. But the university team members, in their role as experts in the use of technology in science education, may feel reluctant about changes that seem contrary to the initial goals of the curriculum design. Similarly, LeTUS teachers sometimes have difficulty understanding why the university seems to be constantly revising the curriculum, making it difficult for them to develop a comfort zone while working with ever-changing materials. Part of the issue is that the university and school district are responding to different sets of standards. Teachers, working to meet district standards, may be satisfied if their students are making progress as measured by local high-stakes tests. University partners, on the other hand, usually design innovations with national standards in mind and evaluate performance across a broad range of indicators. Ideally, evaluation frameworks would be aligned at all levels, but this is not yet the case.

Finally, some challenges to collaboration come from the nature of the organizations involved. Many urban school districts experience changes in leadership every few years, which can disrupt ongoing initiatives (Fuhrman, 1994). A champion who can maintain continuity through such changes is key to helping the innovation survive evolving capability, policy and management, and cultural changes. Within universities, it can be difficult to build coalitions of expertise needed to work with schools successfully. In hi-ce, for example, faculty from science education, computer science, educational psychology, learning technologies, and literacy all collaborate on the LeTUS effort, each bringing different expertise. Such cross-disciplinary collaboration is unusual in university settings, which tend to emphasize individual effort and publication. A related problem is that long-term collaborations often blur the distinction between research and service, which poses identity problems for faculty at research-oriented institutions. Universities need to reconsider how faculty are organized and rewarded in order to encourage the complex organization building that is necessary to promote long-term collaborations with schools.

Conclusion

The heart of this chapter consists of an argument that innovations don't simply work in some school contexts and not in others. The scaling up of innovations is not about creating an instance of something and then encouraging others to take it and use it. Instead, the process begins with creating innovations that are usable in school contexts. This requires compromise between the vision of school practice represented by the innovation in its ideal state and the norms of the adopting school context. For instructional technology innovations to be used successfully, it is necessary to engage collaboratively with schools in a process of reform that ultimately alters both normal practice and aspects of the innovation. The notion of usability emphasizes adaptability, so that potential adopters and the innovation's developers can modify the innovation to produce a better fit with the capability, policy and management, and culture of the adopting district. Such modifications are more likely to be effective when made collaboratively.

It is tempting to draw conclusions about scale in terms of the raw numbers of teachers or schools that are using a particular innovation. However, even when large numbers of users are recruited, a given innovation may not have a measurable impact in any particular setting. A more productive approach, at least when one is fundamentally concerned with issues of standards-based systemic reform, is to focus on the level of adoption within particular contexts, such as a school district or state. When collaboration produces truly usable innovations for particular contexts, it becomes possible to move beyond the innovators and early adopters and foster adoption by the majority. Only when that happens will learning technology innovations have a broad impact on teaching and learning in K–12 education.

REFERENCES

Anderson, J. R., Corbett, A. T., Koedinger, K., & Pelletier, R. (1995). Cognitive tutors: Lessons learned. *Journal of the Learning Sciences, 4,* 167–207.

Anderson, R. E., & Ronnkvist, A. (1999). *The presence of computers in American schools* (Report No. 2). Irvine, CA: Center for Research on Information Technology and Organizations, University of California at Irvine and University of Minnesota. Retrieved March 25, 2003, from http://www.crito.uci.edu/TLC/findings/Internet-Use/startpage.htm

Ball, D. L., & Cohen, D. K. (1996). Reform by the book: What is—or might be—the role of curriculum materials in teacher learning and instructional reform? *Educational Researcher, 25*(9), 6–8.

Becker, H. J., Wong, Y., & Ravitz, J. L. (1999). *Computer use and pedagogy in Co-NECT schools: A comparative study* (Teaching, Learning, and Computing 1998 National Survey Report No. 8). Irvine, CA: Center for Research on Information Technology and Organizations, University of California at Irvine and University of Minnesota. Retrieved July 14, 2003, from http://www.crito.uci.edu/tlc/findings/report_8/REPORT_8.PDF

Blumenfeld, P., Fishman, B. J., Krajcik, J. S., Marx, R. W., & Soloway, E. (2000). Creating usable innovations in systemic reform: Scaling up technology-embedded project-based science in urban schools. *Educational Psychologist, 35*(3), 149–164.

Blumenfeld, P., Soloway, E., Marx, R. W., Krajcik, J. S., Guzdial, M., & Palincsar, A. (1991). Motivating project-based learning: Sustaining the doing, supporting the learning. *Educational Psychologist, 26*(3–4), 369–398.

Bransford, J. D., Brown, A. L., & Cocking, R. R. (Eds.). (1999). *How people learn: Brain, mind, experience, and school.* Washington, DC: National Academy Press.

Cobb, P., Confrey, J., diSessa, A., Lehrer, R., & Schauble, L. (2003). Design experiments in educational research. *Educational Researcher, 32*(1), 9–13.

Cuban, L. (1986). *Teachers and machines: The classroom use of technology since 1920*. New York: Teachers College Press.

Cuban, L., Kirkpatrick, H., & Peck, C. (2001). High access and low use of technologies in high school classrooms: Explaining an apparent paradox. *American Educational Research Journal, 38*(4), 813–834.

Fishman, B. (2003). Linking on-line video and curriculum to leverage community knowledge. In J. Brophy (Ed.), *Advances in research on teaching: Using video in teacher education* (Vol. 10, pp. 201–234). New York: Elsevier Science.

Fishman, B., & Gomez, L. (2000). New technologies and the challenge for school leadership. In M. Honey & C. Shookhoff (Eds.), *The Wingspread Conference on Technology's Role in Urban School Reform: Achieving Equity and Quality* (pp. 13–21). Racine, WI: The Joyce Foundation, The Johnson Foundation, and the EDC Center for Children and Technology.

Fishman, B., Marx, R., Best, S., & Tal, R. (2003). Linking teacher and student learning to improve professional development in systemic reform. *Teaching and Teacher Education, 19*(6), 643–658.

Fuhrman, S. H. (1994). *Challenges in systemic education reform* (CPRE Policy Brief No. RB-14). Philadelphia: Center for Policy Research in Education. Retrieved July 14, 2003, from http://www.cpre.org/Publications/rb14.pdf

Hodas, S. (1993). Technology refusal and the organizational culture of schools. *Education Policy Analysis Archives, 1*(10). Retrieved March 25, 2003, from http://olam.ed.asu.edu/epaa/v1n10.html

Krajcik, J. S., Blumenfeld, P., Marx, R. W., & Soloway, E. (1994). A collaborative model for helping middle grade science teachers learn project-based instruction. *Elementary School Journal, 94*(5), 483–497.

Krajcik, J. S., Blumenfeld, P., Marx, R. W., & Soloway, E. (2000). Instructional, curricular, and technological supports for inquiry in science classrooms. In J. Minstrell & E.H.V. Zee (Eds.), *Inquiring into inquiry learning and teaching in science* (pp. 283–315). Washington, DC: American Association for the Advancement of Science.

Linn, M. C., & Hsi, S. (2000). *Computers, teachers, peers*. Mahwah, NJ: Erlbaum.

Moje, E. B., Collazo, T., Carrillo, R., & Marx, R. W. (2001). "Maestro, what is 'quality'?": Language, literacy, and discourse in project-based science. *Journal of Research in Science Teaching, 38*(4), 469–498.

Moore, G. A. (1999). *Crossing the chasm* (Rev. ed.). New York: Harper Perennial.

Nielsen, J. (1993). *Usability engineering*. San Francisco: Morgan Kaufmann.

Rice, R., & Rogers, E. M. (1980). Reinvention in the innovation process. *Knowledge: Creation, Diffusion, and Utilization, 1*(4), 499–514.

Rogers, E. M. (1995). *Diffusion of innovations* (4th ed.). New York: Free Press.

Roschelle, J. M., Pea, R. D., Hoadley, C. M., Gordin, D. N., & Means, B. M. (2000). Changing how and what children learn in school with computer-based technologies. *The Future of Children: Children and Computer Technology, 10*(2), 76–101.

Scardamalia, M., & Bereiter, C. (1991). Higher levels of agency for children in knowledge building: A challenge for the design of new knowledge media. *Journal of the Learning Sciences, 1*(1), 37–68.

Schneider, R. M., & Krajcik, J. S. (2000, April). *The role of educative curriculum materials in reforming science education.* Paper presented at the annual meeting of the American Educational Research Association, New Orleans, LA.

Shepard, L. A. (2000). The role of assessment in a learning culture. *Educational Researcher, 29*(7), 4–14.

Smith, M. S., & O'Day, J. (1991). Systemic school reform. In S. H. Fuhrman & B. Malen (Eds.), *The politics of curriculum and testing* (pp. 233–267). New York: Falmer.

Soloway, E., Norris, C., Blumenfeld, P., Fishman, B., Krajcik, J. S., & Marx, R. W. (2001, June). Handheld devices are ready at hand. *Communications of the ACM, 44,* 15–20.

Wallace, R., Bos, N., Hoffman, J., Hunter, H. E., Krajcik, J. S., Soloway, E., Kiskis, D., Klann, E., Peters, G., Richardson, D., & Ronen, O. (1998). ARTEMIS: Learner-centered design of an information seeking environment for K–12 education. In C.-M. Karat, A. Lund, J. Coutaz, & J. Karat (Eds.), *Computer Human Interaction '98* (pp. 195–202). Los Angeles: Association of Computing Machinery.

Wallace, R., Kupperman, J., Krajcik, J. S., & Soloway, E. (2000). Science on the Web: Students online in a sixth-grade classroom. *Journal of the Learning Sciences, 9*(1), 75–104.

Wenglinsky, H. (1998). *Does it compute? The relationship between educational technology and student achievement in mathematics* (Policy Information Report). Princeton, NJ: Educational Testing Service.

4

DESIGNING FOR SCALABLE EDUCATIONAL IMPROVEMENT

PROCESSES OF INQUIRY IN PRACTICE

Susan R. Goldman

The Schools for Thought curriculum innovation in Nashville reveals lessons in design principles, collaboration, and the political challenges of scaling up.

IN THIS CHAPTER, I first propose a set of design principles for scalable educational improvement. These principles have been derived from my own experiences as well as those of other researchers and professional developers as we have worked in various parts of the United States with a variety of reform efforts. The design principles are an attempt to capture and reflect the convergence in the lessons learned across these improvement efforts. Ten principles deal with change at three levels in a multi-tiered system: four deal with the change process itself, three with organizational change, and three with individual change. The change process at all levels requires new thinking about learning, social contexts of learning, collaboration among individuals and groups that have traditionally been isolated from one another, and ongoing inquiry and reflection targeted at the multiple levels of the educational system, ranging from student learning to federal policies. Critical to furthering our understanding of educational change and scaling up is the commitment to documenting and analyzing specific educational improvement efforts so that we can build a systematic knowledge base that will inform future efforts.

To exemplify the kinds of experiences and lessons learned from contemporary educational improvement efforts, the second part of the chapter describes a specific case of educational change that I participated in for almost ten years. Over the course of that time, the program experienced a variety of changes, some stimulated by internal forces and others by external ones. These lessons point to issues of goal alignment and coherence in implementation within the innovation, the educational system, and the multiple stakeholders as well as across these three areas. The case is not offered as proof of the utility of the design principles. To the contrary, the design principles serve as a set of hypotheses about what's needed for educational improvement to be both sustainable and scalable.

The concluding section of the chapter raises some general issues for consideration in efforts to create and scale up educational improvement. One issue concerns the meaning of concepts central to the process, including that of improvement itself. A second concerns flexibility and adaptability, which are critical to successful educational improvement models and their adoption by others.

Design Principles for Educational Improvement: A Proposal

The design principles I propose in this chapter draw on my own work and that of numerous other colleagues working on and writing about educational reform efforts and effective professional development in that context (Elmore, 2002; Fullan, 1999; Fullan and Miles, 1992; Murphy and Hallinger, 1993; Zech, Gause-Vega, Bray, Secules, and Goldman, 2000). Specifically, during 2001 and 2002, a number of individuals who had been working in different parts of the country came together informally to consider designs for educational improvement in reading, mathematics, and science for Chicago Public Schools. These discussions brought to light many similarities in the lessons we had learned and in their implications for the design of effective educational improvement efforts. The design principles that I propose draw on those conversations and our collaboration on various proposals written to support educational improvement work in Chicago.

The design principles are offered as a set of working hypotheses rather than as tried-and-true claims. As yet, no formal tests, not even at the level of a demonstration project, provide evidence that this set of principles will result in successful and scalable educational improvement. However, they are a set of reasoned principles that are consistent not only with what we as a community have been learning through lived experiences with reform but also with research devoted to understanding how individuals and organizations learn.

Design principles for sustainable and scalable educational improvement need to address all levels of the educational system, from levels most proximal to students and their learning to those more distal, such as state and federal policies and regulations. The design principles proposed here pertain to the change process itself, to organizational change, and to individual change. They address cognitive and social processes of learning in individuals and organizations.

Principles of the Educational Improvement Change Process

1. *Educational improvement must be an ongoing systems-level activity, especially if it is to be scaled up.* At the heart of change for educational improvement is an inquiry orientation that undergirds a continuous improvement process. Inquiry involves access to information, analysis of information, and actions aimed at supporting what is going well and improving what is not (Senge, 1990, 1999, 2000). Inquiry creates knowledge that informs both individual and organizational change processes. Ongoing, iterative inquiry provides the basis for sustaining and enhancing educational improvement throughout the system.

2. *Educational improvement must occur at multiple levels, with alignment across levels.* Educational improvement efforts need the active support of participants at multiple levels within the educational system and the larger communities within which they are situated. Educational improvement must take into account the multiple, embedded contexts in which students learn, teachers teach, principals administer, and superintendents manage school systems, and it must encompass local, state, and federal systems (McLaughlin and Talbert, 1993). Goal alignment across levels and multiple stakeholders is critical to successful implementation (Pressman and Wildavsky, 1974). The goals of educational improvement need to be aligned with policies and regulations that exist in the political and economic contexts in which educational systems are embedded. For example, when conflicts or inconsistencies exist among federal, state, and district policies and regulations, the success of district-level educational improvement efforts is hampered (Holland, 1998; Mirel, 1994). Within schools, instructional coherence is a critical predictor of school improvement (Newmann, Smith, Allensworth, and Bryk, 2001).

3. *Collaborations and partnerships are critical to educational improvement, but they are hard work.* Principles 1 and 2 imply that successful educational improvement must be a collaboration among organizations

and individuals with a variety of perspectives, areas of expertise, cultures, norms, and operating procedures. As in any multicultural situation, opportunities for misunderstanding and miscommunication abound. For example, the word *improvement* can mean different things to a district superintendent, a learning scientist, and a local businessperson. But participants have to establish a culture of collaboration and mutual respect, and develop shared meanings, goals, and norms for interaction. This process takes a great deal of effort to launch and then to sustain (Little, Gearhart, Curry, and Kafka, 2003).

4. *Educational improvement efforts need to be studied and documented, so that they can contribute to the development of a systematic knowledge base about efforts to innovate, scale up innovations, and then sustain them.* Implementation efforts are a natural setting for use-oriented research (Stokes, 1997). Studying and documenting implementation efforts provides a systematic basis for identifying key principles that undergird success and those that create barriers to instructional transformations (Murphy and Hallinger, 1993). Such a knowledge base can help address one of the commonly cited reasons for failures to sustain and scale change: insufficient attention to situational variations in educational systems and differences across schools, districts, and regions (Elmore, 1995; Fullan, 2002; Fullan and Miles, 1992). Improved understanding of circumstances that facilitate and impede change can be fed into the design of future efforts to promote and sustain educational improvements.

Principles of Organizational Change

Organizations are composed of individuals for whom roles and responsibilities are defined in the context of an overall management structure and organizational culture. That culture is often unresponsive to changing conditions and new challenges, a situation that can threaten the very existence of the organization. Senge (1990) argued that organizations, including educational institutions, in contrast to traditional organizations, need the capacity to learn: to be generative and create new ways of looking at themselves, planning, and making decisions (Senge, 1999, 2000). Generativity depends on opportunities for individual and team learning through inquiry into current models and assumptions, shared vision, and systems thinking. The design principles for organizational change derive from Senge's analysis of learning organizations.

5. *The core of educational improvement is building human capacity for effective performance at all levels of the educational system, but especially*

at those levels most proximal to students. For students to learn and achieve, they must have access to effective learning opportunities. In turn, effective instruction, instructional leadership, and administration depend on teachers and principals having content knowledge, pedagogical content knowledge, and material resources that enable effective instruction, including resources for assessment (Darling-Hammond, 1998; Desimone, 2002; Little, 1993; Senk and Thompson, 2003). Assessment must be aligned with curriculum and instruction as well as with external accountability systems (Webb, 1997). Knowledgeable and supportive leadership at both district and school levels is critical (Elmore 1996; Fullan, 2002; Senge, 2000).

6. *Change is initiated, sustained, and carried through systems by people.* In many cases of successful educational improvement, there is a key individual without whom the reform would not have succeeded (Chapters One and Three of this volume; Honey, McMillan-Culp, and Carrigg, 1999). Such change leaders engage with others in ongoing inquiry into teaching and learning, creating new cohorts of change leaders. This process builds a culture of collaborative inquiry that gradually spreads throughout the system, expanding its capacity as a whole.

7. *Social structures such as learning communities, practitioners' networks, and study groups can facilitate change.* Social interactions in which individuals share their thinking can facilitate changes in thinking and facilitate learning (Brown and Campione, 1990, 1996; Gauvain and Rogoff, 1989; Mugny, Perret-Clermont, and Doise, 1981; Rogoff and Toma, 1997; Vygotsky, 1981). Different views are expressed, and ideas are challenged and questioned, pushing individuals to examine, explore, and explain their own thinking and ideas (Anderson and others, 2001; Kuhn, 1992; Kuhn, Shaw, and Felton, 1997; Vye and others, 1997). Such efforts to explain one's thinking and resolve inconsistencies are the kind of thinking that lead to deep conceptual change (Carey, 1985).

Through collaborative inquiry, teachers have opportunities to participate in learning experiences that parallel effective student learning experiences. Collaborative inquiry also provides a supportive context for sustained reflection on teaching practices and student understanding (Cochran-Smith and Lytle, 1999; Darling-Hammond and Ball, 1997; Louis, Kruse, and Bryk, 1995; Lieberman, 1996; Little, 1993; Little, Gearhart, Curry, and Kafka, 2003; McLaughlin, 1993; Reiser and others, 2000).

Principles of Individual Change

Within their organizations, individuals can be agents of change who act upon the systems in which they are embedded (Adams, 2000; Senge,

1990). To do so, they need learning experiences that facilitate the development of knowledge of content, content-related pedagogy, and assessment; opportunities to try new practices and reflect on them; and organizational contexts that support these efforts on an ongoing and extended basis. The design principles in this cluster elaborate on these themes.

8. *Educational practitioners need opportunities to learn with understanding, so that they grasp the principles of educational improvement efforts and not just the practices and procedures.* Teachers' and administrators' knowledge of content, content-related pedagogy, and assessment must go beyond surface-level enactment of procedures and routines. According to a recent National Research Council publication on how people learn (Donovan, Bransford, and Pellegrino, 1999), learning with understanding means that facts, ideas, and instructional routines are located in a conceptual framework and organized in meaningful patterns. These patterns facilitate retrieval and application in situations different from the context of the original learning. Learning with understanding leads to usable knowledge that is flexible, that can be adapted to meet the needs of diverse students, and that can work with a variety of instructional materials and assessments. In short, usable knowledge makes sense.

9. *Inquiry-based approaches to professional development build knowledge that makes sense.* Inquiry-based approaches to how students learn and what it takes to support and foster that learning help teachers develop knowledge about teaching and learning that makes sense to them (Anders and Richardson, 1994; Cochran-Smith and Lytle, 1999; National Research Council, 2000; Zech and others, 2000). Important processes in inquiry include developing questions, gathering evidence, and reflecting on what the evidence indicates about instructional decision making and further inquiry questions.

Educators are more willing to invest in inquiry and reflection when they see it as relevant to problems of practice and the realities of their schools and classrooms (Anders and Richardson, 1994; Cochran-Smith and Lytle, 1999; Franke, Fennema, and Carpenter, 1997; Zech and others, 2000). There are multiple ways of grounding inquiry in problems of practice—for example, through the design and adaptation of curriculum units, the design of authentic tasks, the analysis of student work, and the development and design of assessments for learning. Where inquiry begins matters less than reaching the desired outcome: inquiry into all facets of learning and teaching.

The inquiry process transforms the way teachers think and learn about their own teaching and learning as well as their students' learning. The process often surfaces tacit theories of learning and epistemological beliefs that are reflected in daily practice (Gause-Vega, 1999; Hofer and Pintrich, 1997). Examining students' understanding in content domains serves as a catalyst for teachers' critical reflection and examination of their own content knowledge and practice. This reflection often leads to self-initiated changes in how they support their students' learning.

10. *Changes in thinking and practice come about through hard work in a context that provides opportunities to try out changes in the classroom and to receive feedback and coaching.* Learners' interpretations of new information depend heavily on their prior beliefs and knowledge (Spillane, Reiser, and Reimer, 2003). There is an overwhelming tendency to assimilate new information to fit current orientations, reject it outright, or fail to notice it at all (Chinn and Brewer, 1993; Piaget, 1970; Rumelhart, 1980; Schank and Abelson, 1977). Learners are most likely to overcome these forms of resistance when they have repeated opportunities to wrestle with information that violates their expectations (Piaget, 1970; Schank, 1986), especially when these opportunities occur over time. For fundamental knowledge restructuring to occur, what is needed is "sustained engagement with a sequence of problematic ideas and an explicit goal of making sense of them and reconsidering what is already 'known'" (Spillane, Reiser, and Reimer, 2003, p. 398).

This process occurs in lesson study, a type of professional development described by Stiegler and Hiebert (1999). One teacher is observed by her colleagues as she enacts a collaboratively planned lesson. In follow-up collaborative reflection on the enacted lesson, the teachers confront discrepancies between lesson plans and expectations and the actual enactments of those plans. Puzzling over the discrepancies may contribute to revisions in lesson plans as well as in teachers' theories of practice. Collaborative discussions also provide opportunities for feedback, a central process in learning (National Research Council, 2000).

Lesson study provides one form of feedback; classroom-based coaching provides another. In classroom-based coaching, teachers get immediate feedback on their efforts to put general principles into operation in their classroom. Coaches observe, facilitate, and provide constructive and immediate feedback to teachers on their attempts to implement new forms of practice. Teachers also need administrators who can tolerate efforts to enact new forms of practice and provide supportive rather than punitive feedback (Elmore, 1996, 1997).

Although they are powerful, changes in thinking and practice not only require hard work but also take time. Thus, it should not be surprising that sustainable changes in knowledge, beliefs, and practices are estimated to take three to five years (Ball and Rundquist, 1993; Cochran-Smith and Lytle, 1999; Hawley and Valli, 1999).

Summary of Design Principles

The ten design principles reflect the complexity of educational improvement processes. Change must permeate every level of a complex system in consistent and coordinated ways over extended periods of time. What happens for students in classrooms depends on individual changes in practices as well as willingness to reflect on the changes and their impact on student understanding. The willingness of individuals to engage in this process depends on how their organization stimulates and reacts to such efforts (Adams, 2000). Learning organizations provide contexts that encourage, facilitate, and support collaborative inquiry and individual change.

An Illustrative Case of Educational Improvement: Schools for Thought

My own thinking on principles that must underlie educational improvement efforts if they are to be sustainable and scalable is based on my participation in one such improvement effort while I was on the faculty at the Learning Technology Center at Vanderbilt University. This effort began in 1993 as a collaboration among several research teams from different institutions and the teachers and school districts with which they each worked. The Nashville version, dubbed Schools for Thought, was subsequently funded to scale up through a Department of Education Technology Innovations Challenge Grant from 1996 to 2001. In this section, I summarize that effort, focusing on the major lessons learned about design principles for educational improvement.

Schools for Thought

In 1993, the James S. McDonnell Foundation funded a small collaborative pilot project for the purpose of developing a research-based curriculum for a new science and math magnet school set to open in St. Louis in 1996. The collaboration brought together three teams of researchers who had been designing innovative learning environments in mathematics, literacy, and science inquiry (Brown and Campione, 1994; Cognition and Technology Group at Vanderbilt, 1994; Scardamalia, Bereiter, and Lamon, 1994). All three projects emphasized problem solving, in-depth study of authentic problems through student research, building on children's thinking, and the integration of technology as a tool for learning (Lamon and others, 1996; Williams and others, 1998). In Nashville, the pilot project began as a collaboration of teachers and researchers who worked toward integrating the principles of the three programs in curriculum units and instructional practices that shifted the focus of instruction from memorizing facts to learning that addressed challenges, dilemmas, and "big questions" in four content areas (Secules, Cottom, Bray, and Miller, 1997). Although initially the project focused on teaching and learning processes at the classroom level, by early 1995, the implementation efforts were informed by research on the political and sociological contexts of education and educational innovation (McLaughlin and Talbert, 1993; Mirel, 1994).

The Evolution of Schools for Thought

Schools for Thought (SFT) was an active educational improvement effort in Nashville Public Schools until 2002. Three clear phases in the development and implementation of SFT can be identified on the basis of major shifts in funding, scale, or governance.

PHASE 1, SUMMER 1993–SUMMER 1996. During phase 1, SFT was a pilot project supported by grants from foundations and Peabody College resources. It grew from two sixth-grade classrooms to thirteen sixth-, seventh-, and eighth-grade classrooms distributed over four schools. University staff provided a variety of in-classroom support for teachers, including modeling SFT participation structures and providing content and technology support, as well as professional development outside the classroom. The amount of in-classroom support decreased as the number of teachers increased, from full-time support for each teacher in 1993–1994 to half a day each day in 1994–1995, to several half-days per week in 1995–1996. Professional development outside the classroom was oriented toward collaborative development of curriculum units by teachers and university SFT staff. The units embodied "big ideas" in the content areas in ways that addressed the district curriculum objectives. (For details, see Lamon et al., 1996; Secules, Cottom, Bray, and Miller, 1997.)

Over the three-year period, unit development increasingly emphasized assessment of student learning before, during, and on completion of the units. In addition, SFT staff developed complex performance assessments of writing, reading comprehension, and mathematics in order to have a means of determining whether children participating in SFT were acquiring the skills and competencies specifically fostered by participation in SFT to a greater degree than students not participating in the program. During the three-year pilot phase, performance on tests administered by SFT staff as well as performance on standardized achievement tests demonstrated that participating in the SFT program had a positive impact. These data, in conjunction with the ways that technology was being used in the classrooms, contributed to the Nashville Public Schools' successfully competing for federal support for scaling up through a Technology Innovations Challenge Grant, awarded in fall 1996.

PHASE 2, FALL 1996–SUMMER 1999. The Technology Innovations Challenge Grant was a five-year grant awarded to the Nashville school district for purposes of scaling up SFT across grades K–8. The grant provided approximately $1 million per year but required substantial matching funds, which were met largely by school district commitments (equipment, substantial in-service funds for professional development) and in-kind contributions from the university (faculty and staff time funded by foundation grants). The challenge grant funding covered five positions to be hired by the school district (one director, two professional developers, and two technology support people) and devoted exclusively to SFT. The university provided subcontracted professional development services and student assessment services, but the grant also required a clear plan for a transition from university-based to district-based expertise in professional development.

During phase 2, SFT expanded to sixty teachers (sixty classrooms), distributed over twenty-five schools and grades K–8. The university-based evaluation research yielded longitudinal data that suggested a neutral or positive impact of SFT participation on standardized test scores, with improvement most noticeable in the early grades. The university also surveyed two randomly drawn parent samples. One sample comprised parents of children who were participating in SFT, and the other consisted of parents of children who were not participating in SFT but were attending the same schools and grade levels as the SFT students. The survey showed that the parents whose children were participating in SFT noticed more positive changes in their children than did parents whose children were not participating.

Phase 2 differed from phase 1 on several contextual dimensions, including the composition of the school board, key personnel (the director of schools resigned and a new director was appointed from within the school system), and policy (new curriculum and accountability guidelines were adopted). In addition, toward the end of phase 2, Nashville achieved unitary status (which meant that it was relieved of court supervision and could make student assignments without external approval) with a new school improvement plan for achieving racial balance in the schools. The plan called for reorganization of school building configurations and attendance patterns and massive staff reassignments to different schools and different grade levels. These changes, as well as the increased numbers of teachers in the SFT program, altered the emphasis and model of professional development from a focus on developing and implementing units to one of engaging in collaborative inquiry into student understanding. Details of this metamorphosis are discussed later in this chapter.

PHASE 3, FALL 1999–SUMMER 2002. Fall 1999 marked the beginning of the fourth year of the challenge grant and the planned transition of major responsibility for professional development from university-based staff to school district staff and teachers. University staff worked with a cadre of experienced SFT teachers to help them develop skill at facilitating and coaching their peers by using a collaborative inquiry model (Bray, Goldman, and Zech, 2001; Goldman, Zech, and Bray, 2001; Zech and Bray, 2001). In the fifth year of the grant, these teachers took over major responsibility for organizing professional development and facilitating teachers' inquiry. Practical considerations limited the role of teacher facilitators to outside-the-classroom meetings of the school and SFT communities. SFT expanded by approximately forty classroom teachers in each of years four and five and by an additional fifty in a no-cost extension year (2001–2002).

A third-party evaluation study that compared classrooms participating in SFT with nonparticipating classrooms within the same school indicated several differences (Ross, Lowther, and Plants, 2000). There were differences in interactions (more student discussion, higher-level questioning and feedback, and more coaching of students by teachers in SFT classrooms); the organization of learning activities (more project-based learning, work centers, and cooperative learning in SFT classrooms); and use of computers (less use for drill and practice but more for locating resources in SFT classrooms).

During phase 3, the first phase of the school improvement plan was enacted, reconfiguring schools and moving principals and teachers all over the district. Mayoral and school board elections resulted in a different constellation of individuals in policy-making positions (1999–2000), the director of schools retired (2001), and a new director of schools was hired from outside the district (2001–2002). A performance audit conducted by order of the mayor in fall 2000 and released in spring 2001 recommended increased funding for schools generally; it also specifically recommended that the SFT program be expanded systemwide, based on its singular success with respect to integrating technology with instruction and learning (reported in the newspaper *The Tennessean*, April 30, 2001).

After a one-year, no-cost extension, federal funding for SFT ended in September 2002, and the SFT program was discontinued, audit recommendations notwithstanding. The remaining SFT-related district staff were reassigned to other departments and roles in the district.

Lessons Learned

We learned many lessons from the effort to develop, scale up, and sustain SFT. In this chapter, only two of those lessons can be developed in any depth, but short descriptions of others are provided. The two discussed in detail had the most pervasive impact on the work and have the broadest implications for understanding the dynamics of educational improvement, scaling up, and success. The first addresses principles of organizational change and the larger process of educational improvement. The second relates to professional development approaches that support individual learning in ways consistent with what we know about how people learn (National Research Council, 2000).

A Lesson About the Process of Educational Change

Education is as much about politics as it is about learning, assessment, and instruction. This simple sentence summarizes a series of changes in the systemic context that had profound effects on the evolution of SFT. These changes reflected the confluence of a complex set of economic, historical, organizational, and personal as well as political factors. The governance structure in Nashville provides an elected school board with each of the nine members representing a different geographic area of the district. The board is responsible for preparing and managing the district's budget and for all hiring decisions, including the one for the director of schools (in Nashville, the superintendent is called the director of schools). However, the mayor and the city council must approve the school budget and appropriate the funds. In 1992, the board hired a new director who viewed himself as a change agent. The new director replaced a thirty-year veteran of the Nashville school system, who retired after serving in that role for eleven years.

The new director was faced with two major mandates: (1) to secure increased funding for capital as well as instructional improvement, and (2) to develop a plan to take Nashville to unitary status, relieving the district of court oversight of desegregation. The majority of Nashville schools were in dire need of repair and refurbishing, with most campuses using portable classrooms to accommodate enrollments. The effect of court-ordered busing, in place since 1971, was that there were almost no neighborhood schools. Students could apply to attend various magnet schools, but parents had to provide transportation. The distribution of grade levels to schools (K; 1–4; 5–6; 7–8; 9–12) meant that students often attended five different schools over the course of their K–12 education. The director, working with central staff and members of the community, developed a plan called Commitment to the Future, intended to accomplish both the capital improvement and desegregation goals. This complex, multifaceted plan involved building new schools, mainly in inner-city neighborhoods; upgrading facilities at a number of existing schools; creating a number of magnet schools with district-supplied transportation; and putting in place a more progressive instructional program. Most of these aims—release from court oversight, retention of systemwide racial diversity, shorter bus rides, fewer schools for each child to attend, smaller classes, more academic choice, and improved student achievement—had wide appeal.

THE SYSTEMIC CONTEXT: SFT PHASE 1 (1993–1996). During phase 1, the systemic context was generally supportive of educational innovation and the SFT program in particular. The director of schools and the school board were supportive, having adopted a district strategic plan that included a goal of creating a learning community, thereby offering a safe context for examining and questioning current practices (Carter and O'Neill, 1995; Holland, 1998; Murphy and Hallinger, 1993; Pressman and Wildavsky, 1974; Sarason, 1982; Senge, 1990, 1999; Wilson and Berne, 1999). Commitment to the Future called for student achievement in areas identified by the U.S. Department of Labor's SCANS report (Secretary's Commission on Achieving Necessary Skills, 1992) as critical for the twenty-first century workforce, such as teamwork, problem solving, and competence with technology. The similarity of those skills to skills emphasized in SFT was clear to the school board as well as the business community. The district was able to take advantage of a state program that provided funding for computer technology.

On an ongoing basis, the SFT pilot project expansion was facilitated by the director of schools and key central office personnel who secured the technology for SFT classrooms. Parents, businesses, and others in the community were supportive of the kinds of experiences children were having in SFT classrooms and were positive about the changes they were noticing in students (Fullan, 1999; Mirel, 1994; Senge, 1999). University staff met regularly with the director of schools and key senior staff to discuss issues of educational improvement beyond the specific SFT pilot, an activity that led to the development of the grant proposal that resulted in the Technology Innovations Challenge Grant award.

CHANGES IN THE SYSTEMIC CONTEXT: SFT PHASE 2 (1996–1999).
Phase 2 was marked by changes in the composition of the school board
and in the funding stream for SFT. Taken together, these created a more
contentious context for SFT. The August 1996 election resulted in a new
board member who described himself as "not easy to please." "We are
going to storm," he said. He considered himself an advocate for improving education for all children, but his method was confrontational.
"Sometimes you've got to kick people to get their attention," he said.
"That's just my personality." He advocated teaching the basics, questioned
any program that emphasized thinking or critical thinking skills, and was,
in his own words, "the board's loudest critic and foe of the board-
approved desegregation plan." He viewed the director of schools as an
advocate for nontraditional instructional programs and subjected district
staff supportive of these programs to belligerent questioning at school
board meetings. His views about SFT were clear; he called the program
"trendy." "It is absolutely not about academic achievement," he said,
arguing that SFT failed to teach the basics (*The Tennessean*, August 2,
1996, and February 11, 1997).

The addition of this voice to the school board was followed two
months later by the award of the federal Technology Innovations Challenge Grant to the district. This award meant that all SFT expenditures
(equipment, positions, and subcontracts) had to be reviewed and
approved by the school board. School board meetings became a public
forum for this new board member to voice his opposition to the program.

During the same time period, the mayor criticized the Commitment to
the Future plan for being too far-reaching and too expensive. Contempo-
raneous with the school board's approval of the plan, the mayor praised
the director's educational vision but described the plan as "a grand design
but hardly a solution when you consider how much money it would take
to fund it. I'm not trying to denigrate the board's work, but they have
dumped the most difficult problem of my term in my lap, and there's a lot
more hard work still to be done" (*The Tennessean*, July 24, 1996).
Nevertheless, throughout the next six months, the director continued
discussions with the mayor aimed at securing the necessary approval
and support for the initiative with its required major capital investment.
The director of schools felt committed to seeing it through: "I feel an obligation to the community to follow through on this very substantial
blueprint for change, to see it funded and implemented. There is a
moment here—with this board, this mayor, this council. We have until June
[1997] to seize the moment, to take the first big step" (*The Tennessean*,
July 24, 1996).

In addition to the political and economic issues involving the municipal government, the director and school board were involved in negotiating a new contract with the teachers union, specifically focused on a requested salary increase. Negotiations became increasingly confrontational and personally targeted at the director of schools. For example, at one point, the teachers union attacked his trustworthiness. The director shared with us his feelings that the personal and vehement nature of the attacks was not only inappropriate but very hurtful to him and his family. He wasn't sure he could get beyond them.

The culmination of these economic, political, and personal issues was that in early January, the director announced that he was considering another director of schools position, and by the end of January, he announced that he was leaving, effective in mid-March. During the director's lame-duck period, the mayor stepped into the leadership vacuum in the school district and put together his own educational agenda, tying its adoption to approval of an adequate budget for the school system. The mayor proposed districtwide implementation of E. D. Hirsch's Core Knowledge Curriculum in grades K–6, to begin in August—just six months away. Guidelines provided by the Core Knowledge Foundation lay out specific and sequenced sets of facts and concepts that children should know at each grade level for each area of the curriculum, month by month. Despite discussion and debate about the wisdom of such rapid deployment, lack of evidence regarding the effectiveness of Core Knowledge in a district as large as Nashville, its assumption that children start at the same place and learn at the same pace, and a district staff that thought that the district already had a good curriculum, the board adopted a resolution that called for using Hirsch's sequence as a starting point to amend the curriculum of the Nashville schools (April 22, 1997). The process began immediately and was completed over five consecutive Saturday meetings in May 1997, by teams made up of a principal and five teachers (one team per grade level). For their participation, the educators received consultant payments authorized by the board.

Over the same period of time, the mayor garnered support for funding the plan. In his State of Metro address (April 1, 1997), titled "Creating a World-Class Public School System: A Back-to-Basics Approach," the mayor called for infusing the school system with a "rigorous, detailed curriculum that sets high expectations for all students." The goal was to establish a common core curriculum that would provide consistency across schools and a level playing field so that every fourth grader in every school would be studying exactly the same curriculum at the same time, while allowing teachers flexibility to try different methods of teaching.

(The staff of the Core Knowledge Foundation claim that they indicate what to teach, not how to teach it.) To fund the program, the mayor would be requesting a tax hike to provide 204 new art and music teachers, 236 new classroom teachers, $191 million in capital improvements, and $400 in pocket money for each teacher to purchase resources needed to implement the new curriculum. Ultimately, a tax increase was approved but for less than half the amount that the mayor had originally proposed. Nevertheless, the school board had adopted Core Knowledge, and it was to be implemented immediately.

The implementation of Core Knowledge made it difficult for other educational improvement projects to continue, because of the very specific and sequenced character of the curriculum guidelines. This was especially true for programs like SFT; its curricula did not fit into the Core Knowledge sequence. As SFT staff worked with teachers to develop new units around the Core Knowledge objectives, they realized that many teachers had a limited grasp of the underlying principles of SFT; the SFT professional development team therefore began rethinking their approach. The result moved away from developing curricula and toward understanding "big ideas" in the content areas, students as learners, assessment, and the role of community in fostering learning (Zech and others, 2000). I elaborate on this in discussing the second set of lessons we learned, those about professional development and teacher learning.

The systemic changes were both traumatic and gut-wrenching for those of us who were personally involved. However, SFT was successfully adapted to these changes, with significant benefits to the program, including a greater appreciation for the multiple goals and perspectives that bear on district-level program decisions, the need for alignment across multiple levels of the system, and the importance of flexibility in implementation.

Lessons About Professional Development and Teacher Learning

In brief, lessons we learned about professional development are consistent with the experiences of others (for example, Hawley and Valli, 1999). Engagement with teachers regarding educational improvement efforts needs to address content knowledge, pedagogical content knowledge, and epistemological orientation. In doing so, it needs to address dilemmas of practice, and it needs to occur in or be close to teachers' contexts of use—that is, their classrooms. Professional development also needs to take place within organizational structures that enable teachers to learn with their peers.

By the end of the SFT project, we had a developed a professional development model called Content-Based Collaborative Inquiry (CBCI) (Zech and others, 2000). We organized professional development sessions as teacher learning communities, although they often included principals as well. The dialectic provided a rich context for learning that was connected to the realities of classrooms and schools. Engagement with colleagues' ideas stimulated examination and deepening of individuals' thinking. Content of the sessions was designed to engage participants in inquiring into their own understanding of content areas, student understanding in content areas, and the implications of both for instructional practices. We often used student work samples to anchor the conversations, because this focus has been shown to deepen teachers' own understanding in content domains (Cobb, Wood, and Yackel, 1990; Franke, Fennema, and Carpenter, 1997; Little, Gearhart, Curry, and Kafka, 2003; Pennell and Firestone, 1996; Rosebery and Warren, 1998; Schifter and Fosnot, 1993). Sometimes teachers contributed these work samples; at other times, professional development staff selected them. A second type of content for the sessions was reflection on the session itself—how we had learned together, what had facilitated learning, what had not. Periodically, groups of teachers would analyze cases of learning communities that we developed and brought in for the specific purpose of generating conversation about the characteristics and functioning of productive learning communities. By reflecting on the sessions themselves, we hoped the teachers would develop new ways to talk about content, student thinking, and their own knowledge of content and pedagogy (Anders and Richardson, 1994; Ball and Cohen, 1999; Richardson, 1990; Rosebery and Warren, 1998; Wilson, Lubienski, and Mattson, 1996). This is not where we started, however.

In 1993, we began the SFT project in the "knowledge in practice" mode (Cochran-Smith and Lytle, 1999), which involved working with teachers to develop curriculum units that would embody the foundational practices and principles of SFT. However, as the number of teachers grew, we could not sustain the kind of in-depth work we had done with the initial teachers, and of necessity, our work with teachers was far more limited. Especially during their first year in SFT, many teachers new to SFT took the already developed units and attempted to mimic the experienced SFT teachers, who were perceived as "doing it right." Surface-level implementations often resulted. Questions were focused on how to teach this or that concept; what resources were needed for a particular unit and where they could be obtained; and whether they were doing it "right." Not surprisingly, teachers related to SFT curriculum units in much the same way that they related to every other new curriculum. Our intention was that as we scaled up, new SFT teachers would actively examine and revise existing SFT curriculum units and thereby come to understand the underlying principles of the content domain, student learning, and assessment. However, only some of the teachers engaged with the curriculum units in this way, in part because as the number of teachers grew, we had to scale back the amount of time for which teachers were released from their classrooms to attend professional development. In the time allotted, the press of planning for the next unit made it difficult to devote time to reflecting on how current units were going or how past units had gone.

In 1996, when district-mandated curriculum changes made it necessary to adapt SFT curriculum units to new scope and sequence requirements, we realized that the focus on developing curriculum units had not led to sufficient understanding of the foundational principles of SFT for teachers to successfully adapt the units (Cognition and Technology Group at Vanderbilt, 2000). Indeed, when we initially attempted to refocus professional development on student understanding in content areas, we found that many SFT teachers had not made a shift away from defining content understanding as the execution of procedures and skills and the accumulation of facts and toward underlying concepts and principles in the content area. Also, as we scaled up SFT to include more teachers and cover more grade levels, there were simply too many units to develop; we could not continue using the curriculum development model with which we had been working.

To deal with these issues of scale and understanding, we ourselves engaged in in-depth reflection on our professional development model, what we had learned from an orientation based on curriculum units, and the results of listening to and observing the teachers both in professional development sessions and in their classrooms. Our group consisted of individuals with different areas of expertise (mathematics, science, social studies, reading and language, learning and developmental sciences, organizational development, teacher education, and school administration), and together we probed what we wanted teachers to focus on and how we could create professional development experiences that would enable this focus. We examined models that others engaged in reform projects were using and the kinds of learning goals they established (for example, Anders and Richardson, 1994; Cobb, Wood, and Yackel, 1990; Franke, Fennema, and Carpenter, 1997; Pappas and Zecker, 1998; Rosebery and Warren, 1998; Schifter and Fosnot, 1993). We decided that we wanted teachers to focus on what students were understanding (a focus on students), what evidence they might look at to understand what students were understanding (assessment), what they wanted students to understand (teachers' knowledge of content understanding), and how to develop instruction and instructional tasks that would make it possible for students to get there (instruction). To engage these issues, we thought teachers needed opportunities to explore their initial ideas about what it meant to understand in math, science, reading, or social studies. We knew that many of them thought of learning in the content areas in traditional ways, so we also wanted to create opportunities for teachers to develop different ways of thinking about content area understanding and learning processes. Finally, for purposes of sustaining the reform effort and an infrastructure for continuing to learn, we added the goal of developing teacher learning communities.

The Content-Based Collaborative Inquiry model reflects a view of teachers' professional learning that is consistent with "knowledge of practice" (Cochran-Smith and Lytle, 1999): in CBCI, teachers engage in inquiry and construct their own knowledge by focusing on student understanding in specific content areas. The knowledge they build represents content, pedagogical content, and general pedagogy (Shulman, 1986) that supports learning with understanding. Through this model, teachers inquired into their own understanding of specific content areas, their students' learning and understanding in specific content areas, and their own teaching and assessment practices (Zech and Bray, 2001; Zech and others, 2000). Inquiry was grounded in the dilemmas they faced in their classrooms, often arising from their own observations and conversations about them with the SFT coaches who visited their classrooms. Some of these issues were discussed at school-site meetings or at cross-site meetings that brought together principals and teachers involved in the SFT project. SFT staff and teacher facilitators ran these meetings during phase 3. At school-site and cross-site meetings, SFT staff facilitated the development of a culture of inquiring together, characterized by being able to disagree and question one another and one's own beliefs and conceptions for the purpose of enhancing the understanding of students, content, instruction, learning, and assessment (Goldman, Zech, and Bray, 2001; Zech and others, 2000). Curriculum materials came into the picture as a result of teachers' inquiry into what it meant to understand a mathematical operation, a historical event, a cause-effect relationship, or patterns in oral or written language. When teachers came to the point of looking for materials that would challenge their students' thinking, the availability of materials that would support this was invaluable.

Additional Lessons Learned

We learned many other important lessons through the SFT project. These lessons speak to the importance of systemic, individual, and research dimensions of educational improvement. Of these, three seem most important to mention briefly here.

PEOPLE MAKE THE DIFFERENCE. At several crucial points in the evolution of SFT, specific individuals made the difference with respect to the fate of SFT. Key among them was the director of schools from 1992 to 1997. His support and commitment to the instruction and learning he saw occurring through SFT created a "safety zone" and garnered support among members of the school board. He advocated for the development of complex performance assessments and their use in conjunction with standardized tests for making accountability determinations. The director's belief in his own need to learn led to the formation of a learning community that was instrumental in developing the proposal for the challenge grant. The director's support made it possible for the director of library, media, and technology services to make sure that SFT classrooms had the technology they needed and to fully and actively support the scaling up of SFT. She served as the communications link between the SFT project and the director of schools. She was always available to talk with university-based SFT staff, assisted with problem solving, and served as liaison with other central office personnel. Finally, she was responsible for coordinating and preparing the challenge grant application for submission.

During phase 2, new forms of interpersonal relationships played a central role in garnering and maintaining support for the continuation of the challenge grant. The director of the SFT program had been in the district for over twenty-five years, had worked with many of the principals and central office staff, and knew several of the board members. During phase 2, she adopted a strategy of inviting and personally escorting individual board members to visit SFT classrooms that were located in their area of the district. Invariably, these visits created friends for SFT.

Finally, relationships among teachers and the quality of the teacher learning community played key roles in enlarging and sustaining the innovation. During phase 1, seeing what the students participating in SFT were doing and how they were engaging with school caused several teachers to seek to become part of the SFT program. During phase 2, we found that the quality of the school community at a site was positively correlated with teacher progress in understanding the SFT approach (as assessed by facilitator ratings) (Goldman and Bray, 1999).

EVALUATION DATA ARE IMPORTANT, BUT SOMETIMES THEY DO NOT SEEM TO MATTER. Throughout the development and scaling up of SFT, university staff developed, collected, and analyzed performance data and standardized test data that were obtained from the school system. These data showed benefits and value added to the educational experiences of students in SFT classrooms. At the request of the school board, we conducted longitudinal analyses of standardized test scores both for students after they left SFT classrooms and, when possible, for students over multiple years in SFT classrooms. (Only a small number of students experienced more than two consecutive years of SFT, in part because the director of schools wished to spread the program far and wide in the district and in part due to teacher mobility.) These data were neutral to positive for SFT. In the face of these findings, the "storming" member of the school board accused the university researchers of not including all the relevant data, in order to make our data look better. (This was not the case.) It is difficult to judge the impact of these data. On one hand, the "stormer" always criticized SFT, regardless of the data; on the other, the board did not rescind permission for the program to operate and carry out the grant. It did, in fact, approve all of the position and equipment purchase requests made by the program.

Two independent evaluations of the program reflected very favorably on what SFT was accomplishing for teachers, students, and the system (Ross, Lowther, and Plants, 2000; *The Tennessean,* April 30, 2001). Although the SFT community was pleased, in the broader context, the results seemed to confirm positive attitudes and leave the negative ones unchanged. These evaluations did not result in the institutionalization of SFT.

EARMARKED FUNDING OVER A SUFFICIENT PERIOD OF TIME PROVIDED CONTINUITY AND A BASIS FOR ESTABLISHING EDUCATORS' TRUST AND SUPPORT. The SFT project was fortunate in having continuous funding over an eight-year period. The five years of challenge grant funding were particularly important in protecting the scaling-up process. Staff at school sites knew that there was a multiyear commitment to a change process and resources to support and facilitate that process. This grant also provided technology support staff in sufficient numbers that SFT teachers felt secure in the knowledge that if equipment was not working, it would get fixed quickly. In addition, SFT staff could develop multiyear plans for recruiting new sites, focusing some years on restricted grade levels (such as K–2) and others on broader spans (such as 3–6).

Lessons Learned from SFT and the Design Principles

The lessons that we learned in the SFT context are very similar to those learned by others engaged in reform and improvement efforts. The set of design principles proposed here attempts to guide future educational improvement efforts by making use of lessons from the past. A central assumption of all of the principles is that contemporary educational improvement efforts are about making change in the underlying fabric of educational systems, not merely in surface manifestations. Accomplishing underlying change that will be long-lasting requires participant ownership of the reform process, not just the reform practice. Addressing the ownership challenge entails professional development models that build the capacity within individuals and organizations to engage in ongoing inquiry into teaching and learning for purposes of identifying what is working well and where change might be needed. Building this capacity serves as the basis for perpetuation and reinvention of principled and effective educational improvement efforts. This is so because educational systems are dynamic rather than static systems: flux is a fact of life, especially in urban areas. High levels of mobility among superintendents, principals, teachers, and students are often the rule rather than the exception. Federal and state policy mandates undergo periodic review and change. In the face of this inevitable but often superficial flux, sustainable educational improvement efforts must adapt to the changing contexts of teaching and learning but not sacrifice the underlying principles of teaching, learning, assessment, and community that are needed to support students in learning with understanding. Building the capacity for inquiry in organizations and individuals acknowledges change as a fact of life and designs for change from the very beginning of educational improvement efforts.

At the same time, these design principles are proposed as a set of hypotheses that await further testing and elaboration. One such effort is under way in Chicago, in the context of an educational improvement effort in reading. At the time that this chapter is being written, the Chicago effort is too young to be used to draw any conclusions about the utility of the design principles.

Issues and Reconsiderations of Scaling Up and Educational Improvement

In concluding, it is useful to examine a kind of "meta-lesson": it is easy for people to use the same words and think that usage means agreement on meaning. This is not a good assumption to make. Educational improvement is complex; it requires bringing together individuals from different disciplinary and professional backgrounds, each with its own norms and language. Coming together as a group focused on a specific educational improvement requires that time be spent negotiating shared meanings or at least surfacing the different meanings that exist among the members of the group.

In the spirit of negotiating meaning, I will close this chapter by considering what we might mean by scaling up. This process can occur along horizontal or vertical dimensions. Horizontal scale means moving the improvement to more students, teachers, schools, districts, and so on. But just as important is vertical scale—going deeper, pursuing more profound understanding and enactment of some improvement strategy, approach, or program. Going deeper may in fact be a requirement for sustaining an educational improvement.

Differences in definitions of scaling up have implications for definitions of success. For some, success and its evidence are to be found only in gains on standardized test scores or in the numbers of teachers, students, schools, or districts involved with the effort, regardless of the quality of enactment. Other stakeholders may have in mind different indicators of success, such as changes in the way teachers relate to one another or to their students. These different meanings may lead stakeholders to posit different and, in some cases, conflicting goals, which in turn compete for limited resources. Failure to negotiate common goals can undermine educational improvement efforts. Goal-related conflicts in reference to a given innovation have long been recognized as a major impediment to enacting and sustaining change (Pressman and Wildavsky, 1974).

There is also something to be learned by examining the assumptions behind the phrase *lessons learned*. We want to avoid the idea that we have acquired a static body of knowledge about what it takes to create and scale educational improvement. On the contrary, we need to regard the lessons as continually being learned. Why? Because even when you have learned something, you must engage the process of applying that knowledge to a new situation. You have to recognize in the new situation the variables and indicators that bear on the lessons you learned in a different context. Because the knowledge is being applied in new situations, we are continually learning new lessons and relearning old ones. How something looks or feels in a new situation in turn enriches knowledge and understanding of that lesson. Thus, we can know that teachers need to be actively involved in some educational improvement effort but completely miss the mark in creating the appropriate context and level of activity. Or we can plan an improvement process that takes heed of known design principles only to have the context change and require adaptation. In other words, even if we have particular lessons and principles in mind, we can't always recognize when our efforts are inconsistent with them. The true challenge of making use of knowledge about educational improvement and scaling processes seems to be maintaining the appropriate balance among fidelity, flexibility, and adaptation.

REFERENCES

Adams, J. E. (2000). *Taking charge of curriculum: Teacher networks and curriculum implementation.* New York: Teachers College Press.

Anders, P. L., & Richardson, V. (1994). Launching a new form of staff development. In V. Richardson (Ed.), *Teacher change and the staff development process: A case in reading instruction* (pp. 1–22). New York: Teachers College Press.

Anderson, R. C., Nghuyen-Jahiel, K., McNurlen, B., Archodidou, A., Kim, S., Reznitskaya, A., Tillmanns, M., & Gilbert, L. (2001). The snowball phenomenon: Spread of ways of talking and ways of thinking across groups of children. *Cognition and Instruction, 19,* 1–46.

Ball, D. L., & Cohen, D. K. (1999). Developing practice, developing practitioners: Toward a practice-based theory of professional education. In L. Darling-Hammond & G. Sykes (Eds.), *Teaching as the learning profession: Handbook of policy and practice* (pp. 3–32). San Francisco: Jossey-Bass.

Ball, D. L., & Rundquist, S. (1993). Collaboration as a context for joining teacher learning with learning about teaching. In D. K. Cohen, M. McLaughlin, & J. Talbert (Eds.), *Teaching for understanding: Challenges for practice, research, and policy* (pp. 13–42). San Francisco: Jossey-Bass.

Bray, M., Goldman, S. R., & Zech, L. (2001, April). *Teacher leadership: Negotiating new understandings.* Paper presented at meeting of the American Educational Research Association, Seattle.

Brown, A. L., & Campione, J. C. (1990). Interactive learning environments and the teaching of science and mathematics. In M. Gardner, J. G. Greeno, F. Reif, A. H. Schoenfeld, A. diSessa, & E. Stage (Eds.), *Toward a scientific practice of science education* (pp. 111–139). Hillsdale, NJ: Erlbaum.

Brown, A. L., & Campione, J. C. (1994). Guided discovery in a community of learners. In K. McGilly (Ed.), *Classroom lessons: Integrating cognitive theory and classroom practice* (pp. 229–270). Cambridge, MA: MIT Press.

Brown, A. L., & Campione, J. C. (1996). Psychological theory and the design of innovative learning environments: On procedures, principles, and systems. In L. Shauble & R. Glaser (Eds.), *Innovations in learning: New environments for education* (pp. 289–325). Mahwah, NJ: Erlbaum.

Carey, S. (1985). *Conceptual change in childhood.* Cambridge, MA: MIT Press.

Carter, D.S.G., & O'Neill, M. H. (1995). *International perspectives on educational reform and policy implementation.* Washington, DC: Falmer Press.

Chinn, C., & Brewer, W. (1993). The role of anomalous data in knowledge acquisition: A theoretical framework and implications for science instruction. *Review of Educational Research, 63,* 1–49.

Cobb, P., Wood, T., & Yackel, E. (1990). Classrooms as learning environments for teachers and researchers. In R. B. Davis, C. A. Mayer, & N. Noddings (Eds.), *Constructivist views on the teaching and learning of mathematics* (pp. 125–146). Reston, VA: National Council of Teachers of Mathematics.

Cochran-Smith, M., & Lytle, S. L. (1999). Relationships of knowledge and practice: Teacher learning in communities. In A. Iran-Nejad and P. D. Pearson (Eds.), *Review of research in education* (pp. 249–305). San Francisco: American Educational Research Association.

Cognition and Technology Group at Vanderbilt. (1994). From visual word problems to learning communities: Changing conceptions of cognitive research. In K. McGilly (Ed.), *Classroom lessons: Integrating cognitive theory and classroom practice* (pp. 157–200). Cambridge, MA: MIT Press.

Cognition and Technology Group at Vanderbilt. (2000). Adventures in anchored instruction: Lessons learned from beyond the ivory tower. In R. Glaser (Ed.), *Advances in instructional psychology* (Vol. 5, pp. 35–99). Mahwah, NJ: Erlbaum.

Darling-Hammond, L. (1998). Strengthening the teaching profession: Teacher learning that supports student learning. *Educational Leadership, 55*(5), 6–11.

Darling-Hammond, L., & Ball, D. L. (1997). *Teaching for high standards: What policymakers need to know and be able to do.* Philadelphia: Consortium for Policy Research in Education, Graduate School of Education, University of Pennsylvania.

Desimone, L. M. (2002). How can comprehensive school reform models be successfully implemented? *Review of Educational Research, 72,* 433–479.

Donovan, S., Bransford, J. D., & Pellegrino, J. W. (1999). *How people learn: Bridging research and practice.* Washington, DC: National Research Council.

Elmore, R. F. (1995). Teaching, learning, and school organization: Principles of practice and the regularities of schooling. *Educational Administration Quarterly, 31,* 355–374.

Elmore, R. F. (1996). Getting to scale with good educational practice. *Harvard Educational Review, 66*(1), 1–26.

Elmore, R. F. (1997). *Investing in teacher learning: Staff development and instructional improvement in Community School District #2, New York City.* New York: National Commission on Teaching and America's Future.

Elmore, R. F. (2002). *Bridging the gap between standards and achievement: The imperative for professional development.* Washington, DC: Albert Shankar Institute.

Franke, M. L., Fennema, E., & Carpenter, T. P. (1997). Teachers creating change: Examining evolving beliefs and classroom practice. In E. Fennema & B. Nelson (Eds.), *Mathematics teachers in transition* (pp. 255–282). Mahwah, NJ: Erlbaum.

Fullan, M. (1999). *Change forces: The sequel.* Philadelphia: Falmer Press.

Fullan, M. (2002). The change leader. *Educational Leadership, 59*(8), 16–20.

Fullan, M. G., & Miles, M. B. (1992). Getting reform right: What works and what doesn't. *Phi Delta Kappan, 73,* 745–752.

Gause-Vega, C. L. (1999). *Epistemological and moral considerations in an unfolding culture of collaborative inquiry: An ethnographic study.* Doctoral dissertation, Peabody College, Vanderbilt University, Nashville, TN.

Gauvain, M., & Rogoff, B. (1989). Collaborative problem solving and children's planning skills. *Developmental Psychology, 25,* 139–151.

Goldman, S. R., & Bray, M. (1999, August). *Learning communities.* Paper presented at the meeting of the European Association for Research on Learning and Instruction, Gotebörg, Sweden.

Goldman, S. R., Zech, L., & Bray, M. (2001, April). *Teachers learning to lead the collaborative inquiry of their peers.* Paper presented at the meeting of the American Educational Research Association, Seattle.

Hawley, W. D., & Valli, L. (1999). The essentials of effective professional development: A new consensus. In L. Darling-Hammond & G. Sykes (Eds.), *Teaching as the learning profession: Handbook of policy and practice* (pp. 127–150). San Francisco: Jossey-Bass.

Hofer, B., & Pintrich, P. (1997). The development of epistemological theories: Beliefs about knowledge and knowing and their relation to learning. *Review of Research in Education, 67*(1), 88–140.

Holland, H. (1998). *Making change: Three educators join the battle for better schools.* Portsmouth, NH: Heinemann.

Honey, M., McMillan-Culp, K., & Carrigg, F. (1999, November/December). Perspectives on technology and education research: Lessons from the past and present. *LNT Perspectives,* no. 12. Available at http://www.edc.org/LNT/news/Issue12/feature1.htm

Kuhn, D. (1992). Thinking as argument. *Harvard Educational Review, 62,* 155–177.

Kuhn, D., Shaw, V., & Felton, M. (1997). Effects of dyadic interaction on argumentative reasoning. *Cognition and Instruction, 15,* 287–315.

Lamon, M., Secules, T., Petrosino, A., Hackett, R., Bransford, J. D., & Goldman, S. R. (1996). Schools for Thought: Overview of the project and lessons learned from one of the sites. In L. Schauble & R. Glaser (Eds.), *Innovations in learning: New environments for education* (pp. 243–288). Mahwah, NJ: Erlbaum.

Lieberman, A. (1996). Practices that support teacher development: Transforming conceptions of professional learning. In M. W. McLaughlin & I. Oberman (Eds.), *Teacher learning: New policies, new practices* (pp. 185–201). New York: Teachers College Press.

Little, J. W. (1993). Teachers' professional development in a climate of educational reform. *Educational Evaluation and Policy Analysis, 15*(2), 129–151.

Little, J. W., Gearhart, M., Curry, M., & Kafka, J. (2003). Looking at student work for teacher learning, teacher community, and school reform. *Phi Delta Kappan, 85*(3), 184–192.

Louis, K. S., Kruse, S., & Bryk, A. (1995). Professionalism and community: What is it and why is it important in urban schools? In K. S. Louis & S. Kruse (Eds.), *Professionalism and community: Strategies for reforming urban schools* (pp. 3–22). Thousand Oaks, CA: Corwin Press.

McLaughlin, M. (1993). What matters most in teachers' workplace context? In J. W. Little & M. McLaughlin (Eds.), *Teachers work* (pp. 79–103). New York: Teachers College Press.

McLaughlin, M. W., & Talbert, J. E. (1993, March). *Contexts that matter for teaching and learning: Strategic opportunities for meeting the nation's educational goals.* Stanford, CA: Center for Research on the Context of Secondary School Teaching, Stanford University.

Mirel, J. (1994). School reform unplugged: The Bensenville New American School Project. *American Educational Research Journal, 31*(3), 481–518.

Mugny, G., Perret-Clermont, A.-N., & Doise, W. (1981). Interpersonal coordinations and social differences in the construction of the intellect. In G. M. Stephenson & J. M. Davis (Eds.), *Progress in applied psychology* (Vol. 1, pp. 315–343). New York: Wiley.

Murphy, J., & Hallinger, P. (1993). *Restructuring schooling: Learning from ongoing efforts.* Newbury Park, CA: Corwin Press.

National Research Council. (2000). *How people learn: Brain, mind, experience, and school.* (J. Bransford, A. L. Brown, & R. R. Cocking, Eds.) Washington, DC: National Academy Press.

Newmann, F. M., Smith, B. S., Allensworth, E., & Bryk, A. S. (2001). Instructional program coherence: What it is and why it should guide school improvement policy. *Educational Evaluation and Policy Analysis, 23*(4), 297–321.

Pappas, C., & Zecker, Z. L. (1998). *Teacher inquiries in literacy teaching-learning: Learning to collaborate in elementary urban classrooms.* Mahwah, NJ: Erlbaum.

Pennell, J. R., & Firestone, W. A. (1996). Changing classroom practices through teacher networks: Matching program features with teacher characteristics and circumstances. *Teachers College Record, 98*(1), 46–76.

Piaget, J. (1970). *Genetic epistemology* (E. Duckworth, Trans.) New York: Columbia University Press.

Pressman, J. L., & Wildavsky, A. B. (1974). *Implementation: How great expectations in Washington are dashed in Oakland.* Berkeley: University of California Press.

Reiser, B. J., Spillane, J. P., Steinmuller, F., Sorsa, D., Carney, K., & Kyza, E. (2000). Investigating the mutual adaptation process in teachers' design of technology-infused curricula. In B. Fishman & S. O'Connor-Divelbiss (Eds.), *Proceedings of the Fourth International Conference of the Learning Sciences* (pp. 342–349). Mahwah, NJ: Erlbaum.

Richardson, V. (1990). Significant and worthwhile change in teaching practice. *Educational Researcher, 19*(7), 10–18.

Rogoff, B., & Toma, C. (1997). Shared thinking: Community and institutional variations. *Discourse Processes, 23,* 471–497.

Rosebery, A., & Warren, B. (Eds.). (1998). *Boats, balloons, and classroom video: Science teaching as inquiry.* Portsmouth, NH: Heinemann.

Ross, S. M., Lowther, D. L., & Plants, R. T. (2000). *Challenge grant evaluation: Final report.* Memphis, TN: University of Memphis.

Rumelhart, D. E. (1980). Schemata: The building blocks of cognition. In R. J. Spiro, B. Bruce, & W. F. Brewer (Eds.), *Theoretical issues in reading and comprehension* (pp. 33–58). Hillsdale, NJ: Erlbaum.

Sarason, S. B. (1982). The *culture of the school and the problem of change* (2nd ed.). Boston: Allyn & Bacon.

Scardamalia, M., Bereiter, C., & Lamon, M. (1994). The CSILE Project: Trying to bring the classroom into World 3. In K. McGilly (Ed.) *Classroom lessons: Integrating cognitive theory and classroom practice* (pp. 201–228). Cambridge, MA: MIT Press.

Schank, R. C. (1986). *Explanation patterns: Understanding mechanically and creatively.* Hillsdale, NJ: Erlbaum.

Schank, R. C., & Abelson, R. P. (1977). *Scripts, plans, goals, and understanding.* Hillsdale, NJ: Erlbaum.

Schifter, D., & Fosnot, C. T. (1993). *Reconstructing mathematics education: Stories of teachers meeting the challenge of reform.* New York: Teachers College Press.

Secretary's Commission on Achieving Necessary Skills. (1992). *Learning a living: A blueprint for high performance, A SCANS report for America 2000.* Washington, DC: U.S. Department of Labor.

Secules, T., Cottom, C., Bray, M. H., & Miller, L. (1997, March). Creating schools for thought. *Educational Leadership, 54*(6), 56–59.

Senge, P. (1990). *The fifth discipline: The art and practice of the learning organization.* New York: Doubleday.

Senge, P. (1999). *The dance of change: The challenges of sustaining momentum in learning organizations.* New York: Doubleday.

Senge, P. (2000). *Schools that learn.* New York: Doubleday.

Senk, S. L., & Thompson, D. R. (Eds.). (2003). *Standards-based school mathematics curricula: What are they? What do students learn?* Mahwah, NJ: Erlbaum.

Shulman, L. S. (1986). Those who understand: Knowledge growth in teaching. *Educational Researcher, 15,* 4–14.

Spillane, J. P., Reiser, B. J., & Reimer, T. (2003). Policy implementation and cognition: Reframing and refocusing implementation research. *Review of Educational Research, 72,* 387–431.

Stiegler, J. W., & Hiebert, J. (1999). *The teaching gap: Best ideas from the world's teachers for improving education in the classroom.* New York: Free Press.

Stokes, D. (1997). *Pasteur's quadrant: Basic science and technological innovation.* Washington DC: Brookings Institution Press.

Vye, N. J., Goldman, S. R., Voss, J. F., Hmelo, C., Williams, S., & the Cognition and Technology Group at Vanderbilt. (1997). Complex mathematical problem solving by individuals and dyads. *Cognition and Instruction, 15,* 435–484.

Vygotsky, L. S. (1981). The genesis of higher-order mental functions. In J. W. Wertsch (Ed.), *The concept of activity in Soviet psychology* (pp. 144–184). Armonk, NY: Sharpe.

Webb, N. L. (1997). *Criteria for alignment of expectations and assessments in mathematics and science education.* (National Institute for Science Education and Council of Chief State School Officers Research Monograph No. 6.) Washington, DC: Council of Chief State School Officers.

Williams, S. M., Burgess, K. L., Bray, M. H., Bransford, J. D., Goldman, S. R., & the Cognition and Technology Group at Vanderbilt (1998). Technology and learning in schools for thought classrooms. In C. Dede (Ed.), *Learning with technology: 1998 yearbook of the Association of Supervision and Curriculum Development* (pp. 97–119). Alexandria, VA: Association of Supervision and Curriculum Development.

Wilson, S. M., & Berne, J. (1999). Teacher learning and the acquisition of professional knowledge: An examination of research on contemporary professional development. In A. Iran-Nejad & P. D. Pearson (Eds.), *Review of research in education* (pp. 173–209). San Francisco: American Educational Research Association.

Wilson, S. M., Lubienski, S. T., & Mattson, S. (1996, April). *What happens to the mathematics: A case study of the challenges facing reform-oriented professional development*. Paper presented at the annual meeting of the American Educational Research Association, New York.

Zech, L., & Bray, M. (2001, April). *Revisioning understanding in mathematics*. Paper presented at the meeting of the American Educational Research Association, Seattle.

Zech, L., Gause-Vega, C., Bray, M. H., Secules, T., & Goldman, S. R. (2000). Content-based collaborative inquiry: Professional development for school reform. *Educational Psychologist, 35*(3), 207–217.

5

SCALING UP PROFESSIONAL DEVELOPMENT IN THE UNITED KINGDOM, SINGAPORE, AND CHILE

Laurence C. Peters

Three countries provide teachers with professional development in information technologies.

THIS CHAPTER discusses what U.S. policymakers might learn from the experiences of the United Kingdom, Singapore, and Chile in their efforts to scale up effective uses of technology. The purpose is not to write a historical account of innovations but rather to highlight some major themes that emerge when comparing these highly centralized systems along one critical dimension—the role accorded to professional development. Professional development has often been the neglected sibling in the push to scale up, with far more resources going into hardware, software, and networking. The experiences of the United Kingdom, Chile, and Singapore can shed light on some reasons why (at least in the United States) helping teachers make use of technology has not proved as compelling as acquiring products that are often heavily marketed. One reason may be the underlying belief systems shared by policymakers and bureaucrats about the nature and function of technology in the classroom. In the United Kingdom, as compared with Chile, helping educators to integrate

97

technology seems to have played a secondary role for policymakers and their bureaucratic servants who play to popular perceptions that technology can transform the learning process without much human intervention (Selwyn and Fritz, 2001). Such a belief can trivialize the work of professional development and define it in terms of simply acquiring skills to operate machines and manipulate software.

In contrast, with the passage of the new federal legislation No Child Left Behind, U.S. school districts may no longer have a choice when it comes to making sufficient provision for professional development: 25 percent of funds used for technology must be devoted to this function. However, educators will have to think harder about what role professional development can play if its goal is truly to integrate technology into the curriculum. Without doubt, that thinking will be heavily influenced by intense accountability pressures on schools resulting from the new requirements for annual testing between third grade and eighth grade. Within this context, the experience of the United Kingdom, with its similar highly public accountability system, can again be instructive. For example, for teachers to become effective users of technology, they need some latitude to experiment and to fail. Classroom teachers must know that they will be supported when venturing out of the safety zone of traditional curriculum and delivery methods. To a greater extent than the United Kingdom, both Chile and Singapore seem to appreciate that using technology often means risk and uncertain results. In the United Kingdom, emphasis on the use of particular approved content materials reinforces the notion that technology merely supplements a traditional curriculum rather than offers opportunities for teachers to go beyond received ways of thinking in their efforts to meet individual learning needs.

One possible conclusion from this cross-national comparison is that there may be two approaches to technology integration. The first sees the challenge primarily in instrumental terms: fitting technology tools and content to curriculum standards and assessments and providing professional development opportunities that focus on skills needed to accomplish these purposes. The other views the task primarily as helping teachers adapt technology tools to their pedagogical purposes. The three cases illustrate the contrast between these approaches.

The United Kingdom's Approach

Prime Minister Tony Blair's placement of educational technology as a top priority of his incoming Labour government meant that the initiative received the lion's share of resources. Between 1998 and 2002, the U.K.

government committed over \$1 billion (£700 million) of matched local education authority funding to connect every one of Britain's thirty thousand schools to the Internet and provided, out of a total federal budget of approximately \$91.4 billion (£64 billion), an additional \$328 million (£230 million) from lottery proceeds for professional development. A key objective, as expressed in 1998 by Blair's education minister, David Blunkett, was to support, "our main goal of driving up standards in schools and delivering material which is of immediate, practical and working use to schools" (U.K. Department of Education and Employment, 1998).

A centerpiece of this investment was the National Grid for Learning (NGfL)—a "meta-depository" for educational artifacts touted by the Department of Education and Employment as "making available to all learners the riches of the world's intellectual, cultural and scientific heritage" (U.K. Department of Education and Employment, 1998). For example, collections from art galleries and museums all over the world would be accessible through the miracle of digital technology. NGfL networks would connect schools, colleges, libraries, and community centers. It included sites for students (the Grid Club), parents (Parents Online), and teachers (Teachernet and the Virtual Teachers Centre). This initiative was portrayed by some as a "walled garden," enabling access to an approved collection of materials and specially created software through an extraordinary public-private partnership that would be unimaginable in the United States.

In December 2001, Tony Blair announced the development of a "groundbreaking service" that would "transform learning in schools" and "help teachers spend more time teaching and motivating pupils" (http://www.egov.vic.gov.au/International/Europe/UnitedKingdom/UKGovtReports/UKGovtRep.htm#curriculumonline). That new initiative was Curriculum Online, a portal site that absorbed the former NGfL initiative. The portal's resources are a mix of free and for-pay content (materials), some with evaluations by Teachers Evaluating Educational Multimedia (TEEM). TEEM evaluators are experienced classroom teachers with a strong history of using software in the classroom who are trained to assess the value of software for classroom teachers. (See http://www.teem.org.uk/ for further details.) Offerings include CD-ROMs, on-line services, pupil assessment software, and interactive videos. E-learning credits—in the form of authorization for schools to purchase digital curriculum resources—are available, together with information and learning management systems developed to "agreed minimum Government standards" (http://edunet.iow.gov.uk/curriculum/ngfl/curricul.asp).

The planning initiatives for entities such as Curriculum Online and its predecessor, the National Grid for Learning, showed great vision. The

British Education Communications and Technology Agency (Becta) was created as a research and evaluation arm to enable the system to continually improve and to offer a critical counterbalance to the centralizing of government authority. The Virtual Teacher Centre provided further depth by offering teachers an on-line network of courses and relevant professional development resources (including Becta reports). The Blair government's overtures to the nascent U.K. software industry were also a brilliant stroke, tapping the skills and knowledge of a vital stakeholder that would otherwise have been left with a much smaller market for its products. Providing teachers with as many as seventeen thousand technology products, including lesson plans, CD-ROMs, and interactive videos that were all designed to support the national standards, obtainable for free or through e-learning credits, makes it difficult for educators to ignore the potential role of technology in the classroom. (Through e-learning credits, the government will give schools about $143 million [£100 million] a year for three years to spend on these products, and 10 percent of them will be available for free.)

Curiously, despite all the investment in making high-quality content accessible, comparatively small resources and attention were given to professional development. Lord Puttnam, the former film director and head of the National Teacher Council, blasted this oversight at a major conference. While acknowledging that more than 237,000 teachers had signed up to take the information and communications technology (ICT) training program, Lord Puttnam said a one-shot course was not "remotely adequate" (Johnston, 2001). In contrast to the other expenditures on technology, the United Kingdom's approach to ICT professional development seems miserly. ICT curriculum training for classroom teachers is being implemented with a one-time lottery payout of $329 million (£230 million)—about $715 (£500) per teacher—including some development awards that will allow teachers to travel. Rather than a means to find time and space in the curriculum for teachers to use new technology or receive continuing support in their learning, professional development is defined largely as a skills issue that pales in comparison to the other more immediate and pressing demands placed on teachers. Preparing for regular outside inspections by the government and for high-stakes assessments diverts teachers' time and attention. For example, teachers may tend to overprepare large volumes of paperwork to avoid being caught out by government inspection teams (National Union of Teachers, 2002). Owen Lynch, chief executive of Becta, agrees that a shift in emphasis from building infrastructure to training does need to occur: "ICT is starting to transform education, but embedding it remains the challenge for the next five years" (Johnston, 2003).

Previous studies (Cox, Rhodes, and Hall, 1988; Cox, 1994) have shown that most courses offered in the United Kingdom to train teachers in the uses of ICT have focused on its technical aspects, with little training on the pedagogical practices required and how to incorporate ICT into the curriculum. A minority of ICT professional development courses are designed to help teachers revise their pedagogical practices so that technology strengths can be fully utilized. Most of the professional development courses, in contrast, may help teachers run certain software packages and fix the printer but do not provide long-term assistance in helping them rethink their teaching. In this regard, the Blair administration planners ignored an entire body of research suggesting that for professional development to be effective, it has to be long-term and integrated into the ways in which teachers solve problems.

Could the United Kingdom have handled the challenge differently? The experiences of Singapore and Chile suggest alternative approaches.

Singapore's Approach

What is remarkable with reference to Singapore's experience is the restraint with which the government handled the 1997 reform act, which did not go quite as far as that of the United Kingdom in dictating to schools how to implement education technology. In Singapore, the central government has enormous power to directly control relatively few schools (377, with 500,000 students and 23,600 teachers).

Differences between Singaporean and British views emerged in an article in the *Times Educational Supplement* that covered a visit of some U.K. educators to the Southeast Asian island. British visitors were surprised to learn that the government there was far more willing to trust teachers to experiment with technology so that they could find their own comfort level as they sought to integrate computer use into the curriculum, an approach described by Tan Yap Kwang, director of the Education Ministry's Educational Technology Division, as a "mandate to make mistakes" (Johnston, 2002). The visitors also learned that to foster a deeper level of experimentation among educators, the "curriculum content was being cut by up to 30 percent in certain subjects to give teachers the time to experiment with ICT and to better teach thinking skills to pupils" (Johnston, 2002). Clare Johnson, a U.K. visitor and principal ICT manager at the Qualifications and Curriculum Authority, commented that the United Kingdom's mistake consisted of "basing plans on the technology itself, rather than thinking about how it can be used to support teaching and learning" (Johnston, 2002).

Johnson's remark indicates the way each government approached the task of integrating technology into the curriculum. For the Singaporean government, an important challenge was capitalizing on the power of information technology to move students from being passive to active learners; its master plan stated that learning "would shift from information receiving toward an emphasis on finding relevant information, learning to apply information to solve problems, and communicating ideas effectively. . . . The rich, interactive capability of IT-based learning resources can also motivate and engage weaker students, and allow them to learn at an appropriate pace" (Singaporean Ministry of Education, 1997). The process of integrating technology in Singapore's educational system was to occur in phases, with the initial focus at the primary level given to English, math, science, and Chinese. At the secondary level, the focus was to include geography, history, English literature, and civics and moral education. Schools that received training were to train others, while the private sector was enlisted to "advise schools on their technology strategies, and help assure a continuous flow of ideas and practices" (Singaporean Ministry of Education, 1997, item 27). The approach was definitively not "one size fits all"; instead, the government clearly acknowledged that "the different approaches to using IT in various schools will be a source of learning to all as we implement the Master Plan" (Johnston, 2002).

Minimum goals called for students, on completion of high school, to have acquired "competencies in desk-top publishing, spreadsheet and database construction, and in sourcing of information from CD-ROMs and on-line resources." (Singaporean Ministry of Education, 1997, item 10). The Ministry of Education would create "strategies for acquiring and developing a range of software relevant to . . . curricula objectives" and serve as a clearinghouse "to source, review and recommend software titles {the Recommended Software List) and Internet sites for schools" (Singaporean Ministry of Education, 1997, item 12). The plan noted that schools would be given autonomy in choosing software and that a system would be established to "provide media clips, web pages and courseware snippets for multimedia resource-based learning" (Singaporean Ministry of Education, 1997, item 13). By 2002, schools were expected to reach national standards for IT infrastructure but were given flexibility to determine how quickly they met the general goal that students would "spend up to 30% of curriculum time using IT" (*Launch of Master Plan,* n.d., p. 7).

What the central government did specify, however, was a pupil-computer ratio of 2:1 for every school by 2002, as well as laptops provided for teachers (also at a 2:1 ratio) and a fan or cascade model of professional development. In U.S. terms, the cascade model would be known as a "train the trainer" model, with the significant difference that unlike what tends to happen in the United States, entire schools' leadership teams rather than individual teachers would be developed through a well-supported, tiered approach. Under the master plan, sixty senior IT specialists would provide the first wave of training. This cadre is responsible for bringing twenty-two demonstration schools into the fold, with department heads in charge of IT and selected teachers from phase 1 schools as well as the first group of senior IT instructors acting as co-trainers for three to four schools each. These schools would then train other schools in a similar fashion.

Chile's Approach: An Alternative to Scaling Up

Similar to the experience in Singapore, for the Chilean government, the challenge presented by networked technology was how it could fundamentally contribute to transforming traditional teaching and learning from a traditional one-size-fits-all pedagogy to one that could begin to appropriately consider individual learning needs and differences. This contrasts with the case of the United Kingdom, where technology was to support an already well developed set of standards and assessments.

Pedro Hepp, the moving force behind Chilean educational reforms, had made clear his belief that expectations for what he refers to as the "transformative effects of technology" in "isolation from teaching and learning were set too high." Accordingly, the Program to Improve the Equity and Quality of Education (later known as ENLACES) began quite modestly as a "trial project" (Hepp's term) in primary schools in the Santiago area, from 1990 to 1992. With the faculty of engineering at the University of Chile as a partner, a team consisting of three engineers, one teacher, and one educational psychologist connected the schools with computers and trained the staff. In this manner, the Ministry of Education team responsible for the program could determine the levels of technical proficiency needed for teachers to feel comfortable with computers in their classrooms and the level of continuing support they required. This knowledge was to inform the early design of a national network of training and support that began in 1992, when the government invited bids from the nation's regional universities for four years of assistance to be provided to one hundred schools.

The initial implementation experience revealed that some teachers felt intimidated by the standard computer interface; therefore, a new one was created, one that would enable a new user to become proficient in basic computer use in thirty minutes or less. At a "virtual town square," users could access specially developed educational software as well as e-mail applications. For the 36 percent of public schools in remote areas with no telephone service, a packet radio system was set up, using ultra-high-frequency channels with the TCP/IP protocol.

By 1996, with the first phase of the program successfully completed, the goal changed to resemble the ambitions of the U.K. and Singapore governments, to reach all secondary schools and half the nation's primary schools by 2000 (covering close to 90 percent of students and teachers of what are known as state "subsidized schools"). Schools competed with other schools for funding by describing how they would use the extra resources to technologically enhance the curriculum. The model of training twenty teachers at each of these selected schools was fully established, with regional universities (known as zone centers) supporting local training and technical assistance. A smaller group of universities (from two to nine, depending on the size of the region) "train the trainers," working with the regional universities to prepare them to implement the ENLACES approach.

The goal of this project was not so much for Chilean schools to look similar in their use of technology, but for each teacher as well as each school to gain its own form of ownership and control over the resources. As Hepp remarks, "The form in which the computers are used in each school depends on its own educational project and its social, cultural and geographical context. In this sense, there are no recipes for universal and automatic application. But there is a wide scope to know, adapt and exchange ideas and educational experiences with other schools of the country and the world. In this sense, the aim is, for example, to exchange working guides between teachers; share curricular activities with the use of technologies and student arrangements" (Hepp, 1999, p. 8). Perhaps the starkest contrast between the approaches of the two other countries so far discussed and the Chilean approach is that, for Hepp, technology provided an opportunity to fundamentally rethink traditional teaching and learning. However, for the United Kingdom and, to a lesser extent, for Singapore, the challenge was more to support existing curricular approaches.

Evaluations of Chilean classrooms implementing the project between 1993 and 1999 show a growth in students' creativity, capacity for gaining knowledge about the world, and reading comprehension levels. One of the important conclusions from the work, noted by a number of authors, is that "innovation must arise out of current pedagogical practices" (Hinostroza, Hepp, and Laral, 2000). ENLACES seeks to show teachers more clearly the multiple ways in which technology can be used, as much in the classroom as in extracurricular activities. The point is not merely to "do the same thing, only with computers, although in the beginning it may seem that way" (Hinostroza, Hepp, and Laral, 2000). The teachers' role is, first, to note changes emerging in the classroom as the students become comfortable with the technology and then to gain confidence in what are termed "more effective strategies" or to adapt "those of other teachers in schools" (Hinostroza, Hepp, and Laral, 2000). This may seem a fairly trivial point, but its weight can be appreciated in the light of the amounts of time and resources that are devoted to training staff—three years of training for twenty teachers in each school, supported by a technical assistance network operated by universities throughout the country.

In comparison, the United Kingdom's approach to IT professional development seems stingy. Compared with the thinking and planning that went into the building of the entire structure of the National Grid for Learning and all that followed, the investment in professional development seems an afterthought, lacking a rationale based in the extensive research literature about teachers' use of technology and the changes it should entail in practice.

Issues for U.S. Policymakers

Clearly, there is not enough evidence to suggest that the U.K. experiment is inherently flawed; the many variables in play preclude drawing firm conclusions. In fact, some positive outcomes have been reported, such as "evidence of positive effects of specific uses of ICT on pupils' attainment in almost all National Curriculum subjects, with the most substantial evidence of these effects in the core subjects of English, mathematics, and science" (Cox and others, 2003). But there is reason to be concerned that major research on sustainable reforms has been ignored. The limited time and resources devoted to professional development in the United Kingdom seem related to the reduction of the teacher's role to selecting from a list of approved technology products. In Singapore and Chile, however, a different set of beliefs concerning teacher efficacy seems to be operating. According to Neil Selwyn (2000), "by constructing the Grid as a carefully sanctioned environment, it can be argued that the autonomy of the teacher will be curtailed rather than bolstered" (pp. 250–251). One way to reframe the issue for U.S. policymakers is to focus professional development plans on how much they are prepared to offer teachers "ownership" of their own practice in the use of technology and how they want to define effective technology integration. If it is defined as enabling students to make deeper gains in learning than might otherwise be available through conventional means rather than simply enabling greater technology facility, it is possible to derive a more sustainable approach.

From the U.S. perspective, the legislative language of Part D of the No Child Left Behind Act—"Enhancing Education Through Technology"—is encouraging from two points of view. First, it mandates that 25 percent of all funds spent on educational technology be devoted to professional development and describes a broad scope for what constitutes "high quality professional development"—namely, that it is to be "ongoing, sustained and intensive." The legislation further specifies that

> The recipient shall provide professional development in the integration of advanced technologies, including emerging technologies, into curricula and instruction and in using those technologies to create new learning environments, such as professional development in the use of technology—
> (A) To access data and resources to develop curricula and instructional materials;
> (B) To enable teachers—
>   (i) to use the Internet and other technology to communicate with parents, other teachers, principals, and administrators; and
>   (ii) To retrieve Internet-based learning resources; and
> (C) To lead to improvements in classroom instruction in the core academic subjects, that effectively prepare students to meet challenging State academic content standards, including increasing student technology literacy, and student academic achievement standards. [Public Law No. 107–110, §2416]

These paragraphs provide a balance between a skills-based approach to professional development, focusing on equipping teachers with the ability to "access data and resources," and an accountability-oriented strategy based on communication with parents and other teachers, with the newer emphasis on helping students "effectively prepare" for "challenging State academic content standards."

How will states and districts balance these different demands? Will the current confusing relationship among decision makers who have responsibility for curriculum, for professional development, and for technology decisions work in favor of the new legislation or against it? How will funded programs be evaluated to achieve the goal of establishing "best practices" that can be "widely replicated in the state" (Public Law No. 107–110, §2413)? The accountability measures contained in No Child

Left Behind legislation certainly focus on the right elements—not student achievement as measured by test scores, but the extent to which activities "are effective in integrating technology into curricula and instruction, increasing the ability of teachers to teach, and enabling students to meet challenging State academic content and student academic achievement standards" (Public Law No. 107–110, §2414). All of these requirements demand major new thinking on the part of states used to accounting for how federal funds are spent simply by delineating the equipment purchased and numbers of teachers provided with training.

How ready will states be to cast off the traditional courses that promote technological literacy, which are the main and sometimes only way in which the success of technology investments are measured (Cox, Preston, and Cox, 1999; Elmore, 1996)? To go to the next step would mean adopting the Chilean position that the challenge is not to supplement existing practice but to go beyond the necessary limitations of traditional teaching. As Hepp (1999) argues, "The point is not to merely do the same thing, only with computers," although in the beginning the opportunities may seem that way. The Chilean perspective helps to shed light on a key condition for success that tends to be overlooked in the United States, the need for both technical assistance and leadership support for the critical work of curriculum redesign that needs to undertaken by all teachers if they are to truly integrate technology into their classrooms. The lack of sufficient computers, the paucity of technical support for teachers, and the domination of the curriculum by high-stakes tests all pose obstacles to the successful integration of technology into the curriculum. However, arguably the most crucial factor is the receptivity of the school culture to the challenge that technology poses to the traditional curriculum and belief systems. These belief systems operated even in the high-tech environments of the Silicon Valley schools that Larry Cuban observed for his influential book *Oversold and Underused*. These educators were not immune to traditional attitudes that kept computers, like old-fashioned filmstrip projectors, sidelined from active engagement with the core of the curriculum (Cuban, 2001).

The schools and communities that seem to be making the most progress in overcoming these obstacles have in common not just enlightened leadership but also effective professional development—transforming this activity from the standard one- or two-day workshop into a teacher-centered menu of activities. These typically are based on faculty priorities (West, 2003) as well as a variety of coaching and mentoring programs in which teachers work to shift their practice from the safety zone of traditional instruction to a more learner-centered classroom (Bennett, 2003; Haney and Wilkins, 2003).

However, schools place multiple demands on teachers' discretionary and nondiscretionary time, so educators need to decide where this work fits within a variety of goals and objectives. Analysis of the British, Singaporean, and Chilean experiences suggests that one key to effective change and scaling up is a deep examination of the underlying belief systems about technology and its role in the classroom. Integrating technology successfully means that pedagogy changes as the teachers' focus shifts to enabling more individualized student learning. For this shift to take place, state and local leadership is vital in articulating why and how high-quality professional development for technology integration matters and in providing teachers with appropriate support as they change their practice.

REFERENCES

Bennett, D. (2003). The impact of technology integration and support from coaches. In A. D. Sheekey (Ed.), *How to ensure that ed/tech is not oversold and underused* (pp. 107–122). Lanham, MD: Scarecrow Press.

Cox, M. J. (1994). An overview of the problems and issues associated with the uptake of computers in the United Kingdom education institutions. In *Visions for teaching and learning: Educomp 1994 proceedings* (pp. 233–247). Penang, Malaysia: Malaysian Council for Computers in Education.

Cox, M., Abbott, C., Webb, M., Blakeley, B., Beauchamp, T., and Rhodes, V. (2003). ICT and attainment. Retrieved from http://www.becta.org.uk/research/cfm?section=1&id=311

Cox, M. J., Preston, C., & Cox, K. (1999, September). *What factors support or prevent teachers from using ICT in their classrooms?* Paper presented at the annual conference of the British Educational Research Association, University of Sussex, Brighton.

Cox, M. J., Rhodes, V., & Hall, J. (1988). The use of computer-assisted learning in primary schools: Some factors affecting the uptake. *Computers and Education 12*(1), 173–178.

Cuban, L. (2001). *Oversold and underused: Computers in the classroom.* Cambridge, MA: Harvard University Press.

Elmore, R. F. (1996). Getting to scale with good educational practice. *Harvard Educational Review, 66,* 1–26.

Haney, M., & Wilkins, E. B. (2003). Using technology to engage students for multiple learning experiences. In A. D. Sheekey (Ed.), *How to ensure that ed/tech is not oversold and underused* (pp. 123–139). Lanham, MD: Scarecrow Press.

Hepp, P. K. (1999). ENLACES: A whole world for Chilean children and young-sters (Latin American and Caribbean Regional Office, World Bank, Trans.). In J. E. Garcia Huidobro (Ed.), *A reforma educacional Chilean* [Chilean Education Reform] (p. 8). Madrid: Editorial Popular. Retrieved from http://www1.worldbank.org/education/secondary/documents/Hepp.htm.

Hinostroza, E., Hepp, P. K., & Laral, K. (2000). *ENLACES: The Chilean ICT experience in education.* Washington, DC: Ernesto Laval Instituto de Informatica Educativa, Universidad de La Frontera.

Johnston, C. (2001, January 1). BETT 2001: Teachers' ICT training inadequate, warns Puttnam. *Times Education Supplement.* Retrieved from http://www.tes.co.uk/search/search_display.asp?section=Breaking+News+Stories&sub_section=Breaking+News&id=276803&Type=0

Johnston, C. (2002, January 4). Learning valuable lessons from the city state. *Times Education Supplement.* Retrieved from http://www.tes.co.uk/search/search_display.asp?section=Archive&sub_section=Online+Education&id=357692&Type=0

Johnston, C. (2003, March 1). Training failure hinders ICT. *Times Education Supplement.* Retrieved from http://www.tes.co.uk/search/search_display.asp?section=Archive&sub_section=Online+Education&id=373272&Type=0

Launch of master plan for IT in education, Singapore. (n.d.) Retrieved from www.watani.org.sa/new/English/F/Launch%20of%20Master%20Plan%20for%20IT%20in%20Education%20in%20Singapore.doc

National Union of Teachers. (2002). *Reducing teachers' workload.* Retrieved from http://education.guardian.co.uk/ofsted/story/0,7348,708924,00.html

Selwyn, N. (2000). The National Grid for Learning: Panacea or panopticon? *British Journal of Sociology, 21*(2), 250–251.

Selwyn, N., & Fritz, J. (2001). The National Grid for Learning: A case study of new Labour education policy-making. *Journal of Education Policy, 16*(2), 127–147.

Singaporean Ministry of Education. (1997). *IT in Education Masterplan Summary.* Retrieved from http://www1.moe.edu.sg/iteducation/masterplan/summary.htm

U.K. Department of Education and Employment. (1998). *Blunkett announces details of biggest ever investment in schools information and communications technology* (Press release 184/98). London: Author.

West, B. (2003). Building the bridge to effective use of technology. In A. D. Sheekey (Ed.), *How to ensure that ed/tech is not oversold and underused* (pp. 53–72). Lanham, MD: Scarecrow Press.

6

TECHNOLOGY AS PROTEUS

DIGITAL INFRASTRUCTURES THAT
EMPOWER SCALING UP

Chris Dede, Robert Nelson

*Complex, multilevel technology innovations help sustain learning
and management in Milwaukee schools.*

THE GREEK SEA DEITY Proteus could overcome challenges by transforming himself, taking on a myriad of forms (such as fish, bird, beast) with
varied attributes and powers. Similarly, information technology can
assume many forms in the service of improved educational outcomes and
organizational effectiveness. Our society is still discovering powerful methods by which emerging interactive media can enable student learning, educators' professional development, efficient administration, links between
schools and communities, and collaborations with distant partners who
provide expertise not available locally. This chapter describes the many
ways in which a single set of core investments in sophisticated computers
and telecommunications has enabled the transfer and scaling up of innovations in the Milwaukee Public Schools (MPS). Research on the MPS
technology infrastructure design and implementation process has developed heuristics that can generalize these protean benefits to other educational settings.

Large Urban School Districts and the Challenge of Scaling Up Innovations

Technology-reliant educational interventions are based on a chord of innovations that harmonize and complement one another and that serve as conditions for success. (An intervention is technology-reliant if the aid of computers or telecommunications is essential to its success; it does not mean that technology is the source of the intervention, which might be, for example, a mentor or a training session.) For example, a technology-reliant instructional intervention might involve the simultaneous introduction of classroom computers, educational software, teacher professional development, and guarantees of technical support. Scaling up such an intervention involves transferring and adapting this set of interrelated innovations to new contexts, resulting in a modified suite of effective practices sustainable across a variety of settings.

An analogy to medical technologies, contrasting an immunization and a controlled longitudinal administration of antibiotics, illustrates how important conditions are to success (Dede, 2001). To be effective, the immunization needs only to take place; it has very simple conditions for success. In contrast, the antibiotics must be taken at the prescribed dosage, at the prescribed time intervals, for the prescribed amount of time. If these more complex conditions are not met, the antibiotics may well be ineffective, even though this medical technology is a powerful intervention when used properly.

The conditions for success of educational technologies in schools are much more complex than those of antibiotics in the treatment of disease. These essential conditions include complementary shifts in curriculum, pedagogy, assessment, professional development, administration, organizational structures, strategies for equity, and partnerships for learning among schools, businesses, homes, and community (Dede, 1998). Moreover, the beliefs, attitudes, and values of users are vital to the effectiveness of learning technologies, as they are in, for example, efforts to maintain public health and personal wellness. Such efforts in the area of health also require the application of research findings to inform everyday practice, a situation that mirrors one of the challenges facing the field of education and its use of technology.

Russell, Bebell, and O'Dwyer (2003) are studying the interrelationships of a variety of factors that are thought to influence the conditions for success of instructional technology in school districts. As Table 6.1 indicates, these factors are in play at different organizational levels. The interrelationships among these factors both within and across organizational levels shape the mutual adaptation of transferred innovations and their new context, and they also influence the fidelity with which technology-reliant educational interventions are implemented.

Research sponsored by the Council of Great City Schools and MRDC Inc. (Snipes, Doolittle, and Herlihy, 2002) documents that large urban school districts confront special challenges in providing conditions for success as they adopt an innovation; adapting the intervention and its district contexts while also retaining fidelity to the intervention's sources of effectiveness can prove difficult. Urban districts that succeed despite these challenges have found some mechanism to provide political and organizational stability over a prolonged period, based on consensus about educational reform strategies (Bascia and Hargreaves, 2000; Datnow, Hubbard, and Mehan, 2002; Snipes, Doolittle, and Herlihy, 2002). Research suggests that a reform movement based on simultaneously combining a substantial

---

Table 6.1. Organization of Factors Influencing Instructional Use of Technology

District	Community attitudes about educational technology
	District vision for technology
	Leadership of technology initiatives
	Resources for technology initiatives
	Support services for technology initiatives
	Infrastructure of computers and telecommunications
	Professional development related to technology
	Relationship between technology and equity
	Technology-related policies and standards
School	Leadership of technology initiatives
	Principal's beliefs about pedagogy
	Principal's beliefs about technology
	Principal's technological preparedness
	School culture
Classroom	Teacher's beliefs about pedagogy
	Teacher's beliefs about technology
	Teacher's technological preparedness
	Teacher's demographic characteristics
	Technological resources
	Students' home access to technological resources
	Students' home usage of technological resources
	Students' comfort with technology
	Students' demographic characteristics

Source: Russell, Bebell, and O'Dwyer, 2003.

number of these strategies is more effective than initiatives that implement a few of these approaches sequentially. Investing in a sophisticated infrastructure of computers and telecommunications, complemented by a sophisticated human capacity for expertise and support, can empower such an overall strategy for educational improvement. Such an investment in technology should not be a primary cause of committing to an effective reform strategy, however. Instead, this protean infrastructure acts as an enabler and makes many improvement processes easier to initiate and sustain.

Scaling Up Successes via Technology: The Milwaukee Public Schools

This section provides a case study about the evolution of technology usage in the Milwaukee Public Schools. Its progression traces how a reform movement, sustained over years through the building of political consensus, increasingly has used computers and telecommunications to enable scaling up a wide variety of innovations.

Today, Milwaukee Public Schools is the twenty-seventh largest school district in the United States, educating over 105,000 students in 161 schools (120 elementary schools, 23 middle schools, and 18 high schools). The enrollment data for 2001–2002, shown in Table 6.2, reflect the ethnically diverse and socially challenging demographics of this urban school district (Grover, 2003).

History

During the early 1990s, declining financial support for the district's business applications of technology threatened to result in administrative meltdown. Howard Fuller, superintendent from 1991 to 1995, designated a

---

Table 6.2. Demographics of Milwaukee Public Schools, 2001–2002

African American	58.9%
Latino	16.5%
White	15.9%
Asian	5.1%
Native American	0.96%
Other nonwhite	2.3%
Students with disabilities	15%
Students with limited English proficiency	7.5%
Students receiving free or reduced lunch	>75%

group of school principals, district department heads, and technology leaders from major Milwaukee area companies to form the Executive Technology Review Committee (ETRC). This group's function was to advise the superintendent and the Milwaukee Board of School Directors regarding strategic technology investments and directions. Intentionally, the school representatives outnumbered the district leaders; the ETRC was chaired by the second author of this chapter, Robert Nelson, then a high school principal.

Early actions of the ETRC supported acquisitions of new software systems to permit processing for traditional business applications within a reasonable time frame. Also, exploration of how to develop instructional technology in K–12 education began. A Big Six consulting firm was hired to help construct a strategic plan for technology at MPS. While this development process and planning document helped establish consensus within MPS about technology needs, the plan fell far short of expectations for linking technology to the core business of MPS: learning. In retrospect, it probably was unreasonable to expect a traditional business-oriented consulting firm to reframe its models to suit this situation. However, Fuller continued to support increasing the role that technology played in the learning experiences of children in Milwaukee. He was intrigued by the mesmerizing effect that technology had on children and believed that equitable access to technology was essential.

Robert Jasna was deputy superintendent during Fuller's tenure and had participated in many of the strategic discussions about technology and its potential roles in K–12 education. When Jasna became superintendent in 1995, one of his early actions was to create the MPS Department of Technology, one of seven district-level departments. Robert Nelson was assigned to direct this new unit.

In terms of partnerships, the University of Wisconsin System administration became interested in and supportive of MPS's technology agenda. Key university leaders began to actively participate in strategic planning and also supported implementation of several demonstration projects. In addition, MPS began participating in several professional organizations, including the Consortium for School Networking, the Education Commission of the States, and the Midwest Higher Education Commission.

At the local level, other events helped shape MPS's technology agenda for the next several years. An ad hoc group of business advisers committed their support for the agenda. Their role was crucial, because Robert Nelson had a good knowledge of schools and MPS but very limited knowledge of technology-driven business processes. This group applied their extensive knowledge of business and strategic planning in support of MPS.

Also, the Department of Technology began developing a new strategic plan for technology at MPS. This plan was generated locally, with extensive input from advisers across the community and state, and was strongly influenced by reports, groups, and individuals that were providing leadership nationally. As part of this plan, a standards-based communications infrastructure was designed to transport data, video, and voice technologies into all MPS classrooms. While the merging of these technologies exceeded the industry standard of the mid-1990s, it was evident that it soon would emerge as the standard. Further, a design requirement of the plan was to select a scalable implementation of this standards-based communications infrastructure based on the eventual delivery of high bandwidth to each classroom.

A continuing challenge was that the MPS student and human resource management systems, like similar software in other organizations, were custom-built and centered on applications. The business community endorsed reengineering the management systems to make them student- and employee-centered, developed on a common relational database platform. Cross-functional teams from schools and departments researched and suggested a selection of new management systems. Their recommendations were advanced to the superintendent and the board by the ETRC.

MPS began providing staff with Internet-based e-mail accounts for twenty-four-hour access. A required initial training program helped set the stage for massive adoption by MPS employees. The district sponsored teacher-led training on a large scale; this was widely accepted. Teachers and other staff enrolled in a twelve-hour training program in exchange for Internet access and e-mail accounts through MPS. This professional development offering transmitted the rationale for the MPS acceptable use policy, provided hands-on examples of effective use of technology in a classroom environment, and gave novice users initial practice with using e-mail and the Internet. An important, immediate impact generated by the inception of this training was that representatives of the Milwaukee Teachers Education Association began to play key, constructive implementation roles in all technology projects.

Over 10,000 staff members have now participated in this required professional development. This training is also available on-line as an alternative to face-to-face instruction. At present, the MPS technology infrastructure is extensively used by students, district educators and staff, and the community. Use of Internet and e-mail access has more than tripled during the past two years (to over 16 million hits per day through the MPS gateway). The number of schools that use interactive video (now over fifty) has experienced similar growth. Over 50,000 students and 10,000 staff members have Internet and e-mail accounts through MPS.

Identifying particular MPS schools to pilot-test special Department of Technology services has proved to be an important means of evolving the services provided. One such strategy was to create "replicable schools," which implement technology innovations in a manner potentially generalizable to the entire district. Principals were offered an opportunity to compete for extra technology resources by identifying how their schools would advance the implementation of the MPS strategic plan for technology. Applications were judged by principals from the ETRC, teachers, and representatives of the business community. This concept allowed local champions intrigued by the possibilities of new strategies and tools to become the initial innovators.

As a culmination of all these efforts, the initial MPS strategic plan for technology was presented to the Milwaukee Board of School Directors in December 1996. This plan, which was primarily a vision statement, reflected how technology could support learning, MPS's core business. The plan featured an important role for schools in Milwaukee as neighborhood technology centers. Most Milwaukee families did not (and still do not) have access to current technologies in their homes. Half of MPS families do not have regular telephone service in their home, and almost none have a second data line available. Developing schools as technology-rich places would provide families in every Milwaukee neighborhood with access to computing and telecommunications.

The conventional organizational procedures, such as the budgeting process, of the school district were not organized to support technology uses like those that MPS was undertaking. This situation created confusion and frustration for many, but the support of the ETRC, the ad hoc advisers, and the superintendent did not waver, and the board voted 9–0 in support of technology initiatives. Very slowly, structural adjustments occurred within district organizations.

Building on this history, a variety of technology initiatives have emerged in MPS as this strategic plan has been implemented. Three principles underpin the technology work in MPS from 1995 to the present:

- The core business of a school district is learning, and MPS has to be better at this than it has been to date.

- Learning in the twenty-first century will become more effective because of capabilities that technology will contribute to the learning process.

- The Department of Technology does not take on a project if a link to learning is not apparent.

The people who best understand the district's core business are the people who work with children in schools. They are the MPS Department of Technology's primary coaches and audience. Parents support this work because intuitively they understand the three premises just given. Targeting schools for proof-of-concept demonstrations that pilot-test an innovation to demonstrate its practicality and value (the result of good advice by seasoned leaders from business and industry) has enabled sophisticated feedback from teachers and school administrators.

Analysis

Milwaukee is typical of large urban districts in confronting the challenges to success that were discussed in detail earlier in this chapter. The historical dynamics described earlier, which led to political and organizational stability over a prolonged period and were based on an emerging consensus about reform strategies, made possible the technological initiatives delineated next in this case study. However, even before computers and telecommunications were widely implemented in the district, the concept of using sophisticated information technologies was a unifying force that helped to create a coalition of stakeholders and a common vision. In this case, shared beliefs and values about the use of technology made a positive contribution—in part by increasing the district's credibility with and buy-in from the business community—even before the technology itself was put in place.

A top-down commitment to reform is not enough to guarantee successful improvement, however. Participants at every level of a district—and all kinds of outside stakeholders—must understand and take ownership of the major themes underlying a strategy for educational innovation (Fullan and Miles, 1992). As the research of Russell, Bebell, and O'Dwyer (2003) documents, this is not simply a matter of intellectual understanding; shared beliefs and values, based on affective and cultural factors as well as reflective cognition, are central to the type of sustained, deep commitment required for participating in educational transformation. In the societal context of the early twenty-first century, information technology as a vehicle for change has an emotional dimension within which many people (rightly or wrongly) find a common purpose. Particularly when the proposed technology use is congruent with fundamental beliefs and experiences about learning and teaching, as the three principles of the MPS Department of Technology exemplify, the theme of technology can become a rallying point for shared commitment and distributed ownership.

Empowering Student Learning via Technology

Some MPS instructional technology projects have attributes of both learning with technology and learning about technology. An example of such a project is the Cisco Network Academy (CNA) program, which uses a scalable, effective-practice example of a Web-based system to deliver its technical content. Students, families, teachers, and principals recognize the leverage this program can provide for students in developing skills and starting a career with higher potential than the jobs available through conventional vocational instruction. MPS launched the CNA program in one high school, then offered it to ten others. After three years, six sites are actively engaged, and the program concept has expanded to include articulation between district high schools, Milwaukee Area Technical College, and the University of Wisconsin–Milwaukee. Because of the Cisco initiative, students (including many who otherwise might not have attended college) are making successful transitions between these academic programs. Now a state-funded competitive grant has facilitated employment for MPS students as technical assistants in city libraries and in individual schools across the district. Their Cisco program teachers provide the technical assistance that students need to add value at their employment site.

Another project that fosters learning with technology is the implementation of "I Can Learn" as a demonstration project for MPS. This program provides a media-rich delivery of curriculum and content for pre-algebra and algebra. Princeton University researchers are conducting a two-year study of the implementation to validate its effectiveness and scalability. Because the district has a shortage of qualified mathematics teachers, one appealing feature of this package is its potential for assisting teachers who have marginal mathematics preparation by providing a more consistent delivery of the curriculum.

In these and similar projects, the district has found that students working in an on-line environment have less opportunity to hide from learning. Changes in teacher behavior are also occurring. Teachers involved in the "I Can Learn" project from five schools are collaborating, centering their discussions on how to help more students achieve success. Users of this innovation envision eventually using this type of academic technology to foster collaboration among educators across the cities in which this package is implemented.

Taking these and other projects to scale requires increased acceptance by the people with traditional responsibility for curriculum and instruction. While there is risk associated with straying from traditional practices, our success rate using conventional methodologies has been poor.

Principals are acutely aware of the declining tolerance for high rates of failure and are willing to try new ways to help more students succeed. Pressure is being placed on principals, not district curriculum experts, to increase student achievement. All the principals approached about these projects welcomed the opportunity to join in. Since their participation required some cost sharing, it did not reflect a casual decision. Should the findings support expansion of demonstration projects, the full participation of district curriculum staff would be required in order to provide sufficient support for a successful implementation.

In its selection of infrastructural technologies and in its classroom uses of computers and telecommunications to aid student learning, MPS has made wise decisions that empower educational improvement on a number of levels. For example, committing to classroom placements of computers rather than isolating educational technologies in labs was an important strategic choice for promoting familiarity and use among teachers. Providing high-quality computers with reliable Internet connections in easily accessible classroom settings is vital in the effective implementation of technology-reliant curricula. Schools' commitment to spending money on equipment, training, and support also influences teachers' decisions on whether to integrate technology into the curriculum (Anderson and Becker, 2001).

Linking school investments in learning technologies to parents' and communities' needs is a powerful method for creating commitment and enhancing equity. Focusing on the career needs of students and vocational opportunities in high-technology industries resonates well with families, businesses, and municipalities. The use of technology-based curricula that aid teachers underprepared in their subject domain addresses a chronic problem in urban school settings.

The first author of this chapter, Chris Dede, studies distributed learning, educational experiences that combine face-to-face teaching with synchronous and asynchronous mediated interaction. The infrastructure that MPS has put in place is now distributing learning across a variety of geographic settings, across time, and across various interactive media. Research shows that the integration of interactive media into learning experiences profoundly shapes students' educational experiences.

In particular, the full range of students' learning styles is undercut when interaction is limited to classroom settings rather than distributed across multiple media (Dede, Whitehouse, and Brown-L'Bahy, 2002). Many students report that the use of asynchronous learning environments positively affects their participation in classes and their individual cognitive processes for engaging with the material. In addition, students indicate that synchronous virtual media (1) help them get to know classmates with whom they otherwise might not individually interact within a classroom setting and (2) provide a clear advantage over asynchronous media in facilitating the work of small groups. Likewise, MPS's video technologies are becoming increasingly practical as a learning tool, now that Internet-based videoconferencing and high-bandwidth telecommunications are maturing and dropping in cost (Dede, 2002). This generation of students is fascinated with video as an expressive medium, an interest the district is well positioned to support.

Empowering Teachers via Technology

The district's sophisticated infrastructure is used by MPS to empower teaching and learning through a number of district initiatives.

Curriculum Design Assistant

The MPS curriculum design assistant (CDA) is a tool that emerged from the district's work with replicable schools. Teachers are asked to blend many agendas into meaningful student work as various directives reach them from the state, the district, professional organizations, their principal, the community, colleagues, their union, and so on. Conventional district curriculum support operations were having little impact in helping teachers deal with these many agendas. To alleviate this problem, the CDA creates a collaborative environment wherein teachers can post and find lessons that support their day-to-day work in classrooms. This tool is Web-based and is accessible twenty-four hours a day, seven days a week (http://www.milwaukee.k12.wi.us/pages/MPS/Teachers_Staff/Tech_Tools/CDA). When used in the creation mode, the CDA guides its users through lesson design options that are research-proven, searchable, and standards-based. State and district standards are readily available in the lesson design process, wherever and whenever the work is taking place.

Early challenges for the CDA included developing a set of blue-ribbon lessons that would draw teachers to this tool. The staff of the replicable schools program, who conceived this idea, were eager to feature their work through the CDA and began to develop the collaborative community they envisioned. The superintendent and senior staff of the district recognized the potential of the CDA and provided early endorsements for this tool as a pivot point that could unify district curriculum messages for schools and teachers. Members of the Milwaukee Board of School Directors participated in a CDA workshop so that they would understand this tool and its broadening base of support.

District in-service experiences were designed to support teachers' embedding lessons in the CDA. Executives from the teachers union were also trained in its use. They quickly recognized that they could support this practice because it advanced effective teaching and did not place their constituency at risk. MPS teachers began featuring their work with the CDA in professional meetings across the state and the nation.

Combinations of strategies were used to scale up the use of the CDA. A PT3 catalyst grant from the U.S. Department of Education was awarded to MPS to assist with this process. Three universities (the University of Wisconsin–Milwaukee, Marquette University, and National Lewis University) were awarded companion PT3 implementation grants to build on the CDA work in MPS. Through these funds, faculty from local colleges and universities were trained in the use of the CDA. The CDA was made available to these institutions so that it could be used as part of their pre-service development programs.

Other school districts in Wisconsin were also provided with access to the CDA, which now can develop a customized view for a given district. Representatives of the Wisconsin Department of Public Instruction were trained in the features and functions of the CDA. Prompted by the legislative mandates of No Child Left Behind, MPS ultimately upgraded the demonstration tool to a mature application capable of supporting a full-scale implementation.

The biggest challenge has been to get the people tasked with curriculum leadership at the district level to use the CDA. They have lagged in their adoption of technologies that support their work and have relied on old methodologies. Organizational tension increased as more schools began employing the CDA in their daily practice. A recent change in district leadership for this area has helped align efforts and change practices.

Professional Support Portal

Students' success largely depends on the effectiveness of their teachers. More than 10 percent of MPS teachers leave each year, and 37 percent of new MPS teachers leave within their first five years, resulting in unacceptable instructional conditions. Students, especially those with the greatest needs, are being taught by rookies year after year. What roles can technology play to advance and accelerate the effectiveness of new teachers, as well as to reduce their attrition rate? This question drives a major professional support portal (PSP) initiative.

MPS spent several months conducting focus groups, asking approximately fifty new teachers about their initial experiences. They identified a host of issues that represented barriers to early success. New teachers also identified district supports that were worth retaining and indicated that making some technology-based tools available could help alleviate some of the problems. These findings were shared with key leaders in the district, who readily endorsed seeking resources to build an MPS professional support portal.

New teachers' needs center on access to high-quality teaching and information resources, frequent interaction with expert mentors and coaches, and ongoing peer support. In response, the portal project has created a convergence of several technology initiatives:

- The CDA provides a ready-made tool that teachers can use to interact about learning and pedagogy.

- Teachscape®, a commercial professional development process based on video case studies, provides examples of standards-based lessons that are being taught in urban elementary classrooms (http://ts2.teachscape.com/html/ts/public/).

- Tapped In®, a nonprofit, multi-user virtual environment for professional development, provides an on-line social context that allows educators to build and sustain communities of practice (http://ti2.sri.com/tappedin/).

The Professional Support Portal Web site will eventually have sections open to the public; at that point, its URL will be http://mpsportal. milwaukee.k12.wi.us. Formative design feedback from new teachers is encouraging.

Through funding from the Joyce Foundation, Chris Dede is orchestrating the availability of distant experts to assist MPS staff with design and implementation of the PSP. Using broadband telecommunications, Internet-based videoconferencing, and collaboration tools, Harvard University and Education Development Center, Inc., are providing these services:

- On-line courses customized by EDC for MPS staff in a cross-section of leadership roles across the district, centering in 2002–2003 on the use of new interactive media in professional development and on data-based decision making

- Videoconference-based guidance from Harvard faculty for a cohort of "rising star" MPS principals who completed the Harvard Principals' Institute in Cambridge, Massachusetts, in the summers of 2002 and 2003 and are now receiving feedback on their attempts to implement leading-edge practices in local settings

- Groupware- and videoconference-based collaborative design of the PSP with interface and knowledge management specialists at Harvard
- Shared development of a pilot graphical multi-user virtual environment to complement the intellectual and social interaction provided in Tapped In
- Consultations with an expert in program evaluation who is helping to design metrics for assessing the complex, interwoven set of activities associated with the PSP
- Analysts who are documenting the process by which the PSP is created and implemented

From a research perspective, the Harvard team is studying the extent to which broadband and Internet2 interactive media can support these complex activities across distance without the necessity of making frequent trips to Milwaukee.

The PSP project is having a significant impact on other departments and divisions in MPS. As content is embedded in the PSP, underlying problems at the district with fragmentation of practices and procedures become apparent. In most cases, administrators view this as an opportunity to improve practices, but some people would rather not bother; working in silos can be comfortable and less complicated. However, district leaders are providing strong support for organizational alignment based on the portal.

Staff Development in Technology Usage

Staff development is a major component of the MPS Department of Technology's work with school and district personnel. Some of this training centers on teaching people how to use productivity tools such as Microsoft Office or the data query tool Brio. Other training teaches staff to use district application systems, such as the student management system. While these initiatives have required person-years of effort, this training enables a wide range of personnel across the district to use technology-supported learning and management tools.

A central component of this training is using technology to support student achievement in reading, writing, and mathematics. The Technology Literacy Challenge Fund (TLCF) grants received by MPS over a number of years resulted in tens of thousands of hours of on-line training. This experience identified new technology leaders from our schools and classrooms, who in turn were asked to assist with delivery of training and development of advanced levels of training. For example, TLCF participants developed lessons to embed in the curriculum design assistant as part of their course requirements.

Now MPS is routinely creating on-line training for experiences that must reach a large number of people. We are learning that lessons developed and delivered in this manner are more rigorous and more effective for the learner. We also see that on-line learning provides an effective strategy for refresher training and for offering training that can be started anytime. Not all training should be done this way, of course, but when the instructional design is done well, this delivery method serves useful purposes unattainable through other approaches.

An emerging priority for MPS is to develop strategies for constructing staff member portfolios. The human resource management system is technically capable of storing this information, but what information is worth collecting? What combinations of experiences constitute useful career development experiences? The Department of Technology will learn some valuable lessons as the professional support portal evolves, but even this resource is limited in not being designed to support classified staff.

Also, MPS's robust infrastructure and technology tools increase the opportunity for employees to work off site, using telecommunications. The district must now develop policies and practices that enable efficient and effective use without compromising data security or increasing liabilities.

Teachers' pedagogical philosophy and their level of preparation in technology shape the potential classroom use of new resources (Becker and Anderson, 2000). In the implementation of the GLOBE curriculum in inquiry-based learning, studies document constellations of practices that contribute to desired student outcomes (Penuel and others, 2002). Some of these practices are routinely implemented by MPS in its CDA partner units:

- Teachers are supported by a school administrator who is positive about the curriculum and can help garner resources, reduce institutional barriers (such as class periods that are too short to permit data collection and analysis), and showcase activities.

- After they've completed their training, teachers can receive support and guidance from a mentor teacher who is familiar with the curriculum.

- Teachers feel that CDA activities are congruent with the content of district standards and state-level high-stakes tests.

- Teachers believe in the benefits of this curriculum for student learning, and this positive attitude means that students are likely to derive more benefit.

A next step for MPS is to analyze CDA units and demonstration projects, using many of the sophisticated evaluation metrics that have been used to analyze curricula such as GLOBE. As discussed earlier, this will involve developing conceptual frameworks that support mutual adaptation of the innovation and its context of use as well as implementation fidelity, so that enactment preserves key aspects of the innovation that generate improvement.

The "expertise across distance" research funded by the Joyce Foundation is important along a number of dimensions. The aid provided is building human capacity within MPS to make the PSP successful in its design, implementation, and evaluation. Also, new teacher retention is a problem shared by many schools, especially in urban districts, a situation that dramatically undercuts students' academic performance (National Commission on Teaching and America's Future, 2003). Because the portal's initial focus is new teacher retention, the involvement of distant partners with expertise aids MPS in this initiative. Studies of the creation and implementation process of the PSP may help in adapting this innovation so that its strengths can be replicated in other settings. In addition, strategies for the successful involvement of geographically remote experts in local improvement efforts could be widely applied as broadband media become uniformly available.

Staffing and Funding Strategies

When major district technology initiatives began in 1995, almost no funding was allocated for this work. After years of insufficient budgets, with frequent leadership and organizational changes, the morale of staff assigned to the Department of Technology was low. This department today is about the same size as it was in 1995 and includes many of the same people, but dramatic changes have occurred in the way they work and in their productivity. Intentionally, MPS was careful to not siphon staff away from schools for district-level technology work, preferring to support school-based leadership in technology whenever practical. Numerous focus groups of these school-based leaders convene regularly in support of the department's work to aid their schools. School technology coordinators, school account managers, school Web masters, interactive video user groups, and a network academy user group meet to share opportunities and challenges. Each of these entities helps extend the department's reach into schools and aids in streamlining support.

Participation in competitive grant programs such as TLCF, PT3, TEACH, and others have helped the district to define the work that needs to be done and to provide funds that advance technology implementations. MPS actively and routinely engages in opportunities to bring in additional funds for infrastructure development; the federal e-rate program and Wisconsin's TEACH program have been essential in this quest. The net result of these external funding sources has been a doubling of the local investment. All these funding efforts are coordinated to support learning in the district and to align with MPS's strategic plan for technology. This plan has been refreshed four times since 1996 and is closely linked to the district's educational mission and goals (see http://www2. milwaukee.k12.wi.us/technology/strat/lead.html).

Continuing Challenges

The biggest challenge to sustaining and scaling up technology-reliant educational innovations in MPS concerns changes in school board members and superintendents. In the past decade, several shifts in school board composition have created discontinuities in political direction. Related to this, from 1995 to 2003, five superintendents have led MPS, each with quite different strategies for educational improvement and dissimilar beliefs about the role of computers and telecommunications. The transition periods cause a loss of momentum; they are followed by a need to reframe work to match the new superintendent's preferred agenda. While the Department of Technology has weathered these transitions so far, continuing the initiatives discussed earlier, the climate of political and organizational instability makes maintaining such progress in the future an uncertain proposition.

A funding shortfall at the state level makes technology investments a prime target for budget cuts. TEACH Wisconsin has ended. Reprioritization at the federal level in relation to the No Child Left Behind Act is prematurely ending funds that encourage technology-related investments. While these policy shifts are not terminating our work, the loss of resources is making success more difficult. Fiscal year 2004 will likely see more than a 20 percent reduction in the funding levels for the MPS Department of Technology.

An organizational preference for "doing things the old way" is another hurdle. Few people would argue that technology won't have a significant role in advancing learning in the twenty-first century, but many people would prefer not to have to change what they do in order to accommodate new ways of working. Technology can aid all aspects of learning and organizational support. Refusal by any individual or unit in the school system to use technology reduces our ability to optimize its impact. To attain the best results, active support of the district administration and the school board is essential.

Another challenge stems from the fact that urban children usually do not have current technology available at home; many do not even have regular telephone service to provide access to on-line resources, even if the district could somehow provide the technology for them to use at home. Schools in neighborhoods across Milwaukee can help mediate the access problem, but declining budgets will limit hours of access and investment in technology tools and support. Just as we have begun to make strides in bridging the digital divide, new barriers are emerging.

A strategy that has been especially effective in transcending these challenges has been the development of the National Technology Advisory Board. One element of MPS's PT3 project was the creation of this board. Two high-profile national leaders, Chris Dede from Harvard and John Morgridge from Cisco, agreed to serve as co-chairs and in turn persuaded other national leaders in educational research and in business to join them. The board's discussions rapidly became focused on two core issues impeding learning in MPS: the lack of active participation by district curriculum leaders in technology innovation efforts and the high turnover among new MPS teachers. A summary report of the work of this committee can be found at http://www.milwaukee.k12.wi.us/pt3/.

MPS's emerging capabilities for data-driven decision making are important in achieving its goals of improved student learning outcomes and better organizational effectiveness. Technology provides many types of leverage in improving student assessment and providing formative, diagnostic information to teachers (Mislevy and others, 2001; Pellegrino, Chudowsky, and Glaser, 2001). Of equal importance, but less understood, are the ways in which sophisticated information systems can aggregate data to enable aligned policy setting across different levels of a large, complex decision-making system. MPS now has the technology infrastructure to develop a sophisticated information system to support data-driven decision making. Creating the human and organizational capabilities to use such a system effectively is the next step. Research is needed on what types of data provide evidence that fosters scalable, sustainable strategies for improvement for practitioners and policymakers.

To enable continual, large-scale educational improvement, all stakeholders in the school system must understand a reform strategy, take ownership of innovation processes, and distribute power and responsibility (Spillane, Halverson, and Diamond, 2001). MPS's approaches to inculcating these types of strategic relationships—both internally and externally—illustrate "leadership without followers" (Dede, 1993). People often see leadership as a combination of meticulous management, adept political maneuvering, and responsive facilitation of others' activities. While each of these is important, the following three attributes are central:

1. Vision is the ability to communicate desirable, achievable futures quite different from the situation toward which the present is drifting. Leaders create and convey compelling images of how our reach is much less than our potential grasp; they redefine people's paradigms about what is possible. Through a long process of dialogue, interweaving top-down, bottom-up, and middle-out initiatives, MPS has developed a complex collective vision.

2. Building trust is crucial for inspiring a group to work toward a shared vision. Projects that involve an investment of many years and millions of dollars before results can be seen require sustained faith that a team of people can overcome all the obstacles to creating a future quite different from the present circumstances. Actualizing a strategic plan involves harnessing people's emotions as well as their minds, developing both understanding and belief. The distributed leadership capacity of MPS, developed through the processes described earlier, provides a communal foundation of trust and faith.

3. Debunking the myth about followers that views them as the bedrock of an organization is also an essential step. According to a destructive myth about leadership, a visionary person gives directions to followers, who execute this plan. Real leaders avoid this mentality, developing in its place a vision that incorporates insights from participants at all levels. True solutions to problems are always based on ideas from multiple perspectives; no individual, however capable, can incorporate the full range of knowledge and experience needed to invent an educational system that fulfills the needs of a diverse community. For a three-year period (1999–2002), key players in MPS (the head of the school board, the director of the Department of Technology, and the superintendent) exemplified this form of leadership.

Given the formidable challenges that MPS now faces (political instability, resource shortfalls, organizational inertia, and impoverished community), this type of distributed leadership is crucial to continuing and expanding the gains that this case study documents. The district's technological infrastructure fosters such leadership through a rich web of virtual communities that complement face-to-face interactions. School technology coordinators, school account managers, school Web masters, interactive video user groups, a network academy user group, the National Technology Advisory Board, and strategic partners from academic and business all supplement direct meetings with mediated dialogue enabled by the district's sophisticated telecommunications.

Implications for Policy and Practice

The MPS story illustrates how stakeholders worked together to create successful educational improvement, with computing and telecommunications fostering a shared vision and supporting partnerships. Studies of the Milwaukee experience provide insights on how the twenty-three classroom, school, and district variables identified by Russell, Bebell, and O'Dwyer (2003) interrelate in the process of technology-reliant educational innovation. This case also extends this conceptual framework to include community, corporate, state, federal, and philanthropic influences.

In the mid-1990s, a consensus about the value of computers and telecommunications enabled joint strategic initiatives between a series of Milwaukee school boards and a sequence of superintendents. This continuing agreement on technology as a priority has become one of the few sources of continuity amid the political instability that is characteristic of MPS as well as other large urban districts. Identified as the primary "customers" of technology services, principals and teachers played a lead role in determining the priorities that should govern MPS's investments in technology and the implementation strategies that would maximize the value of computers and telecommunications. These educators' decision-making role in the implementation of technology generalized to produce a strong bottom-up and middle-out leadership style across the district.

Corporate involvement in MPS was motivated by the potential of educational technology, and improving the district's investments in and use of management technologies provided common ground on which business and district leaders could form alliances. A shared interest in the potential power of computers and telecommunications also prompted academic institutions in the Milwaukee region to work with MPS on strategic planning initiatives that rapidly encompassed more than technology-related issues. The public has supported the district's technology work in part because school-based infrastructure led to community learning centers; these in turn have fostered a broader dialogue about instructional improvement among parents, taxpayers, and educators. Links to regional

and national resources on technology-reliant innovations, the creation of
the National Technology Advisory Board, and the expertise-across-distance
project funded by the Joyce Foundation have resulted in an influx of external insights on all aspects of educational innovation.

Technology-reliant innovations in MPS have generated a strong record
of increased student motivation and higher academic achievement. In particular, urban students who would typically leave school equipped only for
low-level vocational jobs now have access to better-paying technical occu-
pations with a career path that can lead to higher education. Technology-
reliant curricular innovations provide support in subject matter for
instructors who lack optimal background in the content they are teaching,
leading to professional growth that enhances their overall ability as educators. Widespread staff involvement with e-mail and the Internet has fostered collaboration between the teachers union and the district leadership
on joint initiatives such as the curriculum design assistant. These successes
are providing leverage to change deeply entrenched, dysfunctional practices on the part of district staff responsible for curriculum, resulting in
benefits for all aspects of instruction.

The professional support portal initiative now under way is prompting
similar redesign of the district's approaches—both high-touch and high-
tech—to new teacher induction and retention, as well as to professional
development for all of its educators. Emerging information systems for data-
driven decision making are starting to aid teachers and administrators in
improving student learning outcomes and maximizing organizational effectiveness. Reports based on this information also provide a means of involving parents more deeply in their children's education.

Overall, MPS is leveraging its computers and telecommunications infrastructure in multiple ways that collectively are transforming the district's
operations. Too often, investments in technology are narrowly judged on
just one type of capability (for example, "The Internet is in every classroom; did test scores go up?"). Elaborate metrics now exist for calculating
the "total cost of ownership" for information technology (Dickard, 2003),
but estimates of total benefit from this investment tend to dramatically
underestimate the full range of potential improvements enabled by a protean districtwide infrastructure.

Union City, New Jersey, is often cited as a school district and community that has succeeded in establishing a substantial, sustainable process
of educational improvement (Center for Children and Technology, 2000).
Their model of scaling up has inspired many, and other districts have successfully applied strategies that Union City developed (see Chapter One).
However, some parts of the Union City story are difficult to generalize to

other settings because the district is relatively small (about 10,000 students). If MPS continues to succeed with the advances described in this chapter, Milwaukee may offer an inspirational outcome that is similar to Union City's in its level of success, but in a district that is about ten times the size of Union City's—big enough for the MPS model to transfer to many large districts.

To generalize heuristics from Milwaukee's successes to other districts, additional research is needed on the conditions for success that enabled the advances discussed here. In particular, understanding the core sources of effectiveness in MPS's innovation model is vital to preserving implementation fidelity in the mutual adaptation process for transferring this suite of strategies to new settings. The themes in scalable, sustainable innovation that this volume synthesizes will aid in identifying research questions and methods to guide such studies.

REFERENCES

Anderson, R. A., & Becker, H. J. (2001). *School investments in instructional technology.* Irvine: Center for Research on Information Technology and Organizations, University of California, Irvine; and Minneapolis: University of Minnesota.

Bascia, N., & Hargreaves, A. (Eds.). (2000). *The sharp edge of educational change: Teaching, leading, and the realities of reform.* New York: Routledge, 2000.

Becker, H. J., & Anderson, R. E. (2000). *Subject and teacher objectives for computer-using classes by school socio-economic status.* Irvine: Center for Research on Information Technology and Organizations, University of California, Irvine; and Minneapolis: University of Minnesota.

Center for Children and Technology. (2000). *The transformation of Union City: 1989 to present.* New York: Center for Children and Technology; and Union City, NJ: Board of Education.

Datnow, A., Hubbard, L., & Mehan, H. (2002). *Extending educational reform: From one school to many.* New York: Routledge and Falmer Press.

Dede, C. (1993). Leadership without followers. In G. Kearsley & W. Lynch (Eds.), *Educational technology: leadership perspectives* (pp. 19–28). Englewood Cliffs, NJ: Educational Technology Publications.

Dede, C. (1998). The scaling-up process for technology-based educational innovations. In C. Dede (Ed.), *Learning with technology: 1998 yearbook of the Association for Supervision and Curriculum Development* (pp. 199–215). Alexandria, VA: Association for Supervision and Curriculum Development.

Dede, C. (2001, May 10). Creating research centers to enhance the effective use of learning technologies. Testimony to the Research Subcommittee, Science Committee, U.S. House of Representatives. Retrieved from http://www.house.gov/science/research/reshearings.htm

Dede, C. (2002). Foreword. In A. Zucker & R. Kozma (Eds.), *The virtual high school: Teaching generation V* (pp. vii–xi). New York: Teachers College Press.

Dede, C., Whitehouse, P., & Brown-L'Bahy, T. (2002). Designing and studying learning experiences that use multiple interactive media to bridge distance and time. In C. Vrasid & G. Glass (Eds.), *Current perspectives on applied information technologies. Vol. 1: Distance education* (pp. 1–30). Greenwich, CN: Information Age Press.

Dickard, N. (Ed.). (2003). *The sustainability challenge: Taking edtech to the next level.* Washington, DC: Benton Foundation.

Fullan, M., & Miles, M. (1992, June). Getting reform right: What works and what doesn't. *Phi Delta Kappan, 73*(10), 745–752.

Grover, S. (2003). *The problem of new teacher retention and the Milwaukee Public Schools professional support portal.* Unpublished manuscript.

Mislevy, R., Steinberg, L., Almond, R., Haertel, G., & Penuel, W. (2001). *Leverage points for improving educational assessment.* CSE technical report. Los Angeles: Center for Research on Evaluation, Standards, and Student Testing.

National Commission on Teaching and America's Future. (2003). *No dream denied: A promise to America's children.* New York: National Commission on Teaching and America's Future.

Pellegrino, J., Chudowsky, N., & Glaser, R. (2001). Knowing what students know: The science and design of educational assessment. Washington, DC: National Academy Press.

Penuel, W. R., Korbak, C., Lewis, A., Shear, L., Toyama, Y., & Yarnell, L. (2002). *GLOBE year 7 evaluation: Exploring student research and inquiry in GLOBE.* Menlo Park, CA: SRI International.

Russell, M., Bebell, D., & O'Dwyer, L. (2003). *Use, support, and effect of instructional technology study: An overview of the USEIT study and the participating districts.* Boston: Technology and Assessment Study Collaborative, Boston College. Retrieved from http://www.bc.edu/research/intasc/studies/USEIT/description.shtml

Snipes, J., Doolittle, F., & Herlihy, C. (2002). *Foundations for success: Case studies of how urban school districts improve student achievement.* Washington, DC: Council of Great City Schools. Retrieved from http://www.cgcs.org/reports/Foundations.html

Spillane, J., Halverson, R., & Diamond, J. (2001). Investigating school leadership practice: A distributed perspective. *Educational Researcher, 30*(3), 23–28.

SCALING UP DATA USE IN CLASSROOMS, SCHOOLS, AND DISTRICTS

Sam Stringfield, Jeffrey C. Wayman,
Mary E. Yakimowski-Srebnick

Software for student data analysis can enhance
classroom learning and streamline data management.

A Vision of the Near Future

Ms. Lockhart, a middle school teacher, arrives at her desk with fifteen minutes to spare before her academic day begins. She checks the control panel on her desktop computer. Fernando and Jamaal will be absent (their parents have phoned in or sent an e-mail message); Susan will return from four days of family vacation. Both Susan and her mother promise that she'll make up her schoolwork over the weekend.

Last night, Ms. Lockhart finished grading her third-period students' projects. She uploaded their grades into her grade book. Projects submitted electronically were uploaded into students' portfolios. On the way to class, she left the other projects at the front desk to be scanned in by a first-period student worker.

Scotty's work had been particularly troubling to her, with odd spelling errors and occasional words left out. This morning, she opens his electronic portfolio and notices similar problems in his third- and fifth-grade products, with substantial variance in achievement test scores over time. Ms. Lockhart doesn't have a lot of time today, so she sends an e-mail to the special education diagnostic team, asking that someone look at the latest document and at Scotty's prior work and test scores.

She quickly opens today's lesson set: English grammar for most students. Three students will be retaking a quiz they failed last week, and three other students will be writing extra-credit book reports.

The bell rings, her students arrive, and first period begins. Janie is absent for the fourth consecutive day. Ms. Lockhart's completion of the electronic roll book will automatically signal the main office to contact Janie's family.

With fifteen minutes to go in the period, Ms. Lockhart informs the students that their homework assignments are both on the screen at the front of the class and in their e-mail files. She checks the three students' retaken quizzes, congratulates two (and enters their new grades in her electronic grade book), and assigns a different type of review to the third student. Ms. Lockhart e-mails the third student's mother, asking her to double-check the boy's homework tonight and to send an e-mail back if she notices anything that the teacher should particularly attend to over the next week.

With two minutes to go in the class, Ms. Lockhart informs students that their end-of-term grades will be available in their Web folders and on paper in a week. She will be asking several students and a few parents to come in for shared problem solving before the next semester begins. Most of the class, she says reassuringly, is doing well, and several students have shown remarkable progress this semester.

A look at her computer desktop reveals a new message: Janie's family moved without giving notice to the school. Ms. Lockhart sighs and writes a brief e-mail to the receiving teacher, attaching a copy of Janie's permanent record. She tells the class that they won't be seeing Janie anymore but that she is well and attending another school in the district. Ms. Lockhart offers to forward any good-bye e-mail messages that anyone would care to send.

Ms. Lockhart uses a few extra minutes at the end of her day to explore some data disaggregation. She finds that those of her students who receive free lunches have improved on both the state and local assessments this year. She is happy about that, since narrowing the achievement gap between her more and less advantaged students is a goal she set at the beginning of the year.

The bell rings, and twenty-eight preteens bound out of their seats and into the hall, talking and laughing and moping and picking on each other, just as their grandparents did fifty years earlier. In several senses, nothing is different about this school scenario. Parents still pull children out of school to visit grandparents or doctors or to go to Disneyland. Teachers still don't have enough time to meet with special education specialists or to go to the office to look through a child's permanent record.

Yet a great deal is different. Ms. Lockhart keeps her attendance and grade books electronically. At a moment's notice, she not only can see students' products from her classes but also can view products from years gone by. She can forward a special education referral to the proper team with a few mouse clicks. Parents can leave messages, and by 9:00 A.M. every day, they can check whether their children actually showed up for class. The technology that assists Ms. Lockhart is doing several of the things technology does best: efficiently storing and retrieving data and moving relevant information to the people who can most professionally act on it. Ms. Lockhart, who was not significantly better prepared to become a teacher than her predecessors of ten years earlier, is nonetheless a significantly more effective, more efficient educational professional.

Scaling Up Student-Data Software

The much-quoted systems theorist Peter Senge (1990) notes that there are three steps along the path to what, for the purposes of this publication, we are calling scaling up. The first is simply an idea. Ideas are wonderful, whether priceless or a dime a dozen. For example, flight is an idea that has captured human imagination throughout recorded history.

The second step is invention. An invention demonstrates that an idea can be actualized in real life. Senge used the Wright brothers' plane as an example of an invention. But although these planes were the products of a remarkable set of technological advances, the planes themselves had marginal practical value.

The third step is innovation. Senge defined an innovation as a system that allows an invention to be brought to widespread practical use at a reasonable price. By Senge's definition, the DC-3, first flown in 1934, was the first innovation in air flight. Seventy years after their introduction, DC-3s are still being flown commercially around the world.

Computer technology to improve educators' effectiveness should be on the verge of being scaled up. The example of Ms. Lockhart doesn't contain a single new idea and would require no inventions in order to be fully realized. All that is missing is innovation, in the form of the total package: software that integrates aspects of the disconnected world of education software in a manner that efficiently responds to the needs of educators. This concept is tantalizingly close, yet in practice, so distant. While the rest of the world advances at the speed of light, education chugs along, using practices and technologies built for a less technical world. Consequently, we hope to use this chapter as a forum to advance some ideas, opinions, and information that will help move computer software closer to scaling up for use in gathering and analyzing student data.

This chapter has three purposes. The first is to make a few generalizations about scaling up student-data software within the relatively abstract field of U.S. education. The second is to describe state-of-the-art features available in today's student-data software and suggest issues that schools should consider in choosing and implementing such software. The third is to muse briefly about possible directions and implications of this type of ongoing innovation in educational technology.

Moving from idea to invention to innovation in the uses of technology in education sounds simple, but in fact, it has proved frustratingly complex. N. L. Gage, editor of the first *Handbook of Research on Teaching* (1963), states that he has been told throughout his long career that "computers are going to totally transform education—it's just around the corner." He reports that a fifty-year corner is something to gaze at in wonder (N. L. Gage, personal communication, 2000). Computers offer a wide array of capabilities and uses that are directly applicable to education, so why have computers not yet transformed education? Why has implementation in our classrooms and schools been slow?

Two conditions are necessary for a product or service to take off: a cost-efficient delivery system and a product that is demonstrably more useful than its predecessors. In the computer world, cost-efficient delivery has arrived. We hardly need discuss the remarkable increase in raw computing power and great reduction in costs that have marked computer development over the past few years. In spite of cost breakthroughs, however, educators have struggled to implement computer solutions that are clearly better and more useful than their predecessors. Small advances in use have occurred, but currently no computer solutions exist that perform functions so beneficial that no school or classroom can afford to be without them. Our research, however, leads us to believe that this may be the decade in which we turn Gage's corner. Inventions have not been lacking in this area of education, but integrative innovations have. That situation is changing rapidly.

We hypothesize that the first area in which computing will experience a full-blown educational innovation will be one in which computing technology is already well established: the use of computers, networks, and

Internet connectivity for the storage, analysis, and display of data for use in decision making. Known broadly by many terms (for example, *information management, knowledge management*), this application is an indispensable staple in noneducational settings such as business, where capable, sophisticated tools for delivering information to those in a position to use it have been widely implemented. Known by other terms in education (for example, *data-based decision making, knowledge-based decision making*), this area holds great promise. Schools have traditionally been data-rich but information-poor; that is, educational systems collect huge quantities of data on students, staff, and organizations, but rarely is this data accessible for improved decision making.

We believe that the last major impediment to widespread implementation of data use is at the software level, and we believe that this hurdle can be cleared soon. Technological advances in data warehousing and delivery have been accomplished in many other areas, and software companies are beginning to focus on the development and marketing of efficient, easy-to-use products for school use. Also, educators are becoming more aware that using data in decision making can benefit students in ways beyond simply fulfilling the requirements of accountability measures such as the No Child Left Behind Act. Thus, we believe the pieces are in place for a true advancement in what information management technology can offer education.

Information Management

In addition to having the advantage of building from well-understood technologies, information management (IM) has several useful applications for school personnel who want to use student data to improve instruction:

- By storing and retrieving varied performance data on individual students, IM technology can substantially increase the information available to professional educators.

- By easily and quickly generating standard reports on classes and schools, IM can provide useful information within and across classes and schools in formats that educators at all levels can quickly share and use to seek best practices.

- By allowing the generation of unique reports fitted to the questions of an individual educator or group, IM technology can aid in knowledge-based decisions tailored to a specific context (such as a particular school or locality, or use by a particular group of teachers).

- By making daily and annual information available to parents, media such as Web-based data presentations and reports can increase parent involvement in everything from nightly homework to long-term educational planning.

- By making a broad range of student data easily available to teachers, IM technology can help teachers become classroom researchers.

- By making a broad range of multilevel aggregated and disaggregated data available to principals and central administrators, IM can provide increased opportunities to examine and understand factors affecting their schools' progress or lack thereof.

- By making available to teachers information previously obtained only through poring over hard copies of student records, IM can enable increased familiarity with students and help inform classroom practice.

- By storing years of students' actual work in diverse areas such as writing, mathematics, and art, IM has the potential to offer a comprehensive, real-time portfolio of student work and progress.

That a comprehensive solution for widespread data use in education is not yet on the market presents a unique opportunity for school stakeholders and educational researchers to help shape the future of this technology. Educational settings present a different set of challenges from business settings, so software companies will have to research the field to provide tools appropriate for widespread use in education. For IM to truly enhance educational decision making, it is imperative that the market for educational IM technology be driven by the needs of education, not vice versa. Educators can participate in IM innovation by becoming discerning consumers, making educated software purchases and helping software developers learn exactly what schools need to provide the best education for our students.

What Should Scaled-Up Software Look Like?

It is both useful and necessary to speculate about the features that ideal software for student-data analysis might present. Many of the available products do very well within their area of concentration, so speculation can build on the knowledge and experience that has informed the development of current software. We believe that educators will have little tolerance for limiting, frustrating, or esoteric solutions, so the best product will be one that provides a set of data analyses to the user in an intuitive, sensible manner, thus promoting data access and increasing educators' desire to pursue the substantial range of information that is available in student data. To truly inform practice, a product must provide student-data analysis for teachers as well as administrators.

The presentation and quality of the data are inextricably connected. Any analysis of student data is worthwhile only to the extent that the data underlying it are worthwhile, and we anticipate that many schools will require assistance in building data sets that aid educational improvement. Problems will crop up if software companies make schools solely respon-sible for the quality of the data; unfortunately, the simple directive "send us your data" is a prescription for failure. Thus, a scalable program should either have the capacity to provide a near-perfect underlying data set or be seamlessly compatible with a separate, affordable solution that provides clean data; the company producing such a program should assist schools and districts with the problems inherent in dealing with school data.

Educators would want to be able to access the software from home or anywhere they might choose to work. Accessing a large database from a distance raises the issue of access speed, since slow response time is likely to cause frustration and almost certainly reduce data use. Therefore, a highly marketable program would be accessible via the Web, so school personnel can have the greatest possible access to data, and would pro-vide a response speed that enables wider and deeper data querying.

To minimize user frustration and hence maximize use, the user inter-face of the software would be intuitive and easy to use. Given the time demands that school personnel face and the fact that many are not com-puter experts, educators will make more and better use of data software if it is presented in a familiar form. For example, the growing use of the Internet has made many users comfortable with elements such as check boxes, pull-down menus, and click-through links. A company that pro-vides a scalable data solution will employ formats that are easily used as well as a user interface that is intuitive, requiring little or no training.

When the user logs on, the ideal interface would provide quick access to important information, and such access would serve as a springboard to other forms of information. Areas of information would be nearly seamless; the underlying database necessarily would contain different areas of data—the more transparent to the user, the easier for navigation. The software should also provide multiple methods of accessing infor-mation, preferably across a range of complexities suitable for every level of user, as well as multiple ways to represent this information through a variety of graphs and tables.

Although query tools often exist for power users, it is equally important that they be provided for less sophisticated users. Certainly, efficiency is gained when users can lean heavily on standard reports for information, but standardized features should not impose limits. Query tools should be simple to use and nonrestrictive, allowing access to a wide range of data and the ability to provide simultaneous analysis of many variables. Broad "drill-down" capabilities (for example, the ability to query a school-level finding to efficiently examine a subset of data at a grade, classroom, or student level) are important features that provide maximum user ease and flexibility. This drill-down capacity should be flexible and available from anywhere in the program; users should be able to click on graphs, tables, or any form of disaggregation in order to gain more granular information at the student level.

The type of data accessible would be comprehensive and relevant. Users are limited when the information available does not answer all of their questions. Users will grow in their analytic abilities only if offered a wide range of information that is fully applicable to their situation. Thus, preformatted reports would be constructed through a process of thorough consultation with school personnel, and user access to data would be provided in a manner that places few limitations on the user's potential to develop as a data consumer. Further, the items available for analysis would rarely leave the user wanting more.

Additional features that would be desirable include the following:

- On-line student work samples. (School personnel should be able to access not only numeric data on a student but also samples of the student's work.)

- The capacity to use many common formats (such as ASCII and Excel) to export data for further analysis.

- The ability to export graphs or other results into processors such as Microsoft Word or Adobe Acrobat.

- Electronic discussion groups or message boards, allowing users from any location to discuss issues relevant to the software. (Yearly or biyearly user-group meetings are also desirable.)

- Easy access to the learning standards that drive local or state assessments.

- The capacity to link a teacher's own student data to data accessed by the system. (For example, a teacher might wish to correlate in-class grades with, say, assessment results from a state test.)

- A price that is affordable to schools and districts. (Areas most in need of the information such systems can provide are often fiscally disadvantaged, operating with few financial resources.)

Currently Available Software

Elsewhere (Wayman, Stringfield, and Yakimowski, 2004), we have reviewed commercially available software that schools can buy to warehouse student data and make it available to teachers and administrators for analysis. Updated reviews are also available on-line (http://www.csos.jhu.edu/ systemics/datause.htm). In our review (Wayman, Stringfield, and Yakimowski, 2004), software was included if it enabled many different levels of school personnel to analyze existing student data for achievement purposes, meaning any data collected and stored by the school, such as achievement test results, demographic data, portfolios, and so on. Thus, software that allowed only district personnel to view student information was not included, nor was software that addressed only school management issues (attendance, absences, and so on) or required ongoing teacher data entry (such as Palm Pilots and data scanning). This chapter can provide only a brief overview.

Table 7.1 lists several programs available for student data analysis as of February 25, 2004, and compares the features they offer. The aims and features of software for analyzing student data are varied, and each company has concentrated on one or two areas. No single piece of software accomplishes everything. Companies may focus on providing reports, easy data access, or assessment data, to name a few examples. For instance, most companies offer preformatted reports of student data that can be generated with a mouse click. Fewer companies offer stored queries, which allow users to perform a customized query, then save that query for their own or others' use. Only three companies offer on-line student work samples or electronically accessible portfolios of student work.

These programs do share some features that a school should expect in software for student-data management. All of the programs in Table 7.1 are Web-based and thus are accessible from any Internet connection (although most implementations of QSP use the desktop version, which is PC-based). All programs offer at least descriptive analyses (for example, means of different groups and subgroups), and all offer the capacity to produce reports based on the disaggregations mandated by the No Child Left Behind Act. All offer some form of ongoing technical support, and all companies are at least aware of the evolving Schools Interoperability Framework (SIF), which we discuss later in this chapter.

Thus, software companies provide some common basic services, but for the most part, today's schools must choose software based on an area of concentration. We anticipate that as the field moves toward scale, schools will be able to select from more comprehensive programs. In the following sections, we discuss several issues that should be carefully considered in order to implement a data analysis system that suits a school's needs.

Table 7.1. Characteristics of Commercially Available Software for Information Management in Education

	Account from SchoolNet	Concert™ Inform from Pearson Digital Learning	Data Miner from Chancery Student Management systems	Data Point from NSSE	Ease-e from TetraData	EDsmart	eScholar	QSP from CRESST	Sagebrush Analytics, powered by Swift-Knowledge	SAMS from Executive Intelligence	Socrates Data System from CRM	STARS from SchoolCity	Virtual EDucation from EDmin
Company focus	Educational technology	Management of assessment data	Student information systems	Educational research	Educational technology	Educational research	Data warehousing	Educational research	Data analysis and reporting	Educational technology	Educational research	Educational technology	Educational Learning management
Version	4.0	2.01	4.1	n/a	4.5	3.2	5.0	4.3	5.1	3.4	2.2	2.7.26	5.5
Preformatted reports	x		x		x	x	x	x	x	x	x	x	
Query tool for less-advanced users													x
Stored queries	x	x	x	x	x	x	x	x	x	x	x	x	x
On-line student work samples			x	x				x					
User discussion boards or user meetings	x				x	x	x	x		x	x		x
Accepts data formats in addition to ASCII	x	x	x		x	x	x	x	x	x	x	x	x

Variable	Account from SchoolNet	Concert™ Inform from Pearson Digital Learning	Data Miner from Chancery	Data Point from NSSE	Ease-e from TetraData	EDsmart	eScholar	QSP from CRESST	Sagebrush Analytics, powered by Swift-Knowledge	SAMS from Executive Intelligence	Socrates Data System from CRM	STARs from SchoolCity	Virtual EDucation from EDmin
Variable set customized to fit school needs		x	x	x	x	x		x	x	x	x	x	x
Company will house data	x	x		x	x	x			x	x	x	x	x
School may house data	x		x		x	x	x	x	x	x	x	x	x
Company helps collect data	x	x	x	x	x	x	x	x	x		x	x	x
Reports SIF compliance	x	x	x	x	x	x	x		x	x	x	x	x
SIF-certified	x		x		x	x	x			x			x
Number of districts in use	40	25[a]	83	15	464	27	750	100	35	20	92	28	110

[a] *Some districts included in this number are operating software under the Scholar Suite name, marketed by Lightspan.*

Considerations in Implementing a Data Analysis System

Issues discussed in this section include a thorough assessment of basic data needs, time to implementation, cost, choosing a vendor, and the Schools Interoperability Framework. In addition, many schools will be faced with the choice of whether to build (use district staff to create and implement the system), buy (purchase a commercially available product and services), or develop a hybrid of the two.

Assessment of Data Needs

The first step a school or district should take toward implementing a student-data analysis system is a thorough assessment of data, needs, and available resources, including an exhaustive inventory of data sources, a survey of analysis needs and goals, and choosing whether to implement the data system using local staff or contracted help.

Data considerations start with an inventory—a catalogue of what data exist and where they are located. It is not uncommon for student data to be stored in different locations, ranging from a main district data store to an Excel spreadsheet on a counselor's computer to loose papers in a teacher's files, so it is important to identify every source and location of data. This exploration necessarily interacts with the running inventory of data that will ultimately be made available for analysis.

No analysis system adds value if the underlying data are inaccurate, and school data invariably contain problems, often large and vexing ones. Therefore, schools should assess the quality of the extant data and estimate the resources required to "clean" them (for example, to correct errors, omissions, and redundancies) so that they can be integrated. Both school districts and vendors report that one immediate benefit of implementing a data analysis system is the opportunity to clean and improve existing data sets. Often, unanticipated benefits emerge when people at different levels become engaged in this cleaning and data-set integration process.

Currently available software presents a wide range of specialization. Some products offer strengths in data efficiency, and others are strong in data presentation or graphics, but no current product offers great strengths in all areas. Therefore, school systems must carefully evaluate their data and analytic needs in order to identify the software that best fits local needs.

A quality school-data analysis system should provide accurate and efficient storage and retrieval along with useful and intuitive presentation.

Systems that provide fantastic presentation of data with slow retrieval or cumbersome data management are not useful; neither are solutions that provide excellent data management and access but poor data presentation.

Schools should also take care to assess the types of data, presentation, and analyses that will be most helpful in making educational decisions in context. A paradox exists here, however; even well-trained professionals seldom know exactly what they will find most useful and what they will need until they are well into their work. Therefore, we suggest that schools cast a wide net in this assessment, seeking input from many different types of school personnel and software implementation personnel. Development of software for analyzing student data is in its infancy, so assessment of software needs will undoubtedly evolve as the capabilities of various options become more widely known. We thus envision software needs assessment as evolutionary in its own right; needs assessment and implementation mutually inform the ongoing decision-making process, and we recommend that schools assess their data needs with an eye toward future expansion and flexibility.

What does this mean for the district or school that wishes to start today? In terms of currently available software, there is no best program because the focuses and features of the software packages vary greatly. However, many programs provide valuable student-data analyses, and it is possible for schools to choose an adequate program today while also planning to take advantage of future technological improvements.

Some schools and systems have relatively clean data or have the human resources necessary to quickly organize and substantially improve the quality of their data sets. Others have data that would require a great deal of attention, and the processes involved in data preparation and cleaning may seem intimidating. For schools and school systems with rougher data sets, it is helpful to know that many districts and software companies have been through this process, so it is possible to learn from the hard-won experience of others. Such help is often available from companies hired to implement a school data warehouse and analysis system.

Third-party assistance is also available in other areas. For instance, many commercial warehousing and analysis companies offer support during the initial data inventory, helping schools identify potential data sources and merge data from dissimilar formats. Although the cost of adequate computing power and data storage capacity continues to drop dramatically, these costs may still be problematic or expensive for some schools or districts. Many commercial warehousing vendors offer options for housing school data, promising fast access on the Internet.

Ultimately, schools and districts must decide whether efforts described in this section can best be handled within the organization or by outside contractors. Our belief is that unless a district is certain that the expertise to deal with data problems quickly and efficiently exists in-house, the experience that an outside organization brings to the process is well worth the cost, especially when time and accuracy are considered.

Time to Implementation

Rapid, successful implementation is important for the long-term development of a data-based decision-making climate. Experiencing early success is a correlate of long-term implementation success in a range of change efforts (Fullan and Miles, 1992). Speedy realization of at least some aspects of a useful information management system will sustain interest and improve education sooner rather than later. Many of those interviewed for this chapter stressed the importance of getting data up and running quickly, even if less than a full orchestra of data or reports is initially available.

The amount of time required to achieve implementation is a major consideration in choosing whether to build or buy a data system. Developed locally, implementation of a data warehouse with reporting and analysis capabilities often takes years, while most commercial vendors promise an established (that is, running and useful) product in a matter of months. Competent commercial vendors can usually bring prior practical experience and specialized staffing, and thus can often get a system established and functional much faster than can school personnel who are building a system from scratch. This is not a criticism of local school technology personnel; it merely reflects the efficiency advantages when an organization or business specializes in a particular product and set of business processes. Thus, schools that choose to build their own product should understand the potential costs associated with extensive time to implementation.

Cost

Unfortunately, for both commercially available and locally built systems, dollar cost structures of currently available software are complicated and are difficult to accurately establish. However, we are able to cast light on a few areas that consumers should consider.

In evaluating the monetary cost of a commercial system, it is important to recognize that the final cost depends on many variables. Depending on

the size of the school and the number of features chosen, the cost for a
school to implement a system can range from as low as two to over ten
dollars per student per year, with a higher cost in the first year of implementation.

The variables that determine cost are numerous. For example, the number of students per year for whom data will be collected and stored is one
such variable; cost breaks are typically available for larger amounts of
students. Opting for help with data collection and cleaning sometimes carries an added cost, as does opting for outside data storage. Some companies charge for consulting time spent with representatives; others build an
estimated amount of consulting time into the per-student structure. In outlining a total dollar amount, vendors may package various options
together for one cost, or many of these features and others (such as access
to state standards information) may be included in the basic system.
Whether these options are bundled together, chosen separately, or
included in the basic system, it is hardly surprising that more features typically translate to higher cost.

Costs for implementing a locally developed system are typically even
more difficult to ascertain. Such costs include deployment of hardware
and other materials, along with salaries and benefits for local employees
used in the project. Not only must local talent be paid (a cash cost), but
the time they spend developing, debugging, and implementing the product is time that could be spent on other projects (an ongoing opportunity
cost). These other projects will then either be ignored or pursued with
other staff, resulting in some real but typically unquantified cost. Data
cleaning presents other cost issues. In our interviews with local educators
and national product developers, we consistently heard that school data
are almost always messier than school personnel anticipate. Schools planning in-house implementation should fully assess the quality of their data
and the ability of the personnel structure to handle this project over the
short and the long term. In addition, there is no guarantee that a locally
developed product will initially work in the ways intended, so development costs past initial implementation often further complicate the picture. Therefore, a clear understanding of the school organization and
issues surrounding implementation of such a system is vital in order to
accurately evaluate the cost of local development.

Time must also be evaluated as a cost from another perspective. Schools
are about the work of education, and in education, lost time carries
costs. Many schools currently possess the data needed to guide educational practice, but not in a practical, usable form. Each day and year that
this data goes unused is a lost opportunity to better diagnose and educate

children. In evaluating costs, school entities must include opportunity cost in the equation.

Schools are often faced with the choice of whether to buy a system or build one using local staff. The buy-versus-build choice often boils down to a trade-off between the seemingly lower cost of a slowly developed local system and the seemingly higher cost but more rapid implementation of a more refined, commercially developed system. Contrasting a less expensive locally built data tool, which takes two years to develop and implement, with a higher-cost commercially built tool, which is implemented in three months, one well might conclude that the locally built product is cheaper. But does the lost opportunity to better diagnose and educate children justify the savings in dollars?

Choosing a Vendor

Should a district choose to purchase a commercially available student-data management and analysis system, there are many products from which to choose. Reviews and discussion of such products are available (Wayman, Stringfield, and Yakimowski, 2004), and product updates can be found on-line (www.csos.jhu.edu/systemics/datause.htm). Software companies focus on different strengths, so no single company currently offers a software package that is strong in every area. Consequently, choosing a vendor entails finding the best fit for the local district's or school's needs.

In choosing a vendor, school systems first should evaluate the range of services they wish to purchase. Some vendors offer services beyond delivery of data, which schools may find useful. For instance, a school in need of help with educational improvement or professional development related to data use might do well to contract with companies that provide these added services.

Given the seriousness and cost of the software-purchasing decision, it is important that decision makers at schools and districts contact others at schools using the software, query them thoroughly, and visit as many as possible in order to get practical feedback. School decision makers should not discount the details related to their own negotiation experience with the vendor: Does the company return calls in a timely manner? Is the company forthright and responsive to information requests? Also, the purchaser would be well advised to establish multiple relationships at the prospective company, especially with management personnel (for example, relationships with both a salesperson and a relatively senior executive or technical specialist). This not only helps school personnel learn about the company but also will provide resources should problems arise.

Finally, decision makers need to consider the long-term viability of software companies. Obviously, making a long-term commitment to a company with an unstable future is problematic, but in any start-up industry, deciding which company will stand the test of time is always a gamble. There are no absolute answers to these questions, so schools and districts should assess these issues within their own context. One possible guide is industry standards, which are currently being explored through the Schools Interoperability Framework, discussed in the next section.

Schools Interoperability Framework

The Schools Interoperability Framework (SIF) is a collaboration of school-data stakeholders that sets data exchange standards in order to enable software packages to communicate without further software intervention. The SIF Web site (www.sifinfo.org) identifies SIF as "an industry initiative to develop an open specification for ensuring that K–12 instructional and administrative software applications work together more effectively."

SIF came into existence because stakeholders in the technology industry recognized that school options for software were growing rapidly and that if no standards were set for intersoftware communication, schools could potentially be handicapped in their options for improving and upgrading their data capabilities over time. When SIF was formed, school personnel were experiencing problems such as redundant data entry, loss of data, and an increasing amount of time spent on data entry and management. It is feared that without industry standards to make communication possible, school systems' ability to send and receive data efficiently (for example, to and from state departments) could be greatly hampered. Consequently, SIF members have engaged in ongoing work to establish industry standards, defining formats for shared data, naming conventions, and rules of interaction among software applications. The current list of SIF members includes educational technology companies, school districts, federal and state government offices, and research organizations, among others.

The SIF initiative is an ongoing project. Accomplishments include the development of a Zone Integration Server that enables software programs to communicate with one another, the establishment of definitions and objects for commonly used student data (such as name, address, and gender), and, most recently, the launch of the SIF compliance program in May 2003. This program allows software applications to be tested by a third-party validation system in order to ensure both schools and vendors that applications developed using the SIF standard will work together. More details of the program, including a list of SIF-compliant applications, can be found at www.opengroup.org/sif/cert/cert_prodlist.tpl. Ongoing efforts include establishing forms and definitions for learning data such as grades and assessment information. SIF is also working with a number of states and the U.S. Department of Education to enable SIF to support district-to-state reporting in support of the No Child Left Behind Act.

The benefit that SIF holds for schools in the process of buying software is the assurance that SIF-compliant applications will be able to communicate with one another. No school wishes to be in the position of depending on a software package that later proves to be incompatible with other software. Consequently, if SIF definitions become the industry standard, buying an application from a company that does not place emphasis on SIF compliance could place a school or system in the awkward position of having to change technologies later.

In general, school personnel should take care to protect their software investment against future isolation by ensuring that the product can communicate with other products. When considering a purchase, school personnel should thoroughly question software vendors about their knowledge of and involvement with SIF and about plans for making gains in compliance. School personnel may access a full set of questions regarding SIF compliance, including language suitable for use in a request for proposals, on the SIF Web site (http://www.sifinfo.org/compliance/compliance_educator.asp). SIF represents a promising initiative, and SIF standards offer a reasonable starting point for evaluating software interaction.

Future Opportunities

This chapter assumes the validity of the following proposition, prevalent in both business management and school effects literature: creating classrooms and schools that are richer in data and information will raise student achievement. Formal research and our own observations indicate that being data-driven is a phenomenon that generally does not occur in the basic structure of the typical school. We believe that the absence of data-informed decision making is not due to educators' aversion to being informed. Rather, the wealth of data potentially available in schools is often stored in ways that make it virtually inaccessible to teachers and principals and generally far from analysis-friendly.

The current state of school data represents an opportunity for a true innovation in education. Given that the current situation intersects with the rapid advances in data warehouse development and advances in data analysis and presentation software, the potential to solve a large, practical problem in public education seems great.

In fact, both local districts and for-profit corporations have spent much of the past decade developing and refining products that facilitate the storage, analysis, and presentation of educational data. We believe that this situation is leading to a series of additional opportunities, some of which are discussed in the following questions:

1. Will the field of education move not just toward achieving better quantitative data and reporting, but also toward making rich areas of student performance information readily available to students, parents, and teachers? Or will data continue their history of primarily serving the higher levels of educational organizations?

2. Which products will be most successful at going to scale? Will they be locally developed and hence, presumably, highly contextually sensitive? Will they be developed by states? Will they be commercially developed?

3. Will schools and districts that opt not to develop their own product tend to buy a range of software to solve different challenges (such as data warehousing and presentation), or will they tend to buy one unified solution to their data needs?

4. To what extent will the combination of technological advances and the reporting requirements of the No Child Left Behind Act accelerate the scaling up of data warehousing and data reporting and presentation mechanisms?

5. Which districts or companies will listen to their customers the most, designing products that create the deepest penetration into schools and classrooms?

6. Which types of standardized reports or query tools will prove the most useful and popular among educators? In other words, what do educators want from their software?

7. If schools are to promote a climate of data-based decision making, how much professional development is needed and available for teachers and other school personnel? How will schools promote a climate of data-based decision making?

8. Can educators incorporate data involvement within current time limitations, or will it represent another burden on already full schedules?

9. What support will teacher preparation programs provide? Today's preservice teachers are excellent candidates for learning to use software, since they belong to the first generation to grow up in a climate of ubiquitous computer use.

10. What support will educational researchers provide? Can educational research provide relevant and cogent contributions that will prove useful as educators learn, refine, and implement these techniques? We hope so, and we hope to join those who answer this question in the affirmative!

REFERENCES

Fullan, M. G., & Miles, M. M. (1992). Getting reform right: What works and what doesn't. *Phi Delta Kappan, 73*(10), 744–752.

Gage, N. L. (Ed.). (1963). *Handbook of research on teaching.* Chicago: Rand McNally.

Senge, P. M. (1990). *The fifth discipline.* New York: Doubleday.

Wayman, J. C., Stringfield, S., & Yakimowski, M. (2004). *Software enabling school improvement through the analysis of student data* (Technical Report #67). Baltimore, MD: Johns Hopkins University Center for Research on the Education of Students Placed at Risk.

FOUNDATIONS FOR SUCCESS IN THE GREAT CITY SCHOOLS

LESSONS FROM SOME
FASTER-IMPROVING DISTRICTS

Michael Casserly, Jason C. Snipes

Political buy-in, curriculum reform, and data-based decision making drive educational change in urban schools.

THE PROBLEM OF HOW TO SCALE UP successful practices in large urban school districts has dogged the educational reform movement almost from the beginning. Over the years, research and reform efforts in urban districts have alternated between attempts to turn around individual schools or pockets of schools and efforts to define programs or models that can raise student achievement. But few studies or reforms have focused on improving the system itself.

Some studies have simply argued that the way to bring about wide-scale improvement is to take what has been learned about each individual school or program and apply it systemwide. This approach has had limited success, however, because it does not help practitioners sort through the numerous programs and strategies that have been successful in one place or another, nor does it address the systemic problems that exist across the schools in a district. Consequently, many schools and districts simply buy, adopt, or implement a variety of programs, hoping that the mixture will work. Or they conclude that if their principals were more like those who have turned around troubled schools, the district would be better off.

The lack of solid information about scaling up has been particularly frustrating for urban school districts, where the pressure to reform is intense. The sixty school districts that constitute the Council of the Great City Schools—a coalition of the nation's largest urban school systems— enroll about 15 percent of the nation's children but about 40 percent of its poor students, English language learners, and students of color. Without wide-scale improvement in these districts, the U.S. public education system will be unable to meet the challenges ahead.

This chapter describes the results of a study conducted by the Council of the Great City Schools and MDRC, Inc., that looked at how urban districts have improved on a systemwide scale. The results were published in the report *Foundations for Success* (Snipes, Doolittle, and Herlihy, 2002). This chapter also discusses the role of technology in these improvements and lays out promising avenues for future investigations.

The council and MDRC, an independent research firm, conducted this analysis for two reasons. First, many urban school leaders were frustrated about how to translate the research on schools and programs into broader systemic reform. From a practical standpoint, these leaders had to identify systemic levers for change—not just school levers—because as district leaders, they were the ones ultimately being held accountable for results. They needed to know what districts could do to boost performance citywide instead of waiting for individual schools to turn around.

Second, urban schools and districts were asking serious questions about whether reforms they had been pursuing since the 1989 Education Summit were making any difference. Some of these reforms, such as site-based management, emerged from urban schools themselves, while others, such as comprehensive school reform models, came from outside. Little serious work had been done, however, to ascertain whether these and other reforms were producing wide-scale improvement.

The council began its work on urban school improvement by asking whether urban schools were improving on a wide enough scale to warrant further study and which urban districts were making the most progress in student achievement (Casserly, Lewis, Jepson, and Ceperich, 2002). *Foundations for Success* built on the council's initial research by exploring what the successful districts did that could account for their broad-scale improvement.

Several key findings emerged from our studies, including the following:

• Urban school districts that have improved performance on a broad scale share certain preconditions for reform, such as political and organizational stability over a prolonged period and agreement among school board members, the superintendent, and community leaders that student achievement is the top priority.

• The district leadership can play a key role in scaling up improvements through strategies such as setting districtwide goals, holding district- and building-level administrators personally accountable for results, adopting uniform curriculum and instructional approaches that apply to every school, and redefining the main role of the central office as one of guiding, supporting, and improving instruction at the school building level.

• Faster-improving urban school districts provide principals and teachers with early and ongoing assessment data, along with training and support to help them use these data to improve teaching and learning.

The rest of this chapter discusses how we conducted this study, the factors that seem to be associated with progress in faster-improving urban districts, how these districts differ from the lower-performing control districts, and some avenues for further research and practice.

Progress in Urban Schools

To determine whether urban school districts were improving on a wide enough scale to warrant a more detailed analysis, we looked at data from the National Assessment of Educational Progress (NAEP) and data from the states' own assessments. The Council of the Great City Schools commissioned researchers from the Rand Corporation to analyze NAEP data on urban student achievement. The researchers found that from 1992 to 1998 (the most recent data available at the time), the reading achievement of central-city fourth-grade and eighth-grade students showed no change. In mathematics, however, the average performance of central-city students increased by 0.92 points per year from 1992 to 1996 (the most recent data available at the time)—a statistically significant gain. In other words, these central-city students showed no progress in reading but made modest gains in math. Trends in NAEP scores for the nation as a whole generally showed the same patterns. (To find out what has happened in more recent years, the council commissioned a second study that analyzed NAEP data through 2003 and that correlated the results with new census data and results of the new NAEP Urban Trial program. This second study showed significant gains in urban NAEP reading scores.)

To obtain more specific data about achievement in individual cities, the council analyzed state test scores for each of its sixty member school districts. Most states now administer their own assessments. We looked at trends in urban district performance, beginning with the first year a particular state assessment was given and ending with spring 2001. (The results are not comparable across state lines because states use different tests.)

Many cities made gains in both reading and math during the time periods studied, although the math gains are stronger (see Table 8.1). About 40 percent of the cities improved average reading scores at every grade tested between the first year of test administration and 2001. About 63 percent of the cities improved math scores at every grade tested. Since the state test trends in math were similar to the central-city NAEP results, we have considerable confidence that these improvements are real. We are less confident about the reading gains, however, since they are less pronounced and are contradicted by the stagnant NAEP reading scores at that time. The NAEP data indicated that math scores had improved on the widest scale possible—nationwide—but offered no evidence of a substantial "urban effect"—in other words, urban trends differed little from those of the nation as a whole.

We were intrigued, however, by patterns in the state test data that suggested the existence of urban outliers—districts that were making reading and math gains at a greater than average rate for their respective states. According to our analysis, about 44 percent of the cities had improved reading scores in at least half the grades tested at a rate faster than their state's average, and about 46 percent had accomplished this in math. But only 11 percent of the cities—six districts—had made faster gains in reading than their state average in every grade tested, and only 9 percent had done so in math. These districts—Charlotte-Mecklenburg, Fort Worth, Houston, Long Beach, Norfolk, and Sacramento—formed the pool for studying this question: Which urban school districts were making the most wide-scale progress in student achievement?

Trying to answer that question is difficult, in part because so few cities use the same tests. We were forced to rely as much on "informed judgment" as on statistics. We asked a group of educational researchers and

Table 8.1. Percentage of Cities and Grades in the Council of Great City Schools That Improved Reading and Math Scores on State Tests, 2001

	Math	Reading
Cities in which all grades improved	63%	40%
Cities in which all grades improved faster than state average	9%	11%
Cities in which at least 50 percent of grades improved	91%	83%
Cities in which at least 50 percent of grades improved faster than state average	46%	44%
Cities that were at least 50 percent above state average	15%	11%
Grades tested that improved	87%	76%
Grades tested that improved faster than state average	43%	44%
Grades tested that declined	10%	18%
Fourth grades that improved	95%	91%
Eighth grades that improved	80%	60%
Fourth grades that closed the gap between whites and African Americans	60%	78%
Fourth grades that closed the gap between whites and Hispanics	60%	61%
Eighth grades that closed the gap between whites and African Americans	65%	55%
Eighth grades that closed the gap between whites and Hispanics	90%	50%
Tenth grades that closed the gap between whites and African Americans	56%	56%
Tenth grades that closed the gap between whites and Hispanics	81%	56%

school leaders to sort through the disparate data and distinguish the faster-improving urban school systems from the others. We were looking for cities that met the following criteria:

- Improvement in both reading and math in all or nearly all grades through spring 2001
- Faster rates of improvement than their respective states had achieved for at least three years
- Simultaneous narrowing of racial-ethnic achievement gaps

We also wanted the districts to represent a range of sizes, demographics, and geographic characteristics. The research team ultimately selected Charlotte-Mecklenburg, Houston, and Sacramento for further study. The chancellor's district of the New York City public schools, which had shown gains in student achievement and some narrowing of racial-ethnic achievement gaps, was eventually added for limited study.

As shown in Tables 8.2 and 8.3, the three main districts have indeed improved academic achievement on a broad scale and reduced racial-ethnic disparities in student test scores. Moreover, their progress has generally outpaced statewide average gains. Improvements are particularly pronounced at the low end of the achievement distribution and are too extensive to merely reflect gains in a small number of schools or "state effects," the impact of state policies, demographic shifts, and so on.

Progress was greatest at the elementary school level, with some evident at the middle school level. But at the high school level, these districts generally had not raised achievement or reduced racial-ethnic achievement gaps.

Table 8.2. Percentage of Third Graders Below Performance Levels in Reading

	1995	1996	1997	1998	1999	2000	2001	Change
Houston Independent (percentage below 25th percentile on SAT-9)								
African American students	—	—	—	40.5	33.0	29.6	30.2	−10.3
Asian students	—	—	—	17.2	18.4	14.6	12.5	−4.7
Hispanic students	—	—	—	39.6	31.3	25.1	26.7	−12.9
White students	—	—	—	13.8	10.0	10.6	8.7	−5.1
All students	—	—	—	35.1	28.6	24.7	25.4	−9.8
Black-white difference	—	—	—	26.7	23.0	19.0	21.5	−5.2
Hispanic-white difference	—	—	—	25.8	21.3	14.5	18.0	−7.8
Sacramento City (percentage below 25th percentile on SAT-9)								
African American students	—	—	—	57.8	41.3	39.9	—	−18.0
Asian students	—	—	—	54.1	41.7	40.5	—	−13.6
Hispanic students	—	—	—	57.8	45.2	41.7	—	−16.1
White students	—	—	—	29.2	21.4	18.0	—	−11.2
All students	—	—	—	49.3	37.1	35.0	—	−14.4
Black-white difference	—	—	—	28.7	20.0	21.9	—	−6.8
Hispanic-white difference	—	—	—	28.7	23.8	23.7	—	−4.9
Charlotte-Mecklenburg (percentage at level 1 or 2 on EOG)								
African American students	63	61	61	48	45	43	40	−23
White students	24	22	19	15	12	13	10	−14
All students	40	39	37	30	28	28	25	−15
Black-white difference	39	39	42	33	33	30	30	−9

Table 8.3. Percentage of Third Graders Below Performance Levels in Math

	1995	1996	1997	1998	1999	2000	2001	Change
Houston Independent (percentage below 25th percentile on SAT-9)								
African American students	—	—	—	44.5	29.9	25.1	22.1	−22.4
Asian students	—	—	—	12.3	8.1	6.9	4.7	−7.6
Hispanic students	—	—	—	38.3	23.6	18.5	17.1	−21.1
White students	—	—	—	14.3	8.8	7.0	6.5	−7.7
All students	—	—	—	36.3	23.8	19.4	17.5	−18.8
Black-white difference	—	—	—	30.3	21.1	18.0	15.6	−14.7
Hispanic-white difference	—	—	—	24.0	14.8	11.5	10.6	−13.4
Sacramento City (percentage below 25th percentile on SAT-9)								
African American students	—	—	—	64.8	44.5	36.3	—	−28.6
Asian students	—	—	—	42.2	24.8	20.3	—	−21.9
Hispanic students	—	—	—	59.8	37.3	32.6	—	−27.2
White students	—	—	—	32.1	18.6	14.2	—	−17.8
All students	—	—	—	49.2	30.9	25.8	—	−23.4
Black-white difference	—	—	—	32.8	25.9	22.1	—	−10.7
Hispanic-white difference	—	—	—	27.7	18.7	18.4	—	−9.3
Charlotte-Mecklenburg (percentage at level 1 or 2 on EOG)								
African American students	62	58	59	58	53	51	47	−15
White students	20	19	16	18	14	14	10	−10
All students	36	36	35	36	32	31	28	−8
Black-white difference	42	39	43	40	39	37	37	−5

Challenges and Successes in Faster-Improving Urban Districts

Once we had identified a pool of districts that had begun to show broad-scale improvement, we turned our attention to how they did it. Our study was exploratory and preliminary; more research needs to take a serious look at what drives broad-scale improvement. The results of our work are not definitive, but they are provocative and suggest new avenues of research.

In this study, we had to overcome several hurdles and address a fair amount of skepticism. We were told that school effects, teacher effects, student effects, and maybe even state effects do exist, but not district effects. We were also mindful of the popular sentiment that districts—particularly urban districts—were the problem, not the solution. Ironically, we came to agree that in many cases, this doubt concerning district effects was warranted. In too many cities, the district administration produced no effect or had a negative impact. But we found enough progress in some cities to convince us that district effects were possible and desirable.

Some observers also doubted that commonalities existed across the faster-improving districts, claiming that the factors that led to achievement gains were unique to each city and could not be generalized. Others believed that the systemwide gains were nothing more than the sum of individual school effects. But though preliminary, our research suggests that there are indeed common themes and that citywide gains are too significant to have been created by individual schools.

In addition to the aforementioned districts, our research included two anonymous comparison districts that had not experienced similar improvements. Because of the exploratory nature of the analysis, the research team chose a case study approach focused on developing hypotheses about reasons for systemic improvement. The comparison districts provided a partial test of these hypotheses and helped pinpoint what was unusual about the districts that were showing gains at scale.

Challenges Facing Urban School Districts

The large urban school districts examined in this study faced a common set of challenges in addition to those confronting their individual schools. They include the following:

• *Unsatisfactory academic achievement.* Before the current period of reform, each of the districts we studied was characterized by low student achievement. In both the case study districts and the comparison districts, achievement for minority and disadvantaged students was noticeably lower than for white and more affluent students. And the differences between racial/ethnic groups and between income groups appeared to widen as students grew older.

• *Political conflict.* Each of the three case study districts had experienced a period of political turmoil involving a factional school board and disputes over resources and influence, including salaries, hiring and firing decisions, student assignments, school closings, and construction—all micromanagement issues that contributed nothing to student learning. Infighting occurred between department heads, between board members, between board members and superintendent, between superintendent and principals, and between principals and teachers; these conflicts often became serious and personal. As a result, district leadership was often not focused on improving student achievement.

- *Inexperienced teaching staff.* Each case study district acknowledged that much of its teaching staff was relatively inexperienced and suffered from high turnover, especially once teachers gained some initial experience. These districts had difficulty recruiting and retaining teachers when neighboring suburban districts could offer higher salaries, better facilities, less challenging students, and less stressful working environments. These difficulties were compounded by the limited training that the districts offered to new teachers.

- *Low expectations and lack of demanding curriculum.* In each district, staff felt overwhelmed at times by the challenges facing many low-income and minority students. This led some teachers to reduce expectations for achievement in the lower grades and attribute students' lack of progress to social conditions. In the higher grades, where instruction and expectations can differ starkly across groups of students, low-income and minority students were underrepresented in college preparatory and advanced placement classes. In some schools that served primarily low-income and minority students, the more demanding classes were offered infrequently or not at all.

- *Lack of instructional coherence.* In all the districts studied, we found that in the past, many different educational initiatives and curricula had been in place in individual schools, and instruction was not well aligned with state standards. Also, experiments with site-based management allowed schools in the same district to use a confusing array of educational strategies. This caused confusion among school-level staff and made it difficult for the district to determine what to support. In addition, professional development was fragmented and unfocused, often consisting of one-shot workshops on a series of topics defined by the individual schools. Finally, each district was weighed down with scores of programs that lacked connection or coordination.

- *High student mobility.* Previous research suggests that learning can be undermined when students move from one school to another; this problem may be exacerbated by variations in instructional approach. District leaders in each of the cities believed that the high rate of student mobility within the district undermined continuity of instruction in core subjects such as reading and math. Some central office staff also noticed higher rates of mobility among low-income and minority students, which presented another challenge in closing racial-ethnic and economic achievement gaps.

- *Unsatisfactory business operations.* One of the greatest frustrations among teachers and principals in ailing urban schools was the lack of basic necessities. All too often, school facilities were poorly maintained or even dangerous, students were taught by substitutes for part or even all of the school year, and teachers lacked an adequate supply of books and materials. At times, district operations were managed by personnel who had been promoted because of tenure rather than qualifications, and administrative systems were often outdated and cumbersome. Also, the direct political influence of school board members and other elected officials frequently affected decisions on hiring, promotions, assignments, and contracts for supplies or services. Finally, school-level staff often viewed the central office as unresponsive, bureaucratic, and characterized by micromanagement rather than dedicated to solving problems or supporting the schools.

Reform Efforts in Faster-Improving Districts

Our study identified several common reforms shared by the urban school districts that had improved student performance on a broad scale. These included what the research team came to call "preconditions" and district reform "strategies."

PRECONDITIONS FOR REFORM. The individual histories of the faster-improving urban school districts suggested that political and organizational stability over a prolonged period and consensus on educational reform strategies were prerequisites to meaningful change. The basic preconditions included the following:

- A new role for the school board, whereby a new board majority (or other governing unit) focused on policy-level decisions that supported improved student achievement rather than day-to-day operations of the district
- A shared vision between the chief executive or superintendent of the school district and the school board regarding the goals and strategies for reform
- A capacity to diagnose instructional problems
- An ability to sell the leadership's vision for reform to city and district stakeholders
- A focus on revamping district operations to serve and support the schools
- Resources to support reform and improvement

DISTRICT STRATEGIES FOR REFORM. The faster-improving urban districts also used the following strategies:

- They focused on student achievement and set specific goals for the district and for individual schools, with a fixed schedule for attaining them and consequences for failing to do so.

- They created accountability systems that exceeded state requirements in order to hold district leadership and building-level staff personally responsible for producing results.

- They adopted or developed districtwide curricula and instructional approaches rather than allowing each school to devise its own strategies, and they aligned curricula with state standards.

- They supported districtwide strategies at the central office through professional development and support for consistent implementation throughout the district.

- They drove reform into the classroom by defining a role for the central office that entailed guiding, supporting, and improving instruction at the building level.

- They committed themselves to data-driven decision making and instruction. They disaggregated data in a variety of ways to better understand patterns in student performance and improved the infrastructure for analyzing and disseminating data throughout the district. And they gave early and ongoing assessment data to principals and teachers and provided training and support to help them use these data to diagnose teacher and student weaknesses and make improvements.

- They focused on the lowest-performing schools by providing additional resources and improving those schools' stock of qualified teachers and administrators.

- They started their reforms at the elementary grade levels instead of trying to fix everything at once.

- They provided intensive instruction in reading and math to middle and high school students, even if it came at the expense of other subjects.

Practices of the Comparison Districts

While the comparison districts claimed to be implementing many of the reforms undertaken by the faster-improving districts, important differences prevented them from achieving similar gains:

- They lacked consensus among key stakeholders about district priorities or an overall strategy for reform.
- They lacked specific, clear standards; achievement goals; time lines; and consequences.

- The district's central office took little or no responsibility for improving instruction or creating a cohesive instructional strategy throughout the district.

- The policies and practices of the central office were not strongly connected to intended changes in teaching and learning in the classrooms.

- The districts gave schools multiple and conflicting curriculum and instructional expectations, which they were left to decipher on their own.

Table 8.4 summarizes these differences.

Barriers to Reform at Scale

The case study districts worked hard to develop and implement the changes outlined in this chapter, but the process was not without setbacks or controversy. This section summarizes the key challenges the districts faced and how they addressed them.

Concern About the Central Office and Staffing

School-level staff in each district often felt skeptical about the ability of central office staff to redefine their roles and support schools in meeting district goals. In fact, substantial barriers stood in the way of building initial support for the this effort: the history of poor support for daily school operations, frequent changes in policy and leadership, and the perception that the central office staff believed the schools existed to support them. The district leadership tried to transform attitudes and foster goodwill by making immediate improvements in facilities and material support, applying new accountability measures to the senior office staff first and cleaning house by firing or demoting ineffective staff.

As the reforms moved forward, certain central office staff and principals were removed from their posts; this inevitably created controversy, but in the case study districts, the school boards reinforced the authority of district administrators to make these decisions and did not intervene. This change in attitude and practice among school boards can be attributed to two factors. First, the superintendents were willing to be held personally accountable for student achievement, and the boards believed that in exchange, superintendents had the right to assemble the leadership team they desired. Second, the superintendents were committed to creating a racially and ethnically diverse leadership team and filled vacancies with many minority administrators.

Table 8.4. Summary of Case Study and Comparison Districts

Key Characteristics Preconditions	Case Study Districts	Comparison Districts
1. School Board Role	Major shakeup of board members. Board role changes to focus on policy.	Reform of school board may not have occurred. Board often focused on day-to-day decisions unrelated to achievement.
	Board sets first priority as raising student achievement.	Board is slower to focus on student achievement or is distracted by other issues.
2. Shared Vision	Board defines initial vision for district. Board seeks superintendent who matches initial vision.	Board is slower to define vision. Board seeks superintendent with own ideas and platform.
	Board seeks superintendent who is willing to be accountable for goals.	Board may not hold superintendent accountable for goals.
	Board and superintendent refine vision and goals jointly.	Board and superintendent may not pursue joint vision and goals.
3. Diagnosing Situation	Board and superintendent analyze factors affecting achievement.	Board and superintendent may not diagnose what affects achievement.
	Board and superintendent assess strengths and weaknesses of district.	Board and superintendent may not assess district strengths and weaknesses.
	Board and superintendent consider district options and strategies.	Superintendent may develop solutions without board involvement.
	Board trusts superintendent to run district.	Board may continue micromanaging administration.

(continued)

Table 8.4. Summary of Case Study and Comparison Districts *(continued)*

Key Characteristics Preconditions	Case Study Districts	Comparison Districts
4. Selling Reform	Board and superintendent build concrete and specific goals for district.	Board and superintendent may not build concrete goals for district.
	Board and superintendent listen extensively to community needs.	Board and superintendent may not listen to or involve community.
	Board and superintendent begin selling goals and plans to schools and community.	Administration may not seek extensive buy-in.
	Board and superintendent emphasize urgency, high standards, and no excuses.	Board and superintendent may not stress urgency or develop new attitude.
5. Improving Operations	Central office revamps business operations to be more effective.	Central office may revamp operations to exclusion of student achievement.
	Central office develops new sense of customer service with schools.	Central office may not have customer orientation.
	Central office moves to fix immediate problems that annoy all.	Central office may not respond to immediate problems.
6. Finding Funds	District pursues funds to initiate reforms and launch priorities.	District may pursue or accept funds unrelated to reforms and priorities.
	District builds confidence in reforms in order to attract funds.	District may pursue funds to fill shortfalls.
	District shifts funds into instructional priorities.	District may shift funds into other priorities, instruction being one.

Key Characteristics Educational Strategies	Case Study Districts	Comparison Districts
1. Setting Goals	District sets specific performance goals and targets for self and schools.	District may set more general goals and lack school targets.
	District uses goals to build consensus and rally support.	District may not move to build consensus or support.
	District spends time considering what works elsewhere ("existence proofs").	District may not seek existence proofs.
	District sets specific timetables for meeting goals and targets.	District lacks specific time lines for meeting goals and targets.
	District focuses relentlessly on goal to improve student achievement.	District is sometimes distracted by other priorities.
2. Creating Accountability	District goes beyond state accountability system.	District does not go beyond state accountability system.
	District puts senior staff on performance contracts tied to goals.	District does not put senior staff on performance contracts.
	District puts principals on performance contracts tied to goals.	District probably does not put principals on performance contracts.
	District creates rewards and recognition for progress on goals and targets.	District has no reward and recognition system for progress on goals.

(continued)

Table 8.4. Summary of Case Study and Comparison Districts (*continued*)

Key Characteristics Educational Strategies	Case Study Districts	Comparison Districts
3. Focusing on Lowest-Performing Schools	District creates system for focusing on lowest-performing schools.	District may lack full system for focusing on lowest-performing schools.
	District uses school improvement process to drive schools forward.	Districts may have more generalized school improvement strategy.
	District has detailed bank of interventions for lowest performers.	District may lack intervention strategies for lowest performers.
	District shifts extra help, funds, programs to lowest performers.	District lacks strategy for handling lowest performers.
	District tries to improve quality of teachers in lowest-performing schools.	District may lack way to improve quality of teachers in lowest-performing schools.
	District closely monitors schools.	District may not closely monitor schools.
4. Unifying Curriculum	District adopts or develops uniform curriculum or framework for instruction.	District has multiple curricula or no framework for instruction.
	District uses more prescriptive reading and math curriculum or tight framework.	District curriculum may be vague or lack unifying framework.
	District curriculum is explicitly aligned with state standards and tests.	District may not have tied curriculum to state standards and tests.
	District has clearer grade-to-grade alignment in curriculum.	District does not align curriculum between grades.
	District uses scientifically based reading curriculum.	District may use older reading curriculum.
	District uses pacing guides that tell teachers when certain skills should be taught.	District may or may not have pacing guides.

Key Characteristics Educational Strategies	Case Study Districts	Comparison Districts
5. Professional development	District pushes for faithful implementation of curriculum.	District may not monitor implementation closely.
	District has uniform professional development built on curriculum.	District may rely more on school-by-school professional development.
	District focuses professional development on classroom practice.	District may not have such focused professional development.
	District provides teacher supports when needed.	District may not have a teacher support mechanism.
6. Pressing Reforms Down	District works to drive reforms all the way into classroom ("reform press").	District may wait for reforms to trickle down.
	District has a system of encouraging or monitoring implementation of reforms.	District has no way to tell whether reforms are being implemented.
	Central office takes responsibility for quality of instruction.	Central office leaves instruction up to individual schools.
7. Using Data	District uses data extensively to monitor system and school progress.	District may not use data for either system or school progress.
	District assesses student progress throughout the school year.	District is more likely to use previous year's performance data.
	District disaggregates data in numerous ways.	District may or may not disaggregate data.
	District uses data to decide where to target interventions.	District does not use data to shape intervention strategy.
	District provides training in meaning and use of test score results.	District training may be voluntary or lack detail.
	District uses data to target professional development.	District does not use data to target professional development.

(continued)

Table 8.4. Summary of Case Study and Comparison Districts (*continued*)

Key Characteristics Educational Strategies	Case Study Districts	Comparison Districts
8. Starting Early	District starts reform efforts in early elementary grades and works up.	District has not defined where to start reforms.
9. Handling Upper Grades	District has at least fledgling strategies for teaching older students.	District has no strategies for teaching older students who are behind.
	District has some middle school and high school interventions.	District lacks intervention strategies at the middle school and high school level.
	District doubles up on teaching basic skills to students who are behind.	District has no strategies for teaching older students.
	District begins expanding advanced placement courses in district high schools.	District lacks AP courses in many high schools.

Gathering and Reporting Data

Each of the districts began the reform process without the data they needed. In some cases, data-processing systems were antiquated; in others, new types of reports were needed. Further, the districts lacked the infrastructure for gathering and distributing data in a useful form and timely fashion, and teachers and rincipals needed to be trained to understand and use the reports. To solve these problems, one district hired a consultant to produce the reports; another had the technology group supplement the work of the research department, which had traditionally produced reports. Over time, each district invested substantial resources in data processing and dissemination.

Support for a Uniform Curriculum

Experienced teachers often put up the most resistance to changes in curriculum, fearful of losing the freedom to use the teaching strategies that they believed worked best. However, data from the case study districts revealed that many of the teachers' favorite lesson plans and activities were not producing gains in student achievement. Later, some experienced teachers reported that they had been skeptical about a uniform, sometimes prescriptive curriculum but were eventually convinced of its merit. District leadership often called on these successful teachers as role models. District staff and principals also provided support so that less experienced teachers could have success with the new curriculum.

Complaints About a Narrow Educational Focus

As they engaged in reform measures, district leaders were often accused of restricting the scope of education. In some districts, for example, expanded instruction in reading and math took time and resources from electives, art and music, field trips, and fun-filled activities. In some cases, critics argued convincingly that in light of the disadvantaged circumstances facing many urban children, schools were the only setting in which they could gain this broader array of knowledge and experience. Nonetheless, the district leadership consistently made the point that children who lacked basic academic skills would be severely hindered later in life. In light of limited resources, district leadership opted to focus on basic academic skills while seeking supplemental funding to expand other offerings.

Concerns About Undercutting the Achievement of Excellence

Many efforts described in this chapter focused on raising the achievement of low-performing schools and the students they represent; they represent the districts' greatest success. But in each district, critics expressed concerns that the emphasis on remedial work diverted attention from students who had already demonstrated academic proficiency, arguing that this trend would tempt families of high-achieving students to seek educational opportunities elsewhere. This effect would undermine broad support for public education.

Yet in each district, the leadership publicized the accomplishments of high-performing schools and students. Academic achievement at some schools exceeded the district average, and special educational offerings to reward excellence remained in place. In Charlotte-Mecklenburg, the leadership directly addressed this issue by expanding academically demanding programs at the high school level, ensuring equal access to these programs, and increasing the number of graduates who successfully met the requirements of these programs. Nevertheless, the leaders of the case study districts readily admit that more efforts are needed to extend higher levels of academic performance across the whole system.

Fatigue and Stress in the Constant Push for Improvement

In the case study districts, principals and teachers reported that their jobs had grown much more demanding and stressful than in the past, taking a toll on emotions and threatening to take the joy out of working with children. District leadership confronted this problem in several ways: improving the quality of facilities, materials, and administrative support for principals and teachers; continually stressing the importance of the mission of educating young people; telling those who did not want to increase their level of effort that it was time to leave; celebrating successes; and being visible in the schools and listening to the staff. Despite these efforts, the work remained grueling, and everyone involved felt the pressure.

The Role of Technology and Other Reforms

Our study did not address several popular and widely discussed reform strategies, such as the precise roles played by technology, parent involvement, class-size reduction, or early childhood education. Instead, we collected the relevant systemwide data, interviewed stakeholders, and let the critical themes that drove improvements rise to the top. This does not mean, however, that these smaller-bore reforms were not significant.

Good preschool programs may, in fact, be important to early grade school performance. Charlotte-Mecklenburg, for instance, had a sizable and substantive early childhood program, but it had not been in operation long enough to produce a measured effect on student achievement. This was also the case in Houston and Sacramento.

Parental involvement has been consistently shown to have a positive relationship with achievement levels in schools of all types. Parental participation did not emerge, however, as a major factor in driving improvement in the case study districts; although it had been critical in galvanizing reforms in Sacramento, the research team did not see the same dynamic in the other districts. It should be noted that only a small number of parents were interviewed by the study team, a limitation of the research.

Based on what the research team saw, technology may, in fact, be a factor in districtwide improvement, but it did not emerge as a major theme. The team might have expected to see technology play a prominent role in three areas: instructional coherence, professional development, and data analysis and assessment. The first two areas did not emerge as dynamic in shaping or implementing reform; the connection to achievement gains using technology lay more in the area of management than instruction. Each faster-improving district used regular assessments and detailed data to drive instructional interventions and improvements; therefore, technology and the infrastructure for managing and disseminating performance data played critical roles. Technology allowed district administrators to assess students before they fell behind, determine what skills students lacked, and decide where to place interventions to assist teachers and students. To make this happen, data on tens of thousands of students and their skills had to be generated, aggregated, and analyzed very quickly—often within a matter of days or a few weeks. This information, moreover, had to be disseminated to teachers and principals in a timely manner. Often, technology upgrades in the case study districts were made with these new functions in mind.

Many other districts have data-management systems similar to those found in the case study districts, but they are not reaping comparable academic gains. Apparently, the data and how people used it, rather than the technology itself, helped improve student performance. Still, technology plays an essential role in this process.

It is likely that technology, early childhood education, and parental involvement play roles that are subservient to the structural and systemic themes that the study identified. Still, considerably more research is needed to draw definitive conclusions.

Conclusion

In many ways, the findings of our study represent good practices for any type of organization seeking broad-scale improvement: set priorities and specific goals; identify appropriate roles for parts of the organization; select or develop the techniques needed to move toward the goals in the given context; collect and use information to track progress; identify needed refinements; and stay on course long enough for the efforts to pay off. But these commonsense steps are strewn with stumbling blocks in the complex world of urban school districts, with their diverse stakeholders, frequent leadership changes, competing priorities, limited resources, and difficult-to-manage bureaucracies. Several factors could help urban school districts accelerate progress and expand its scale:

• The study offers two main hypotheses about the political preconditions that seem critical to improvement. First, school board members, community leaders, and superintendents must make improved student achievement their top priority. Second, a common vision must be developed and supported by a stable majority of the board. The school community and general public should also provide feedback and support.

• A coherent approach to curriculum and instruction appears to be vital in helping city school districts address a variety of problems. Support from the central office, a clearly defined approach to elementary-level instruction, extensive professional development for teachers, and incentives to bring experienced staff to low-performing schools are essential building blocks.

• The role of data in decision making invites several hypotheses: (1) teachers can use achievement data to improve instructional practice, diagnose students' specific instructional needs, and increase student learning, but teachers and principals need to receive this type of data at regular intervals from the start of the academic year, along with training in using these data to diagnose areas of weakness; (2) students may be assigned to more beneficial classroom situations if administrators carefully use assessment data in placement decisions, and this practice may also increase the odds that disadvantaged and minority students will qualify for high-level classes; and (3) making all these changes together can have a much larger impact than a single one undertaken alone; indeed, unless a district works to reform its entire system, trying any one of these approaches may be a wasted effort.

• The federal No Child Left Behind legislation requires that states identify low-performing school districts and provide them with technical assistance and other interventions. Our study suggests two possible approaches.

First, a "theory of change" approach would involve translating the findings from the *Foundations for Success* report into a coherent theory of system-level improvement and then assessing a district's progress and needs in light of this theory. Second, a "gap analysis" approach would involve measuring the differences in practices between faster-improving districts and those that are the target of technical assistance.

• Concern about how to sustain progress in the future, move beyond basic levels of proficiency to achieve excellence, and extend reforms from the elementary level to the middle school and high school levels will likely require different strategies for different districts. Many challenges remain.

In the end, our study underscores the importance of the district as a unit of analysis for research and as a level of intervention in bringing reforms to scale. An important next step is to refine the hypotheses about promising district-level practices and establish a strong empirical basis for understanding the relationship between these educational improvement strategies and changes in teaching, learning, and student achievement in large urban school systems. The findings also highlight the importance of testing these strategies in widely diverse settings, in order to see how well they apply to systems with the greatest need for reform.

REFERENCES

Casserly, M., Lewis, S., Jepson, J., & Ceperich, J. (2002, June). *Beating the odds II: A city-by-city analysis of student performance and achievement gaps on state assessments.* Washington, DC: Council of the Great City Schools.

Snipes, J., Doolittle, F., & Herlihy, C. (2002). *Foundations for success: Case studies of how urban school districts improve student achievement.* Washington, DC: Council of the Great City Schools. Retrieved from http://www.cgcs.org/reports/Foundations.html

SCALING UP TECHNOLOGY-BASED EDUCATIONAL INNOVATIONS

Barbara Means, William R. Penuel

Research on the use of an Internet-based science inquiry program reveals the problems and promise of studying broad-scale use of learning technology.

FEDERAL POLICYMAKERS are calling on the education research community to use rigorous methods to evaluate and clearly articulate the answer to this question: "What works?" Although appealing, this seemingly straightforward approach is an incomplete basis for scaling up educational interventions, particularly those involving sophisticated uses of technology. Instead, scaling up of complex educational interventions should be informed by research that sheds light on a more complex question: "What works when, and how?" This alternative statement of the problem draws attention to issues of implementation and context in research design, which are often neglected by studies focused on main effects, or comparison of treatment and control group means. After reviewing aspects of technology-based educational innovations that make them highly dependent on implementation processes and contextual factors, we describe strategies for evaluating technology-supported educational innovations to inform scaling up. We illustrate the application of those strategies with the Center for Technology in Learning's evaluation of GLOBE, a Web-based environmental education program. We conclude with thoughts on the relationship between evaluative research and the scaling up of innovations.

Research to Support Scaling Up

At the federal level, educational policy clearly reflects a new emphasis on research and evaluation focused on treatment effects and on communication of research findings in terms of "what works." This emphasis is manifested in the recent authorization of the Institute of Education Sciences (the successor to the Office of Educational Research and Improvement), with the goal of reshaping the field of education research into an enterprise that will "use scientifically rigorous randomized trials to provide definitive evidence of what works and what doesn't" (Whitehurst, 2002). The ability to identify and scale up practices that can be justified on the basis of research is a cornerstone of the No Child Left Behind legislation. To support this effort, the administration has funded the What Works Clearinghouse, "which will vet the evidence from research on education and make it available to decision-makers in easily understood forms" (Whitehurst, 2002).

This approach is an important step forward in encouraging the development of a research base for practice, but it risks overlooking important factors, and interactions among factors, that need to be considered when scaling up educational interventions, especially those involving sophisticated uses of technology. Scaling up reform necessarily involves adaptation by local actors to local contexts; some of these adaptations will undoubtedly make innovations less effective, while others may result in creative transformations that enhance the program overall (Brown and Edelson, 1998; McLaughlin, 1987; Spillane and Jennings, 1997). The research base needed for scaling up goes beyond the question "What works?" to include research that sheds light on a more complex question: "What works when, and how?" Rather than an average effect size, local decision makers need research findings that shed light on the expected effects under different circumstances and on the contextual and implementation factors that are likely to influence success. An emphasis on average effects can be counterproductive if it results in inattention to these critical factors.

Limitations of Main Effects Studies

The Education Sciences Reform Act of 2002 and the evaluation criteria for the What Works Clearinghouse treat the random-assignment experiment as the "gold standard" for establishing that an intervention can cause the desired effects. We would agree that in research that concerns a well-defined intervention and primarily asks a question about causality ("Does treatment A cause outcome B?"), a random-assignment experiment (also called a randomized field trial) is the strongest design from a technical standpoint; it is the best option when experiments are socially and politically feasible to implement.

Critics of random-assignment experiments have raised practical, political, and ethical objections to their use in education (Cronbach, 1982; Cronbach and others, 1980). We will not repeat those arguments here. (Also see Cook, 2002, for a summary of the criticisms and a rebuttal.) Rather, we want to raise the question of random-assignment experiments' utility for supporting the decisions of state and local policymakers and practitioners considering large-scale implementation of a technology-based innovation.

In creating research designs to test the hypothesis that treatment A causes outcome B, experimentalists recognize the complexity of the real world in which schools and classrooms operate but dismiss this complexity with the qualifier ceteris paribus (other things being equal). In real life, however, all other things never really are equal, and we care about the influences of those differences. The power of random assignment lies in its ability to create treatment and control groups that are, on average, equivalent prior to introduction of the treatment. But that very power invites neglect of relationships between context variables and the intervention. The particular context in which we try out treatment A and the way in which we implement it will shape enactment at the classroom level. Moreover, the treatment may interact with some aspect of the classroom context, producing side effects that would be unlikely in control classrooms.

To take a simple example, classrooms with multiple computers with high-speed Internet connections and teachers who are experienced technology users and well trained in the pedagogy and content that are part of our intended instructional treatment will surely execute different teaching and learning activities than will teachers in classrooms where these qualities are present to lesser degrees or not at all. Students' and teachers' knowledge and experiences will shape the way an innovation unfolds and will also be affected by it. The teacher who finds that a certain kind of analysis is stressed in a new piece of software may direct students to apply the same analysis technique in other teaching contexts when that software is not being used, for example. As in this illustration, causal relationships in educational settings are typically determined by multiple influences rather than a single one, and technology's role is typically that of a support for teaching and learning activities rather than their sole purveyor. This complexity has led Lesgold (2003) to argue that technology should not be thought of as a potential causal agent but rather as a magnifier of the effects of other aspects of an intervention. If technology is not thought of as the causal agent, experimental designs geared toward testing causal hypotheses are of questionable relevance.

We can overcome this objection to some extent by defining the treatment as something broader than the technology per se. This expanded definition would generally include the software used, curriculum content, and the assignment or instructions given to students. If these are in fact fully specified and consistently enacted, we can design an experiment to test the effects of this treatment package. But most innovations, if they are designed to affect instruction in a wide range of contexts, will need to be flexible enough to allow for variation in implementation. The teacher's goals in enacting the intervention, the way she sets up the activity, the conceptual and motivational context provided for it, the teacher's knowledge of relevant content, the ways that students work with the technology (individually or in groups), the kinds of supports provided as students are using the technology, the amount of time students spend on the activity, and a host of other variables that may or may not have been specified by the organization disseminating the software become part of the treatment for any given set of students. Moreover, variations in the treatment should not necessarily be considered negative (as is implied by the concept of implementation fidelity). Differences in students' prior knowledge and interests and in local resources and constraints may make adaptations advisable, if not mandatory. Typically, so much variability characterizes implementation of technology-supported innovations that we must be cautious about assuming that the same treatment is being enacted in different contexts.

But even when it is reasonable to assume that treatment consistency exists, in many cases in education, the primary question does not concern causation. Often, a culturally valued practice or a politically popular intervention will be implemented regardless of the outcome of any research. In such cases, the policymaker or practitioner would like to know how best to implement treatment A to produce positive outcomes and minimize unanticipated, undesirable side effects. For many communities, we would claim, computer and Internet technologies fit this category. For example, the large number of districts and states that have invested in laptop programs have done so largely to increase equity of access to tools believed to be necessary for all students to master in the new century (Penuel and others, 2001).

Finally, even when a decision is pending as to whether to implement a technology-supported intervention, the random-assignment experiment can support the research base but by itself does not provide enough information to support good local decisions. This design is primarily a tool for identifying main effects—that is, on average, that the application of treatment A will result in an improvement in outcome B. At state and local levels, policymakers and practitioners care not so much about averages as about specific cases and particular kinds of students and contexts—urban classrooms, immigrant English language learners from Mexico, and so on. Even the strongest proponents of experimental designs recognize that in the face of resource limitations that restrict sample sizes, they generally are unable to establish any but the strongest and most straightforward interactions between treatment efficacy and the characteristics of the students, teachers, or settings in which the treatment is implemented, let alone variables associated with the way in which it is implemented (Cook, 2002). Without such knowledge, the local policymaker is still making decisions in the dark.

The policymaker or practitioner needs not only knowledge that some intervention has been shown to be effective on average but also knowledge that can permit a reasonable judgment concerning (1) whether the intervention would prove effective with the students, teachers, and schools for which that person is responsible; (2) an understanding of the supporting conditions necessary for success in these settings; and (3) the range of adaptations that can occur under local conditions without compromising the intervention's essential principles or reducing its efficacy.

Context can make all the difference. To take an example, the rigorous experimental test of the effects of class-size reduction in Tennessee found strong positive impacts, especially for disadvantaged students (Finn, 2002). Although sizable, the experiment in Tennessee was conducted in selected districts and involved too few teachers to affect the education labor market. When California legislators, impressed by the Tennessee findings, instituted class-size reduction in grades K–3 statewide in California, they were instituting one of the "most expensive state education reforms in U.S. history" (Bohrnstedt and Stecher, 2002, p. 18). With the wisdom of hindsight, we can see that scaling up this intervention in a new context, though tremendously popular, was not well informed by the experimental research. After four years and billions of dollars, there were no significant positive impacts on student achievement (Stecher and Bohrnstedt, 2002). The best-documented impact of the program, implemented at a time when California was suffering from a severe teacher shortage, was an increase in the gap between teacher qualifications in schools serving low-income students and those serving the more affluent. By thinking about the California context as a complex system, we can appreciate that treatment A (small class size) is not a discrete intervention in practice but rather a change that will have both direct and indirect influences on many parts of the system. Generalizing the results of an experiment in one setting (or sample of settings) to other complex settings with some similarities to the experiment setting but also many differences is a risky practice.

Reframing the Question

We argue that educational research in general, and certainly research on scaling up, requires much more emphasis on context and enactment variables than is common in random-assignment experiments. To give the policymaker or practitioner a knowledge base for making decisions concerning the likely benefit of an educational intervention in the settings they care about and concerning the way in which the intervention should be implemented to maximize the likelihood of positive outcomes, we need to study the intervention in multiple contexts and to understand how it plays out in those contexts—the factors that support, hinder, and shape its enactment in classrooms. Thus, we believe we need to tackle that more complicated question: "What works when, and how?"

Studying Technology-Supported Innovations

After spending the past decade studying attempts to change the nature of school teaching and learning and enhance student learning with technology-supported interventions, we argue that the case for emphasizing contextual and implementation variables is particularly crucial. Studies of how technology-based interventions actually get implemented (or fail to get implemented) in classrooms show repeatedly that context does matter. The location and quality of Internet-connected computers, the reliability of connections, and the amount of time students have to use the technology all make a great difference, as does the way in which teachers frame the technology-based activity (Blumenfeld and others, 2000; Means, Penuel, and Padilla, 2001). Teachers' pedagogical philosophy and experience and comfort with technology will influence the way they use it in their teaching (Becker and Anderson, 2000). Likewise, school expenditures on equipment, training, and support also shape teachers' decisions on how to use technology in school (Anderson and Becker, 2001).

Another issue for studies of technology-supported learning is the high likelihood of a mismatch between the intended outcomes of the intervention and the most commonly used and readily available measures of student learning. While the emphasis on standardized test scores in accountability systems cannot be ignored (and has only gotten stronger with the No Child Left Behind legislation), many interventions target learning outcomes that are not tapped in these tests. Even in cases with apparent alignment between tests and desired outcomes, the overlap is usually only partial, making it difficult to interpret the results. As learning technology innovators seek to use technology's affordances to make possible the acquisition of understandings and skills that could not exist without technology, the evaluative researcher is challenged to find new ways of measuring the intended learning outcomes.

An Illustration: Implementing and Evaluating the GLOBE Program

To illustrate the importance of addressing the learning outcomes issue (and measuring appropriate student outcomes) and of examining context and implementation variables, we present an example of a technology-supported innovation that has gone to scale and some of our research on the program. This discussion draws on findings from multiple years of evaluation; we do so not to imply that our own research is a model but rather to use a scaled-up innovation that we know well to illustrate some of the context and implementation information that scaling-up efforts require.

Program Description

The GLOBE program was established in 1994 as an international environmental science and education program. GLOBE seeks to strike a balance between its scientific objective—to obtain accurate and reliable data to enhance our scientific understanding of earth systems—and its educational goal—to promote science and mathematics education and environmental awareness. For more information about the GLOBE program, visit http://www.globe.gov.

A distinctive feature of the program is that GLOBE students collect data not only as part of an isolated laboratory experience but also as contributors to actual scientific studies. Through submission to the program's Web site, student-collected data become part of a large repository of worldwide environmental science data. GLOBE scientists use these student-collected data in their own investigations, such as the verification of remotely sensed global precipitation (Postawko, Morrissey, Green, and Mirsky, 2001), assessment of the accuracy of images from the Landsat satellite program (Congalton, Rowe, and Becker, 2001), and modeling of relationships among earth systems (Robin, Levine, and Riha, 2001). The

GLOBE program has hired educators to organize training—initially for teachers and then for GLOBE's various partner organizations (usually universities), which now provide teacher training under a "train the trainers" model. Other than requiring careful adherence to the environmental data collection protocols, GLOBE gives schools complete latitude in determining the K–12 grade levels and classes in which to implement the program, the educational activities to provide, and the way in which the program will fit into the local curriculum. SRI's Center for Technology in Learning began studying this program in 1995.

GLOBE clearly is an example of a technology-supported education program at scale. By 2002, GLOBE had reached 104 countries, and students had submitted over 8 million measurements to the GLOBE Web site. As of July 2002, more than 20,000 teachers from more than 12,000 schools had completed GLOBE training. Based on responses to our recent teacher surveys, we estimate that between 153,000 and 244,000 students have engaged in GLOBE activities at schools that have reported data to the GLOBE Web site in the past three years (Penuel and others, 2002).

While such numbers suggest that the GLOBE program is indeed widespread, they can be misleading if taken at face value. As in most programs, teachers may go through GLOBE training without implementing what they have learned. Enactment of an innovation such as GLOBE may involve a wholesale change in a teacher's course or teaching method, or merely a day's passing activity. Mere numbers of teachers who have received training mean little without information on depth and persistence of implementation in a variety of contexts.

Articulating a Theory of Change

As the foregoing description suggests, the GLOBE program is multifaceted; technology forms only a small piece of the program (albeit an essential enabler), and the GLOBE classroom-level activities are neither completely specified nor controlled by the program. The program's efforts to ensure implementation fidelity have focused on fidelity to scientific protocols and to accurate and consistent data reporting rather than classroom enactment (Penuel and Means, 2004). Moreover, the program's student learning objectives were framed at a very generic level. When the program was launched, the kinds of activities that students would undertake were delineated to some extent (that is, students would collect and report environmental data), but the logical connection between these activities and the program's stated goals for impact on student learning was not worked out beyond the intuitive sense that "doing real science" would be good for kids.

Before we could design the evaluation, we needed to work with the program to better understand the specific kinds of learning that GLOBE was intended to support and to think through the mechanisms by which learning could be expected to take place. As part of this work, we sought to identify not only points of agreement among program designers about desired outcomes and implementation patterns but also possible points where the elements of the program design might not work, given the constraints of the contexts in which the program would be implemented. Furthermore, we sought to find early evidence about the validity of the claims of GLOBE's potential for improving learning, through direct observation of students as they collected, reported, and discussed environmental data.

Our observations of GLOBE classrooms in action suggested that the program had the potential to provide experiences that help students understand the reason for using standardized equipment and procedures within a scientific investigation. GLOBE activities also could introduce students to the reasoning and mathematics skills related to sampling, central tendency, reliability, and data accuracy. At the same time, it was clear that nothing in the data protocols themselves or the first GLOBE teacher's guide provided this instructionally rich context. In its original design, the GLOBE program simply relied on teachers to provide a meaningful context and tie GLOBE activities to their goals for student learning. The training model that prepared teachers to implement GLOBE focused nearly exclusively on accurate collection of data according to the protocols, giving little time to discussion of classroom enactment issues (Means and others, 1999).

As we worked with program staff to form a clearer and more realistic understanding of the kinds of learning they wanted GLOBE to promote, we also worked backward to specify the kinds of classroom and field experiences that would support the learning goals (Wiggins and McTighe, 1998). Clearly, just collecting the data according to the protocols would not be enough to produce an understanding of concepts such as sampling and measurement error, for example. Students and their teachers need to discuss reasons for the inclusion of particular protocols (why, for example, they took multiple Global Positioning System readings of a location's latitude and longitude and then averaged those readings rather than just reporting the first one) and to examine, analyze, and discuss the data they had collected. The potential for very different enactments (both good and bad) in different contexts is enormous.

It became clear that additional elements were needed in the GLOBE training program, data collection activities, and teacher's guide in order to stimulate and equip teachers not only to train their students to collect valid and reliable data but also to provide a fully rounded experience, incorporating the posing of questions, the interpretation of evidence, and the communication aspects of scientific inquiry. If teachers are supposed to implement these activities, the program's technology supports and teacher training should help them do so. As we worked with the program office to articulate the missing links in the program's theory of change, the staff clarified the kinds of learning activities they wanted to include in the next edition of the teacher's guide as well as new emphases in teacher training. In particular, they redesigned both the program's teacher training and school materials to give much greater weight to scientific inquiry, student-designed investigations, and data analysis.

Documenting Implementation and Context Variables

GLOBE is implemented differently in different settings and by different teachers. Although the program office had originally hoped that teachers, at least at the middle school and high school levels, would implement all the data collection protocols, teachers have in fact chosen from GLOBE's offerings those they find congruent with their goals and feasible to implement. Given the purposely flexible nature of the program and the fact that it includes content and activities running the gamut from those for kids in primary grades to those for advanced secondary school students, the kind of "fidelity of implementation" standard customarily used in evaluation studies did not seem to fit. We felt the need to obtain information about multiple specific features of implementation in multiple contexts where there is no one normative implementation model.

Not surprisingly, the extent to which teachers have multiple opportunities to learn about GLOBE influences the level and nature of implementation. One motive behind GLOBE's move to a "train the trainer" model was the assumption that a local organization could provide both locally relevant implementation guidance (for example, coastal South Carolina soil is so sandy that the standard GLOBE procedure for taking soil samples must be modified) and more extensive posttraining follow-up. In practice, training partner organizations have varied widely in the nature and quantity of posttraining support they provide. In our analyses, we have found that teachers' receipt of certain posttraining supports for implementing GLOBE is associated with higher levels of program implementation. Having someone from the organization that provided GLOBE training visit the teacher's school appears to be especially effective, as are partner-provided supplementary educational materials and specific incentives for data reporting. Listservs, newsletters, and other communication strategies have been insufficient unless accompanied by these other supports and inducements.

Also, student and school characteristics are associated with tremendous variation in GLOBE enactment. GLOBE activities are much harder to implement in urban settings than in suburban or rural ones. Urban schools are challenged not only by a lack of nearby study sites (a stream or a tree canopy may not be present in the neighborhood) but also by heightened security problems for GLOBE equipment and district restrictions about transporting students in cars driven by parents or students. In contrast, many rural schools that participate in GLOBE not only have accessible study sites but also enjoy the extensive involvement of community members, who help out with taking measurements on weekends and summers, a practice the GLOBE program encourages.

We discovered early that different patterns of technology access affected GLOBE teachers' decisions about enactment, especially data reporting. In surveys conducted as recently as spring 2002, a number of teachers cited limited technology access as a main reason for their inability to report GLOBE data to the Web site. In site visits to schools, we have frequently observed teachers who gather stacks of paper records of student-collected environmental data and then wait for a turn at the computer lab before these data can be entered. In many cases, the amount of data that accumulates becomes daunting, and the data are never entered.

The nature of the classes that implement GLOBE varies with grade level and constitutes another major influence on the GLOBE experience. Some schools regard GLOBE as most appropriate for honors students who are ready to take on more responsibility; others think the hands-on approach makes the program ideal for less academically inclined students because it gets them motivated. In middle school, environmental science is often a portion of a general science class or an advanced elective. In high school, environmental science classes may be the alternative for students who are not planning to attend colleges that require the full sequence of biology, chemistry, and physics.

Enactment patterns themselves vary considerably across classrooms and schools as well. Classrooms vary with respect to how many weeks per year they implement GLOBE; some use it for just a few weeks a year, while others implement the program year-round (Means, Coleman, and Lewis, 1998). Classrooms also vary with respect to teachers' engagement of their students in the activities of data collection, data reporting, and data analysis (Penuel and others, 2002; Yarnall and Penuel, 2002). Some teachers use the data collection protocols but do not implement the associated learning activities from the teacher's guide; still others use the learning activities but do not implement the data collection protocols (Penuel and others, 2002). We have developed detailed instruments to capture the context and enactment of GLOBE in classrooms participating in studies of student learning associated with GLOBE participation. The information about implementation is used in our data analysis and helps make sense of the patterns of student performance, which will be discussed next.

Studying Sites with High and Average Levels of Implementation

Innovation developers typically would like their evaluators to focus on those locations where the program is implemented as intended. Such sites can provide evidence of what an innovation can potentially do. Our understanding of the program would not be complete, however, if we did not also look at sites where enactment is average and even weak. We need to document the nature of the program in these sites if we are to paint a representative picture of the innovation as implemented. Moreover, by studying these sites, we can identify barriers to more active or well-conceived enactments, providing a basis for recommendations to the program office for ways to address them.

Because a significant component of GLOBE is collecting environmental data that are contributed to the data archive, we have a handy proxy for intensity of GLOBE enactment. If a school is submitting data to the GLOBE data site on a regular basis, we know that GLOBE activities are going on there. Thus, the fact that an essential part of GLOBE is technology-based gives us a window into the activities of classrooms around the world. Teacher survey responses (collected nearly annually) provide additional information about the way in which the program is implemented (for example, the frequency with which the class engages in analysis of data from the GLOBE data archive) and the contexts of enactment. We have supplemented these data sources with on-site observations and interviews of GLOBE teachers.

Over the years, we've conducted mini–case studies of more than a score of GLOBE schools. In schools where observers see GLOBE being implemented in a meaningful way, certain conditions are usually present:

- Teachers at these schools are supported by an administrator who is positive about the program and can help garner resources, reduce institutional barriers (such as securing transportation to study sites), and showcase activities.
- Teachers have benefited from support and mentoring from a GLOBE training partner after they've completed their training.
- Teachers either feel less pressure from district and state accountability systems or feel that GLOBE activities are congruent with the content of standards and high-stakes tests.

- Teachers make GLOBE content more personally relevant for their students by designing or supporting students' design of local investigations using GLOBE measurements or concepts.
- Teachers emphasize analysis and interpretation of GLOBE data.

Developing Instructionally Relevant Measures of Learning Outcomes

Our work in better defining GLOBE's learning objectives made it clear that most standardized tests have few if any items related to those objectives. The feasibility of analyzing test performance as an approach for evaluating national programs like GLOBE is further complicated by the fact that states have adopted different standards and diverse assessment instruments to test progress against them. While some enthusiastic program promoters argued that GLOBE would increase standardized test scores for students in their state, we advised the program against promoting GLOBE on this basis.

We have conducted a variety of studies that focus on the learning outcomes for GLOBE students. The goal is not so much to determine whether GLOBE participation causes an increase in student learning but rather to identify which GLOBE activities contribute to students' understanding of GLOBE concepts and skills. Thus, these studies shed light on the relationship between selected implementation practices and learning outcomes. Knowing that different teachers implement different components of the program in different settings and with different goals, we have investigated common forms of practice rather than a single GLOBE "treatment." Such findings are especially important to the GLOBE program and its partners in identifying areas in which additional training and materials support could enhance GLOBE. Such findings also help GLOBE teachers make decisions about which components of GLOBE to implement with their students. In each of these studies, we have assessed learning both within GLOBE classrooms and in comparison classrooms. However, we have not randomly assigned teachers or students to GLOBE and non-GLOBE conditions because the program's philosophy has so strongly emphasized teacher choice in enactment, and that philosophy is likely to remain a condition of GLOBE participation for the foreseeable future. Our goal has been to measure learning with GLOBE when the program is implemented to a specified (reasonable but not exemplary) extent, to learn more about its potential effects, and to provide the program staff with data about which components are associated with which outcomes.

GLOBE Study #1

For the first of our assessment studies, we developed item banks at elementary, middle school, and high school levels that contained three types of items. The first set of items was closely related to the content of the GLOBE measurement protocols. As far as possible, with paper-and-pencil instruments, we tried to simulate the taking of environmental measurements. For example, one item showed a detailed picture of a min/max thermometer and asked the student to indicate the minimum, maximum, and current temperatures shown on the thermometer. The second set of items involved general principles of sampling and measurement (such as the greater accuracy of an average of multiple measurements compared with that of a single measurement). The third set of items asked students to interpret data shown in a graph or table or to answer inference questions dealing with earth science concepts. The first set of items was developed by SRI staff working with GLOBE content. The other two sets were adopted or adapted from a broad group of standardized tests, including released (publicly available) science items from the National Assessment of Educational Progress (NAEP) and the Third International Mathematics and Science Survey (TIMSS). Whereas any single standardized test typically includes only a few items on GLOBE-related topics, we identified a sizable set of relevant items by drawing from multiple tests.

We administered these assessments to fourth-grade and seventh-grade classes engaged in GLOBE and in classes of teachers registered for GLOBE training but who had not yet completed the training or started implementing GLOBE with their students. Not surprisingly, the greatest advantage for GLOBE students occurred on items concerning how to take the kinds of measurements used in GLOBE. However, GLOBE students scored significantly better than students in the comparison classes on all three sets of items (measurement taking, principles of sampling and measurement, and data interpretation and application). The differences on items dealing with data interpretation and applying earth science concepts were relatively small, however.

The importance of the instructional context for a technology-supported innovation was suggested by another component of this study. Each of the teachers whose students participated in the assessment also filled out a survey concerning their science teaching for the year. For each of thirteen environmental science topics related to the assessment, the teacher was asked to report whether it had been covered in class, and if so, what students had been expected to do (learn vocabulary and verbal concepts, perform measurements or observations, apply concepts, or interpret data).

Students who had received instruction on the topics covered by the assessment items and who had experience in taking measurements, applying concepts, and interpreting data scored best on the items related to taking environmental measurements and the sampling and measurement assessment items. In contrast, the items on data interpretation and concept application, taken from standardized tests, appeared to tap skills that are independent of receipt of instruction on the environmental science topics. Students who had not received instruction on the topics involved in the data tables or charts contained in these test items performed just as well as those who had. Thus, these items did not appear to be sensitive to instruction. While GLOBE participation had a modest positive effect on performance on these items, teachers' coverage of the content area related to the charts and graphs had none.

The self-reports of the teachers whose students took the assessment revealed interesting patterns: GLOBE teachers were more likely than non-GLOBE teachers to have had their students go beyond learning science vocabulary and verbal concepts to take measurements or observations, apply concepts, and interpret data for nine of the thirteen environmental science topics on which teachers were queried. Non-GLOBE teachers were more likely to report that a topic's coverage in their class was confined to learning vocabulary and verbal definitions. On the student survey, pupils corroborated what their teachers had reported. Non-GLOBE students were more likely than their GLOBE counterparts to report spending science class time "learning new words" most or all of the time. These findings demonstrate that measuring context and enactment variables helps the evaluator make sense of student performance data and can corroborate the intervention's theory of change by demonstrating the association between processes or interim outcomes (in this case, a change in teaching practice) and the student learning outcomes that are the goal of the intervention.

GLOBE Study #2

Later, we developed on-line performance-oriented assessments for the GLOBE program. One of these attempted to capture findings related to the GLOBE program's environmental awareness goal. In this assessment, students view a photograph of a complex environmental scene, using the World Wide Web. Initially, they are given a very open-ended prompt ("Think about what you have learned in science this year as you look at this picture of Mt. Hood. Describe what is happening in this environment."). Students typed their responses into a text box in the Web interface. These responses were later scored for the number of statements that went beyond mere description ("Those trees must be evergreen") to address one of the "big ideas" that subject-matter experts have identified as central to understanding the environment (specifically, interdependence, adaptation, cycles, ecosystems, and pollutants). An example of such a response is "As the clouds collect more and more water droplets, they begin to release precipitation."

We also developed a Web-based performance assessment that attempted to capture students' ability to derive meaning from environmental data, use data to make a decision, and present a logical argument supported by data. Given a set of environmental criteria for selecting a site for the Winter Olympics and climate data about five cities, students were asked to identify the best site and prepare a presentation, with data graphs, supporting their selection. Students' performance on this task was scored for the number of data graphs they developed, the consistency between the argument they were making ("Flagstaff is more likely to be sunny at the base than Salt Lake City") and the data they showed in their graphs, and whether they identified the one city which did in fact meet all of the Olympic Committee's criteria.

These two Web-based assessments were given to three groups: students from GLOBE classes that were above average in number of submissions to the GLOBE data archive; students from GLOBE classes that were average in number of submissions; and students of teachers who had signed up for GLOBE training but had not yet received it or been certified to implement the program. On the environmental awareness task, GLOBE students generated more environmental and water-cycle concepts than did students in the classes that had not yet implemented GLOBE, but students in the GLOBE classes that were above average in number of data submissions did no better than students in classes that were average. On the second performance task, which required data-driven problem solving, students from the classes that had submitted above average amounts of GLOBE data did better than those in GLOBE classes that had submitted average amounts of data, who were similar to those in the classes that had not yet implemented GLOBE. Teacher survey data indicated that the classes that were above average in number of data submissions were also more likely than the second group to have engaged in data analysis activities in the context of GLOBE. Considered together, these Web-based performance assessments suggest that different components of GLOBE (data collection and data analysis) support different learning outcomes.

GLOBE Study #3

During the 2001–2002 school year, 292 students from fifteen classrooms implementing activities within the atmosphere-investigation area of GLOBE participated in another student assessment. Students completed an assessment of their background knowledge concerning Earth's atmosphere, a performance task requiring them to demonstrate their science inquiry skills using atmospheric data, and a survey containing items about their attitude toward science and activities in their classroom. These students' teachers completed an inventory describing the nature and extent of their GLOBE-related activities, as well as a self-report of their science teaching practices.

Student performance on the conceptual knowledge measure was predicted by their teachers' belief in GLOBE's centrality for their science learning goals, students' attitude toward science, coverage of atmosphere topics in the curriculum, and the frequency with which their classroom engaged in analysis of GLOBE data. The more central the teacher considered GLOBE to students' science learning, the higher the students scored on this assessment. Scores on the inquiry portion of the assessment were predicted to a significant extent by the coverage of topics on the atmosphere, participation in inquiry activities across the curriculum, and the extent to which students analyzed GLOBE data (but not the extent to which they collected or reported data).

What GLOBE Implementation Data Tell Program Staff, Partners, and Teachers

Data about program enactment in different settings have provided GLOBE program staff with important insights into their own assumptions about how the program would function. In some cases, those assumptions have held up: it does appear that many teachers can and do report environmental data consistently and over multiple years, and partners have been successful in getting hundreds of schools up and running with GLOBE by providing training and support to new program teachers. At the same time, evaluation data show that many schools fail to report data from year to year and that technology access remains a big barrier for many schools. Evaluation data also show that GLOBE training partners vary with respect to the particular posttraining supports they offer and that teachers' receipt of these offerings is associated with higher rates of data reporting. Both of these sets of findings have given pause to GLOBE program staff, as well as GLOBE training partners, and recent years have witnessed a redoubled effort to focus partners' efforts on finding effective strategies to help teachers implement GLOBE after their initial training has been completed.

These data also provide program designers with input on how to modify specific components of the program, such that the diverse needs of teachers within the program can be better addressed. Early evaluation data pointed to the need for more supports for teacher enactment of GLOBE, as well as for helping teachers situate data collection in the context of meaningful inquiry. Over the years, program staff members have provided training partners with more materials to support deep implementation, which they in turn pass on to teachers. The focus of training has shifted as well; just this year, specialized sessions for training partners have been developed that will focus entirely on program enactment rather than reporting of environmental data.

Perhaps one of the most significant contributions of evaluation data about context and enactment in GLOBE has been the identification of constellations or networks of practices that together contribute to desired student outcomes. We know that content coverage matters: students need multiple opportunities to learn the concepts that are part of GLOBE, whether in the context of data collection activities or as part of teachers' regular curriculum. Evidence from a number of student learning studies shows that the combination of data collection and data analysis activities is associated with higher scores on tests of students' conceptual knowledge, environmental awareness, and inquiry skills. Data also suggest that engaging students in inquiry with GLOBE—that is, building student investigations around GLOBE data—is associated with higher scores on students' inquiry skills. Finally, we have data about teachers' attitudes and student outcomes: the extent to which teachers believe in the benefits of GLOBE for student learning affects the benefits that their students are likely to derive, as evidenced by performance on our assessment tasks. (Such data suggest that a mandated GLOBE program would likely be less effective than the voluntary implementations.) Together, these findings constitute information that teachers can use in deciding when to implement GLOBE and which elements of the program to use, and these findings are increasingly becoming part of training partners' own presentations to teachers.

For researchers, the availability of broad and detailed data on context and enactment variables has led to the development of more refined studies of GLOBE's effects. At the outset of the evaluation, we focused on simple comparisons of performance of students from GLOBE and non-GLOBE schools on our assessment measures. Over time, we have used enactment data to revise these measures to better reflect the range of expected student opportunities to learn in GLOBE; we have also used enactment data to develop more sophisticated sampling procedures, recruitment techniques, and scheduling of assessments to maximize study participation rates. We have developed a range of assessments that are more specifically aligned with the hands-on inquiry that students encounter in GLOBE. We have posed more refined hypotheses about

student learning and adopted techniques for statistical modeling of enactment variables to test those hypotheses, without having to adopt a
"kitchen sink" approach to investigating all possible predictors of student
learning.

Conclusion

Returning to the issue of the strengths and limitations of random-
assignment experiments, we can think about what such a study design
could provide for the GLOBE program. To make a randomized trial of
GLOBE's efficacy feasible, we would need to limit our experiment to specified grade levels and course contexts (for example, general elementary
classrooms or middle school environmental science classes) and employ
an experimental protocol that mandates selected, well-specified program
components (such as atmospheric data collection or hydrology learning
activities). Assuming that schools could be persuaded to participate in the
experiment and that teachers would stick with their randomly assigned
condition, we would gain evidence concerning the impact of the selected
GLOBE components in the contexts that were studied on the selected outcome measures. The case for GLOBE as the causal agent for student learning in these contexts would be stronger than that provided by the
quasi-experiments we have used in the past. However, we would not be
justified in extrapolating the results to different contexts or components
of GLOBE, nor would the experiment per se help us understand how to
improve the program.

The broader implications of this discussion concern the primacy now
being given to random-assignment experiments by federal education
research agencies. Not only in new sponsored research but also in sum-
marizing prior research studies for the field, heavy emphasis is given to
random-assignment experiments. While we agree that this experimental
design is an important and often neglected tool in the education
researcher's tool kit, we do not think that a single type of design can
answer all of the important and legitimate research questions surrounding educational improvement. Random-assignment experiments are
appropriate when the central question is one of treatment effects, the
treatment is well-specified, and the time required for treatment implementation is short enough that fidelity to the experimental protocol is a
reasonable expectation (Means and Haertel, 2003). These conditions
rarely apply to the kinds of systemwide reforms discussed elsewhere in
this volume. Moreover, as Smith (2004) notes, school administrators and
parents are sometimes more concerned with issues of social justice and

program sustainability than with causal effects. The ability of the research field to examine these issues in a way that leads to the accumulation of knowledge across different localities will be hampered if federal agencies sponsoring education research fail to recognize the value of and provide support for this kind of study as well as experimental investigations.

Context and enactment data provide valuable information about the range of contexts where scaling up is taking place and where it is not: Who are the participants? In what kinds of districts, schools, and classrooms is the program implemented? What kinds of participants find the innovation easy to implement? When and where is the innovation hard to implement well? These data will provide program designers with input on how to modify specific components of a program, such that the diverse needs of students and teachers within it can be better addressed. If, for example, evaluation research data show that principals are particularly important to the success of an innovation, program designers might require evidence of principal buy-in before accepting teachers for training or design a new program component to enhance principal support. Similarly, if research data suggest that a training component is less effective in yielding high-quality enactment than trainer site visits to schools, more resources could be devoted to the site visits. Thus, we conclude that while random-assignment experiments are powerful tools in adding to education's knowledge base, those interested in scaling innovations across a range of contexts need additional kinds of studies—those that help us understand when and how the innovation produces positive outcomes.

REFERENCES

Anderson, R. A., & Becker, H. J. (2001). *School investments in instructional technology.* Irvine: Center for Research on Information Technology and Organizations, University of California, Irvine; and Minneapolis: University of Minnesota.

Becker, H. J., & Anderson, R. E. (2000). *Subject and teacher objectives for computer-using classes by school socio-economic status.* Irvine: Center for Research on Information Technology and Organizations, University of California, Irvine; and Minneapolis: University of Minnesota.

Blumenfeld, P., Fishman, B. J., Krajcik, J. S., Marx, R. W., & Soloway, E. (2000). Creating usable innovations in systemic reform: Scaling up technology-embedded project-based science in urban schools. *Educational Psychologist, 35*(3), 149–164.

Bohrnstedt, G. W., & Stecher, B. M. (2002). *What we have learned about class-size reduction in California.* Sacramento: California Department of Education.

Brown, M., & Edelson, D. C. (1998). Software in context: Designing for students, teachers, and classroom enactment. In A. Ram (Ed.), *Proceedings of ICLS 98: International Conference on the Learning Sciences* (pp. 63–69). Charlottesville, VA: Association for the Advancement of Computing in Education.

Congalton, R. G., Rowe, R., & Becker, M. (2001, July). Using GLOBE student-collected MUC-A-THON data to aid in assessing the accuracy of a Landsat Thematic Mapper–derived land cover map of Dutchess County, New York. Paper presented at the Sixth Annual GLOBE Conference, Blaine, WA.

Cook, T. D. (2002). Randomized experiments in education: Why are they so rare? *Educational Evaluation and Policy Analysis, 24*(3), 175–199.

Cronbach, L. J. (1982). *Designing evaluations of educational and social programs.* San Francisco: Jossey-Bass.

Cronbach, L. J., Ambron, S. R., Dornbusch, S. M., Hess, R. D., Hornik, R. C., Phillips, D. C., Walker, D. F., and Weiner, S. S. (1980). *Toward reform of program evaluation.* San Francisco: Jossey-Bass.

Finn, J. D. (2002). Class-size reduction in grades K–3. In A. Molnar (Ed.), *School reform proposals: The research evidence* (pp. 15–24). Tempe: Education Policy Research Unit, Arizona State University.

Lesgold, A. (2003). Detecting technology's effects in complex school environments. In G. D. Haertel & B. Means (Eds.), *Evaluating educational technology: Effective research designs for improving learning* (pp. 38–74). New York: Teachers College Press.

McLaughlin, M. W. (1987). Learning from experience: Lessons from policy implementation. *Educational Evaluation and Policy Analysis, 9,* 171–178.

Means, B., Coleman, E. B., Baisden, K., Haertel, G. D., Korbak, C., & Lewis, A. (1999). *GLOBE Year 4 evaluation: Evolving implementation practices.* Menlo Park, CA: SRI International.

Means, B., Coleman, E. B., & Lewis, A. (1998). *GLOBE Year 3 evaluation: Implementation and progress.* Menlo Park, CA: SRI International.

Means, B., & Haertel, G. D. (Eds.). (2003). *Evaluating educational technology: Effective research designs for improving learning.* New York: Teachers College Press.

Means, B., Penuel, W. R., & Padilla, C. (2001). *The connected school: Technology and learning in high school.* San Francisco: Jossey-Bass.

Penuel, W. R., Kim, D. Y., Michalchik, V., Lewis, S., Means, B., and Murphy, R. (2001). *Using technology to enhance connections between home and school: A research synthesis.* Menlo Park, CA: SRI International.

Penuel, W. R., Korbak, C., Lewis, A., Shear, L., Toyama, Y., & Yarnall, L. (2002). *GLOBE Year 7 evaluation: Exploring student research and inquiry in GLOBE.* Menlo Park, CA: SRI International.

Penuel, W. R., & Means, B. (2004). Implementation variation and fidelity in an inquiry science program: An analysis of GLOBE data reporting patterns. *Journal of Research in Science Teaching, 41*(3), 294–315.

Postawko, S., Morrissey, M., Green, J. S., & Mirsky, N. (2001, July). *Using GLOBE student data for surface verification of remotely sensed global precipitation.* Paper presented at the Sixth Annual GLOBE Conference, Blaine, WA.

Robin, J., Levine, E., & Riha, S. (2001, July). *GLOBE meets GAPS: Utilizing student data to model the atmosphere-plant-soil system.* Paper presented at the Sixth Annual GLOBE Conference, Blaine, WA.

Smith, N. (2004). Research designs to evaluate technology innovations. In B. Means & G. D. Haertel (Eds.), *Using technology evaluation to enhance student learning* (pp. 33–40). New York: Teachers College Press.

Spillane, J. P., & Jennings, N. E. (1997). Aligned instructional policy and ambitious pedagogy: Exploring instructional reform from the classroom perspective. *Teachers College Record, 98,* 449–481.

Stecher, B. M., & Bohrnstedt, G. A. (Eds.). (2002). *Class size reduction in California: Findings from 1999–2001 and 2000–2001.* Sacramento: California Department of Education.

Whitehurst, G. G. (2002, June 25). Statement before the Senate Committee on Health, Education, Labor and Pensions.

Wiggins, G., & McTighe, J. (1998). *Understanding by design.* Alexandria, VA: ASCD.

Yarnall, L., & Penuel, W. R. (2002). Structuring group learning within a Web-based science inquiry program. In G. Stahl (Ed.), *Proceedings of the Computer Support for Collaborative Learning Conference 2002* (pp. 577–578). Boulder: University of Colorado.

CRITIQUING AND IMPROVING THE USE OF DATA FROM HIGH-STAKES TESTS WITH THE AID OF DYNAMIC STATISTICS SOFTWARE

Jere Confrey, Katie M. Makar

Data analysis can lay the groundwork for improved portrayal and interpretation of student performance.

ACROSS THE COUNTRY, proponents extol the potential use of data from high-stakes tests to improve instruction (Eisenhower National Clearinghouse, 2003). Drawing from models of business, the argument suggests that by a careful examination of overall data reports and the disaggregation of data by subgroup (race/ethnicity, socioeconomic status, gender, language group, and educational status) practitioners can monitor the overall progress in the system and devise appropriate strategies for instructional improvement tailored to local settings. In this chapter, we use a case study and subsequent work to illustrate how these approaches to disaggregation may shed some light on the relevant issues of performance differences but lack the robust application of statistical concepts and relevant theories of equity and assessment to ensure that data use is valid and fair. We outline approaches that would support scaling up through the use of more accurate and fair ways of examining distribution and difference that are still easily accessible to policymakers, teachers, and community members. Moreover, we demonstrate the value of providing teachers with professional development experiences in conducting similar inquiries of their own, using real data and dynamic statistics software.

In Texas, schools are provided with data on the overall performance of their students scaled to the Texas Learning Index (TLI), a scaled score that is linked to the process of test equating from year to year. These scores can be compared to districtwide performance or state performance. Groups like Just for the Kids (now the National Center for Educational Accountability, www.nc4ea.org) provide schools with profiles of the highest-achieving comparison schools in the state that share the same demographics. Their summaries report on total student populations as well as totals for individual students who have been enrolled in the school for three or more years. Schools also receive these same data for a number of subgroups, including ethnic groups (African American, Hispanic, white, and Asian), economically disadvantaged students, students with limited English proficiency, and special education students. All data are reported as percentages passing. We wish to demonstrate that separating the data into groups and reporting the percentage passing on scaled scores present an inadequate representation of the situation. Using the statistical concepts of distribution, sampling variation, significant differences, and variability of performance by objective, we use data representations to demonstrate weaknesses in schools' current system of data use.

This work is particularly important when one considers that the approach to school reform in the No Child Left Behind Act is consistent with the design of the accountability system in Texas, and its regulations are modeled closely after the Texas system. Our argument is part of a larger exploration under development in a book that Confrey is writing called *Systemic Crossfire,* in which she argues that the national model of linking standards and accountability systems into a "bookends" approach to reform masks an underlying controversy about issues of content and of equity. These conflicts produce incoherence and conflict at the classroom level, and because the model is relatively silent on practice in the instructional core (teaching, learning, and formative assessment), it leaves the public blaming the failure of the system on teachers and students, rather than on the naïveté, incompleteness, and underfinanced aspects of the model, including poor funding of professional development. In this chapter, our investigations focus on how the use of feedback in that model of systemic reform suffers from inadequate approaches to the employment of data. Particularly problematic is the role of data analysis in ensuring that the system is properly attending to issues of fairness and consequential validity (Messick, 1995).

Nancy Love (2003) has undertaken some of the most well regarded studies of the use of data. She advises teachers and administrators to learn what they can from standardized tests and warns that the summary data reported to the public does not provide teachers with the information they need to guide instruction. She recommends digging further into disaggregated data to search for potential gaps between genders, socioeconomic levels, special education designations, and ethnic or racial groups—gaps in performance that are hidden by summary statistics. While we agree that examination of data needs to go beyond aggregate data, we have found that schools draw hasty and erroneous conclusions based on even disaggregated summary statistics. In this chapter, we outline and demonstrate why current methodologies for the distribution and analysis of data are insufficient from the perspective of fairness and thus lack the validity to lead to the careful design of revised instructional practices.

Background

For five years (1996–2000), our research team partnered with Tree High School (not the school's real name), a high-poverty urban school in Austin, with 71 percent Hispanic, 11 percent African American, 16 percent Caucasian, and 2 percent Asian and others, as well as 43 percent economically disadvantaged students. At the end of a five-year period of working with the entire mathematics department on the use of replacement units (short curricular units used by a set of teachers to experiment with or build a transition to a new approach) in algebra, our research collaborative had seen a 25 percent increase in the passing rate on the state exit test, called Texas Assessment of Academic Skills (TAAS), in mathematics. Students are required to pass TAAS in order to graduate, and schools are held accountable for their students' performance. Overall scores (for about 300 students tested per year) had increased from 48.4 percent passing to 73.4 percent over our five years of working with the school. This was in comparison with a 13 percent gain at the state level and 15 percent district gains (see Figure 10.1).

The results of the 2000 TAAS revealed that the performance of the school's African American students had dropped below acceptable levels in mathematics. The school data were reported to staff, parents, and community members in a chart (Table 10.1), which presented the percentage of students passing TAAS, disaggregated by subgroup.

Since less than half of the African American students (15 out of 31) had passed the test, based on the state accountability system, the school was labeled as low-performing. A number of obligatory steps followed. The

Figure 10.1. Longitudinal Pass Rates on TAAS Math Test for Tenth Graders at Tree High School, Austin Independent School District, and the State of Texas, 1996–2000

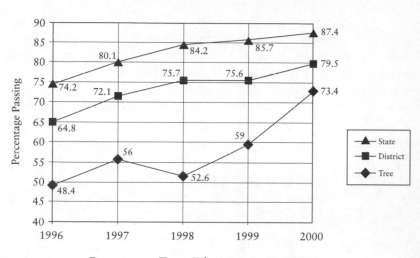

Data source: *Texas Education Agency, 2000a.*

teachers were called to a one-day meeting with district administrators and curriculum supervisors at which the school data were compared to the district and state data in tables that summarized the students' performance. The motto for the day was "The clearer the focus, the greater the achievement." The district administrators, including the area superintendent, the special projects director, and the mathematics supervisor, provided state, district, and school data summaries, raw data by objective on TAAS and the new algebra end-of-course exam, and an item analysis of TAAS. Teachers were promised additional resources and training to address the weaknesses in their students' performance. The meeting included virtually no discussion of the 49 Hispanic or the 6 white students who had also failed the exam.

The teachers identified what they saw as the school's problems, which, ranked from highest to lowest, included a lack of high expectations, poor attendance, lack of formative assessment, the need for challenging math problems, the need for smaller class size, language barriers, disruptive student behavior, gaps in students' competencies in mathematics, and a lack of diverse cultural representations and role models. The district ruled out the possibility of changes to class size and attendance patterns and focused

Table 10.1. Percentage of Students Passing the TAAS Math Test, 1999-2000

	State	District	Campus Group	Campus	African American	Hispanic	White	Native American	Asian and Pacific Islander	Male	Female	Economically Disadvantaged	Special Education
2000	86.8	81.7	82.3	73.4	48.4	74.5	85.7	—	83.3	80.4	65.6	71.3	42.9
1999	81.6	73.9	75.5	59.0	58.1	55.7	73.9	*	80.0	54.9	63.5	58.3	40.0

* Sample size was too small for the State to report results

Data source: Texas Education Agency, 2000b.

the teachers on two questions: (1) How are you using data to focus instruction? and (2) How are you differentiating your program for students who are members of the underperforming group? At that meeting, no attention was given to the distribution of scores of the African Americans in order to explore the depth of the problem, nor did any examination of the performance of the students as a whole or by subgroup over time take place. Later, the research team met with the district administrators and pointed out that the teachers' substantial progress over the past few years, as reflected in the scores of all students, had not been acknowledged adequately. Furthermore, the analysis of the performance of African American students had not been placed in time longitudinally, nor had the district examined the distribution of scores.

After the meeting, the discussions continued at the campus, culminating in a campus improvement plan (CIP). The campus plan included the following action plans regarding mathematics: "Need a systematic concentrated effort to teach/reinforce TAAS objectives. . . . Need to address specific learning needs of special populations—how populations are defined, legal requirements, and programs/resources available for each group" (Tree High School's *2000–2001 Campus Improvement Plan,* p. 6).

One priority stated in the plan was "To increase the student passing rate of the African American TAAS subgroup to at least 60%" (Tree High School's *2000–2001 Campus Improvement Plan,* p. 39). The key strategies to obtain this goal were identified: "To provide the faculty with staff development training targeting the subgroup found in the 'condition of performance,'" "to identify all African-American students in the 9th and 10th grade and assign them a peer tutor," and to "identify and address TAAS objectives which were below 50%" (Tree High School's *2000–2001 Campus Improvement Plan,* p. 39). Also included in the CIP was a stated plan to meet with teachers from a neighboring high school in the wealthier part of town, who had eliminated low performance by requiring that all African American students attend mandatory lunchtime tutoring programs.

In response, the research team wrote a letter to the new principal and the department, which stated,

> Our concern [is] that the CIP, as currently written, unfairly targets African-American students for specific interventions when such interventions would more appropriately be directed at all low-performing students at [Tree] High School. Although TAAS results are reported by racial/ethnic group for purposes of the Texas accountability system and schools can be labeled as low performing based on the TAAS scores of one subgroup on one subtest, we believe it is important that

resources and services be targeted primarily based on student performance, not race. If racism against African Americans is a schoolwide
problem, we agree it merits schoolwide attention with regard to the
whole target group. However, initiatives like assigning mentors or providing pullout treatments should not be done for an entire group. Finer
distinctions would be more helpful. [letter from J. Confrey to Tree
High School principal, October 13, 2000]

In her response to this letter (October 30, 2000, p. 1), the principal agreed
to change the wording in the CIP to "low-performing students" but
added, "we will still focus on our target population in order to adequately
address the anticipated questions from the Texas Education Agency and
in order to ensure all of our students' needs are being met."

During this time period, the research team and its partners watched in
frustration as the new principal and her collaborators at the district level,
curriculum coordinators, and district special programs directors disman-
tled the partnership with the university research team. The research team
engaged in an effort to interview students to document their responses to
the programs; in so doing, evidence surfaced showing that at least one
African American student had been reassigned to special education status
before the 2001 TAAS test by counselors, without his or his parents'
knowledge, and was thereby exempted from testing requirements. Our
interviews increased the tensions between the research team and the
school personnel. At a tense meeting in the spring of 2001, the research
team asked the teachers if they wished to continue the collaboration.
When the teachers decided to discontinue the projects, the research team
expressed a combination of relief and disappointment at the ending of the
partnership, agreeing that our involvement in the school's activities was
no longer productive.

This experience left our research team puzzled and disturbed. We began
to consider critically what had happened and sought to understand how,
in a system that professes to support standards-based instruction, such a
result could lead to the demise of a program that was showing steady
improvement and success in relation to the high-stakes tests and was consistent with the recommendations of the National Council of Teachers of
Mathematics standards movement. We helplessly watched as the program
was replaced by a program of test preparation and pull-out programs for
particular students, primarily students of color. In subsequent years, the
school's performance continued to rise, with 77 percent of all students
and 71 percent of African American students at the school passing in
2002; however, the number of African American students taking the test

had dropped below accountability requirements in both 2001 and 2002. State and district performance also continued to rise.

Based on our observations, the school district had made a number of questionable decisions in implementing the accountability system. First, they did not look at the data in a systematic way to examine how this data point fit into the long-term trajectory, nor did they examine the distribution of the subgroup's scores and compare its performance to that of the larger population of students. Second, their treatment program was heavily oriented toward treating the students in this group as a problem to be fixed, giving little attention to other factors in the systematic treatment of African Americans in the school that might need examination. Third, the approach of "fixing" the students revealed a view of remediation that was poorly connected with a larger vision of curricular progress; it simply focused on bringing these students across the threshold of a passing score. And finally, it appeared likely that the school had adopted a strategy of ensuring that it was not designated as low-performing in the following year. Tactics included assigning students to special education or holding them back a grade, to keep small the numbers of students in certain subgroups in order to keep the school from being held accountable for their performance. This case led our team to question the implications and approaches drawn from the disaggregation of data and the design of the accountability system in the case of small populations. It made us aware of schools' neglect of distribution, sampling variation, and inferences of statistical difference in the use of data from TAAS.

The project director presented evidence to the district administration that decisions had been based on an incomplete assessment of indicators. However, the administrators would not consider the longitudinal trajectory of the whole tenth grade or the fact that the pass rate for that year was the second highest of the past five years. Had the administration pursued a more robust study of the statistics behind the data, they would have seen a different story. First, the long-term trajectory of student performance had continued to rise during the partnership (Figure 10.1). Second, the African American subgroup continued to be on the same trajectory as the district and state when examined longitudinally, based on a least-squares fit of the data (Figure 10.2). Third, the drop in performance of the African American subgroup was not unusually large, given the high variability of past performance of the subgroup. We found that the residual of the 2000 drop in performance was still within one standard deviation of their projected pass rate of 54 percent (based on the least-squares regression line). Given the small size of the subgroup, our simulations indicate that if we accept the trajectory of performance of the

African American population over the seven years since the partnership began in 1996, the subgroup had more than a 30 percent chance of falling below 50 percent passing just by chance (Figure 10.3). Even if the district had based their decisions only on the 1996–1999 data available at the time, the 2000 drop in scores was still not statistically significant. Furthermore, in an examination of the distribution of scores of the African Americans, we found that a number of students were close to passing; in fact, if one student had answered one or two more questions correctly, the school would not have been labeled as low-performing. We demonstrate the probability of the low-performing score by using a simulation rather than a *t* test because simulation is easily supported by the software we used and because it produces a visual display that gives a spread of outcomes from a diverse set of samples and makes the point more vigorously that variation in sampling distributions is expected. Finally, in our attempt to verify the scores of the 31 African American students at the school as reported by the state, we found that only 20 were still enrolled.

Figure 10.2. Longitudinal Performance Trajectories of African American Students on the TAAS Math Test in the State of Texas, Austin Independent School District, and Tree High School, 1996–2002

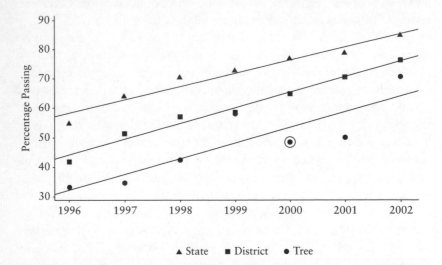

Note: *The 2000 drop in performance of African Americans at Tree High School is circled. The 1999 performance of the African Americans at Tree High School overlaps with that of the district.*

Figure 10.3. Simulation Showing Variation of Pass Rates for a Subgroup of Thirty-One Students When Projected Pass Rate Is on Trajectory (53.6 percent)

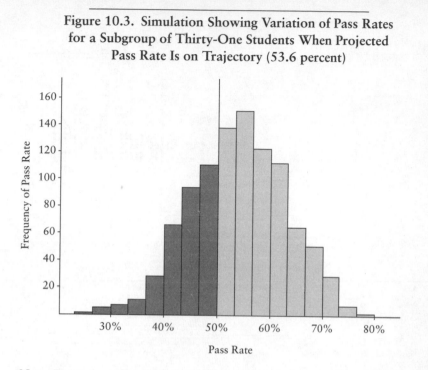

Note: *Due to sampling variation, in more than 30 percent of the 1,000 cases in the simulation, the subgroup of 31 students had a pass rate below 50 percent.*

In order to see a more accurate and complete picture of the performance of the African American subgroup at Tree High School, we present first a figure showing the African American students' distribution in relation to the distribution of the whole school (Figure 10.4). We represent the same data in the form of box plots as well, to assist the reader in considering how different representations support different pictures of student performance. For example, the box plot allows easier comparison of unequally sized groups, particularly of the variation in student outcomes by performance level noted by the quartiles. The dot plot, on the other hand, does not obscure the group sizes, which are needed to determine whether differences in performance may be due to sampling variation based on the size of the groups. Because these data were not available publicly, we requested them from the area superintendent. We tried to corroborate the presence of the 31 African American students by matching identification numbers but were able to find only 20 of them.

**Figure 10.4. Performance of African American
Tenth Graders on the TAAS Math Test Compared with the
Rest of the Student Population at Tree High School, 2000**

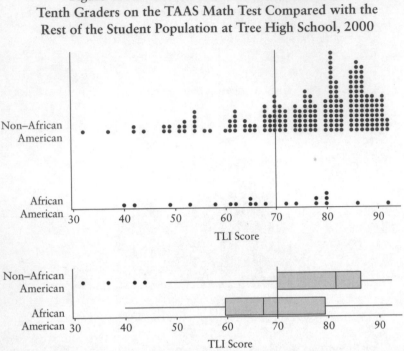

Note: *The same data is shown as a pair of dot plots (top) and a pair
of box plots (bottom). The passing standard (TLI score = 70) is marked
on each plot. In the box plots, the length of the box encompasses the
second and third quartiles and the vertical line shows the median.*

The conclusions we draw from these analyses are twofold. First, we
believe it is essential to provide a comprehensive picture of the scores of
the whole student body and the identified subgroups in terms of (1) percentage passing, (2) median or mean score, and (3) distributions marked
by standard deviation or quartiles. The relationships between these sets
of scores must be displayed in order to show the variation among members of subgroups and examine the significance of differences in the measures of central tendency.

Second, we emphasize that scores of students represent only an estimate
of their ability to perform on a test. There is inherent sampling error in any
measurement taken. In particular, small subgroups demonstrate much greater
variability in performance than do larger subgroups. This suggests that plac-
ing a school in the low-performing category on the basis of a subgroup of

30 students may fail to take into account expected variations in scores. While we certainly recognize that a pass rate of only half the students is cause for concern and significant intervention efforts, we believe that the policy should be based on better-informed ideas of variation and distribution.

As a result of the dissolution of our partnership, we began to ask other questions about the testing system and its use of data, particularly in relation to distributions and variation. Over the past three years, we have worked with teachers to make more informed analyses of their school's assessment data (Confrey and Makar, 2002; Makar and Confrey, 2002; Makar and Confrey, 2004). In our work with teachers and data, we discovered other issues that are neglected in consideration of summary data.

State policy tends to encourage schools to focus on indicators of success rather than improvements in learning for all students. In Texas, the accountability system uses percentage passing rather than mean score as an indicator of a school's success. This leads schools to focus their energy where it will have the greatest impact on this indicator: students who are close to passing. These "bubble kids" are given additional remediation and test preparation, while other students are neglected. The statewide impact of this emphasis becomes apparent when one compares two longitudinal state-level graphs: percentage passing and average scaled score (Figure 10.5). In the percentage passing graph, the achievement gap appears to be closing as one looks at the differences in the scores of higher and lower performers over time, from left to right. However, this feature is less apparent when one examines the average TLI of subgroups over the same time period, in which the same differences narrow only slightly.

If one were to graph the individual student-level scores used to calculate the summary data in Figure 10.5 as a set of longitudinal box plots, the progress by quartiles over time would become apparent. However, the data needed to produce such a graph are not reported to the public. Analyzing this representation, one could see that the idea that forms the basis of the No Child Left Behind accountability system is faulty. Teachers and schools are not held accountable for improving the performance of the bottom portion of the scoring distribution. Attending to only the top 50 percent allows schools to avoid categorization as low-performing. Schools are also held accountable for keeping the dropout rate tolerably low, but this is not equivalent to being obliged to teach all students successfully.

Based on this analysis of distribution of scores, we argue that performance of state-designated subgroups (based on ethnicity, language proficiency, socioeconomic status, and gender) are not the only sets of student subgroups that need to be considered. For example, the lowest-testing 30 percent of students at a school are often neglected, particularly if they fall well below the passing standard. We propose that a standard be set for

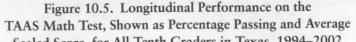

Figure 10.5. Longitudinal Performance on the
TAAS Math Test, Shown as Percentage Passing and Average
Scaled Score, for All Tenth Graders in Texas, 1994–2002

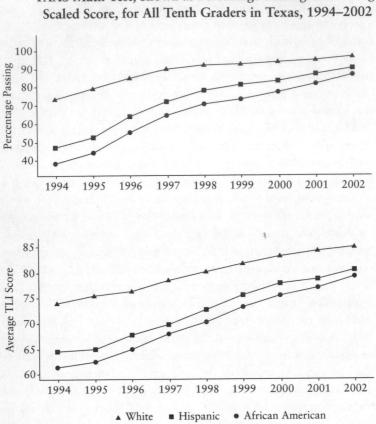

▲ White   ■ Hispanic   ● African American

Note: *The upper graph shows a closing of the performance gap between tenth
graders of different races over time when performance is viewed in terms of the
percentage of students who passed the math portion of the TAAS exit exam.
However, when performance is viewed as the average TLI score on the same
exam, narrowing of the gap between subgroups is less apparent.*
Data source: *Texas Education Agency, 2002b.*

the improvement of each quartile rather than a simple report of percentage passing; if indeed there is a commitment to the adage "all students
can learn," such measures should be compulsory.

   In addition to focusing on the variation in scores during a single year,
it is important to look at the performance of individual students over time
to see the extent to which students' performances change within the
distributions. For example, in the pair of graphs in Figure 10.6, the

performance of students on the TAAS exam in sixth grade are compared
with the performance of the same students in seventh grade. One might
assume that an individual student's performance relative to the group
would remain somewhat the same from year to year—that is, students
who are clustered close to passing in seventh grade would be the same
ones who had scores close to passing in sixth grade.

A dynamic software program, Fathom (Finzer and Swenson, 2001), can
help in such analyses. A feature of Fathom is the ability to select a subset
within one distribution and show the same sample highlighted within
other distributions. Using this feature, we can see that in fact, the students
in the highlighted cluster in seventh grade came from a wide range of
scores in sixth grade (Figure 10.6). This variation in the performance of
particular students raised significant questions about what is being measured for these students each year. Conducting similar analyses across students from different percentiles may reveal that test results vary more
among particular subgroups of students on the basis of test motivation.
Theories to explain such differences could lead to intervention practices
that go well beyond simple practice test items. Representations available
through Fathom can highlight such neglected issues and can provide
teachers with the resources to more completely analyze their own data
and conduct their own inquiries.

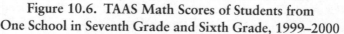

Figure 10.6. TAAS Math Scores of Students from
One School in Seventh Grade and Sixth Grade, 1999–2000

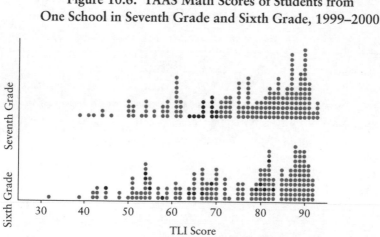

Note: *Students' scores in seventh grade are compared with their scores the year
before. Fourteen students who were close to passing in seventh grade are highlighted in order to investigate their previous performance. Over one-third of
them were high performers the previous year.*

Similarly, Figure 10.7 shows the performance of students on TAAS across two test administrations from the eighth to the tenth grades. The students who fall below the line $y = x$ scored lower on the tenth-grade test than on the eighth-grade test. These graphs suggest that quite a few students perform differently on TAAS across the grades. These data suggest that one would be particularly incorrect to assume that lower-performing students maintain their performance level as a group over time. Though many students lost ground over the two-year period, a significant number also performed substantially better. These two figures support a variety of interpretations, all of which, we suggest, should be considered in the professional work of school personnel serving students.

Examining data in terms of distributions raises the question of whether school personnel have been adequately prepared to draw conclusions concerning differences between groups. For example, how would they know whether a two-point difference in means between genders on the TAAS in math is a significant difference or simply due to issues of natural variability (Figure 10.8)? A permutation test can be used to compare a measure in the actual data with its likelihood of being due to random variation. The process randomly shuffles the comparison attribute (for example, gender) in the data to simulate a null hypothesis, then calculates the measure in question for the shuffled data. This is repeated multiple times, and these calculated measures are plotted as a sampling distribution

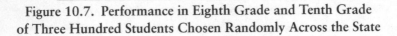

Figure 10.7. Performance in Eighth Grade and Tenth Grade of Three Hundred Students Chosen Randomly Across the State

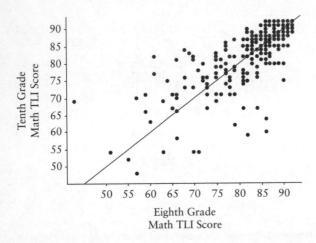

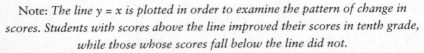

Note: *The line y = x is plotted in order to examine the pattern of change in scores. Students with scores above the line improved their scores in tenth grade, while those whose scores fall below the line did not.*

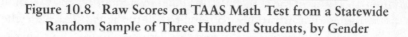

Figure 10.8. Raw Scores on TAAS Math Test from a Statewide Random Sample of Three Hundred Students, by Gender

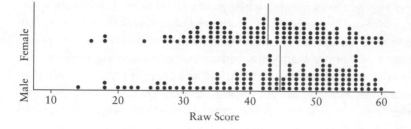

to get a sense of their variability, so that one can compare the original measure within this sampling distribution. The Fathom software makes this process very easy to visualize. Running permutation tests multiple times, with the gender of students randomly scrambled, and noting the difference in means gives an idea of the variability one can expect. By running this type of simulation, as opposed to simply a *t* test, one can plot a graph similar to the one in Figure 10.3 (except that the horizontal access would show the difference between the means of each simulation instead of passing rate) and thus visually identify the likelihood that the two-point difference between the two groups is due to chance variation. Examining distributions without taking random variation into account or considering sample size can lead to an interpretation of a two-point difference as meaningful when it may just be due to random variation. In this case, for example, running the simulation five hundred times (similar to what was done in the simulation discussed in Figure 10.3) indicates that males performed at least two points higher than females in only about 25 percent of the cases.

To understand differences between groups, practitioners need to understand that even with statistically significant differences, there are often large amounts of overlap between the distributions of the two groups, and thus it is an act of stereotyping to assume that all members of a population perform at the lower or higher mean. Statistical significance is more easily obtained with higher sample sizes, and decisions in practice still require an interpretation of whether those differences constitute not just statistical but also educational significance. Finally, it must always be kept in mind, as we discussed in the example concerning African American students, that sampling variation can produce the appearance of difference, but this finding may not hold up under close examination of the variance of the sampling distribution.

So far, our discussions of distribution and variation have concerned differences in students' total scores. Yet there is also the key question of variation of scores on the objectives of a single test and perhaps variation in the performance of subgroups on the different objectives. Teachers who focus on teaching particular topics find this data by objective particularly compelling in helping them to make instructional decisions. In fact, at the retreat with our research group, district administrators spent a great deal of time identifying the lowest performances by objectives and stressing that the teachers needed to concentrate on teaching these topics to the low-performing subgroup. In addition, the campus improvement plan identified this as a critical area for intervention. However, objective-level data are reported as the average number of questions pegged to a particular objective that students answered correctly, based on a raw score. Because the difficulty levels of the questions vary from year to year, comparing these averages can be exceedingly misleading for teachers (see Figure 10.9). How can they know whether students' drop in performance is due to difficulty with division or due to more difficult questions presented under this objective? Conversely, there is no way for teachers to know whether performance gains are due to their increased instructional efforts or due to easier questions (Confrey and Carrejo, 2002). Figure 10.9 illustrates this problem; it shows the difficulty of questions (based on the percentage of students that answered each question correctly) under objective 9 (division) over time.

Variable difficulty of items is a key issue in data use. If the data are scaled only as a total score, then significant amounts of information that is crucial to the curriculum are lost. We argue that it is indefensible to provide teachers with unscaled data by objective if the items on those objectives are not sampled consistently from the various levels of difficulty (which could be ascertained by field testing). Not to provide teachers with valid and reliable data by objective is also unacceptable because it renders teachers unable to direct instruction and curricular treatment toward the topics for which students need additional help. This dilemma is a very serious one that is examined further in a related paper (Confrey and Carrejo, 2002) that asks questions about the validity of the psychometric construction and analysis of TAAS.

To examine the external validity of TAAS, we also conducted a brief analysis of the TAAS scores in relation to scores on the Iowa Test of Basic Skills (ITBS). The ITBS is a nationally norm-referenced, standardized test that reports student performance as estimated grade level ability. For example, an ITBS score of 8.3 indicates that the student performs at the median level of a student in the third month of grade 8. Figure 10.10 indicates a strong ceiling effect on TAAS for students performing at or above

Figure 10.9. Variation in Difficulty of the Questions on Objective 9 (Division) of the TAAS Math Test

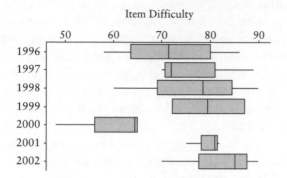

Note: *The box plot shows the difficulty level (percentage of students answering each question correctly) of the four questions on objective 9 for each year from 1996 to 2002; it shows high variability in difficulty from year to year.*

Figure 10.10. Performance of Eighth Graders at One School on the Math Portion of TAAS and the Math Portion of the Iowa Test of Basic Skills, 2000

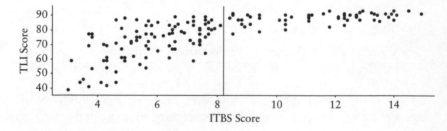

Note: *Grade level = 8.2.*

grade level on ITBS. However, it also indicates a weaker relationship between student performance on ITBS and TAAS for students who are below grade level. This weak relationship could indicate that one or both tests are not producing accurate readings at the lower scores or that at the lower scores, the tests are not measuring the same aspects of achievement and learning.

Discussion of Data and Results

The examples presented here demonstrate how the common forms of reporting data from high-stakes testing (for example, see Table 10.1) provide overly simplistic and potentially misleading information. Furthermore, we argue that by presenting the results on percentage passing by subgroup, without reports of central tendency and standard deviation or by quartiles, the state of Texas increases the likelihood that schools will treat low-performing subgroups as deficits to the school, contributing to racial or class stereotyping. While we recognize that the policy was intended to increase fair and equitable treatment across groups, we suggest that the failure to develop a more sophisticated view of distribution and variation is having a negative impact on racial and cross-class relations.

Interventions with little educational merit, such as those outlined in the case, are more likely to follow from this simplistic presentation of disaggregation; such interventions include the following:

- Treatment of certain conditions based on race rather than performance level
- Pull-out programs targeted at particular students that detract from their overall education
- Special efforts focused on "bubble kids" whose performance may not show consistency over time and hence may not need incremental improvement
- Overuse of practice tests
- A tendency to ignore the lowest-scoring and most needy students until high school, at which point they are denied diplomas

Since school practitioners are not held accountable for all students, the lowest-performing group over time is not required to improve. By the time this group reaches high school, expectations for remediation have become increasingly unrealistic. There is considerable debate about how many of these students drop out (Supik and Johnson, 1999) and how to calculate the number of dropouts in systems marked by high student mobility. Current predictions by the National Center for Education Statistics rank Texas twenty-sixth out of forty-seven states that reported, setting the rate of dropouts at 5 percent per year, which would translate into approximately 19 percent per high school cohort. This number has been reported to be as low as 9 percent by the Texas Education Agency and as high as 42 percent by the Intercultural Development Research Association (Supik and Johnson, 1999). According to the current accountability model, students denied diplomas due to results of high-stakes exams do not count as dropouts. As shown in Figure 10.6, considerable variation characterizes the performance of the "bubble kids" from one year to the next, variation that may be an indicator of children who are not consistent in their engagement and identification with the system. Their scores may be a function of the degree of alienation from school that they feel, an expression of a lack of confidence, the result of low expectations, or the result of differences in instructional quality. It may represent anxiety about or ease with test taking or detachment from the technologies of school testing. Whatever the explanation is, only by systematically examining the data for variation as well as the distribution of the data, as demonstrated in the preceding examples, can we make better conjectures and build more successful, focused approaches.

Finally, it is in the failure of the system to provide valid and reliable data at the level of specific curricular objectives that we see the most disturbing aspects of a lack of examination of distribution. There is no way to use the current system to gauge students' and schools' progress at the level of particular curricular objectives. Three losses accrue from this predicament: (1) we cannot use the results by objective to improve instruction; (2) when summed across objectives, a student's score may represent a kind of overall capacity to collect superficial math skills rather than real proficiency, reflecting general school competence rather than precise mathematical reasoning; and (3) we are thereby unable to truly determine whether the system is improving. When one sees that on TAAS, the correlation between the math and reading tests is $r = 0.68$ (Texas Education Agency, 2002a), concern about the second claim is strengthened. And the refusal of the testing companies to release publicly the items they use for test equating makes it impossible to determine whether the system is improving or whether, through equating and narrowness of item sampling, there is so much drift toward predictability in the system that only improved test performance and not growth in knowledge is occurring.

The failures of the system to recognize, diagnose, and treat these problems may have produced a system in which some educational leaders can claim success and progress, but the imminent implementation of a new test, the Texas Assessment of Knowledge and Skills (TAKS), will reveal the cost of an improperly designed system of accountability.

TAKS is a more difficult exam; the math portion tests high school students' knowledge of algebra, geometry, probability and statistics, and ratio reasoning. In addition to the math test, students must pass the other three tests in science (physical science, biology, chemistry, and physics), history, and English language arts in order to graduate from high school. The projected failure rates are alarming. In the fall of 2002, the Texas Education Agency's Passing Standards Panels recommended a passing score of 33 out of 60 items, or 55 percent correct on the TAKS mathematics exit exam, which is administered to eleventh-grade students. If the State Board of Education had passed this 55-percent standard, the field test data indicated that 173,600 out of 280,000 students, or 62 percent, would have failed the mathematics test, which is required for graduation. For African Americans, the predicted failure rate was 80 percent; for Hispanic students, 73 percent; for whites, 53 percent. Economically disadvantaged students' failure rate was predicted to be 75 percent. Experience with the TAAS exam suggested that under high-stakes conditions, scores would improve by approximately 15 percent. The board relaxed the standard for the 2003–2004 year to 41.7 percent correct, or a score of 25 out of 60, for which a failure rate of 117,600 students, or 42 percent, was predicted. These results raise serious questions as to whether the previous system has moved Texas into a state of readiness for new tests. At the standard-setting meeting of the State Board of Education and the Texas Education Agency on November 15, 2002, Sandy Kress, a White House adviser in education, testified in favor of implementing the passing scores as recommended by the panels and offered the following response to a board member's question about why the scores on the field tests were so low:

> I will be candid with you. The board set the TAKS curricula five years ago, but, candidly, I don't think it's been truly taught. I think it's beginning to be taught, but I think that we can make the argument that these new standards should have been set a year or two ago, that we may be late, not early. Once our teachers, our parents, and our community understand what's expected, they'll rise to the occasion, just as they did on TAAS. So my first answer is that you probably haven't seen the implementation of TAKS. My judgment is that if you postpone setting standards, you will have the inadvertent effect of further delay before implementation of TAKS. We have to get on down the road. We have to pass standards.

Later, Kress added,

> We've gotten there together because we put pressure on ourselves. There was a lot of pressure when TAAS came out. The passing rates were worse than the ones we are talking about now, and we responded, and Texas has done better because of it. Now is not the time to lose heart. Now is not the time to stop climbing up the mountain. I don't know where the bell curve is. I don't know where the right answer is. I believe this board has said this curriculum ought to be mastered by all children.

Our question to an administration that is so publicly committed to the use of scientifically proven programs is this: Are the data in fact being used accurately, fairly, and completely to ascertain the consequential validity of test results? Our interpretation of the situation is that flaws in the construction of the previous tests (Confrey & Carrejo, 2002) and the poor quality of released summary data have contributed to the *appearance* of widespread progress across the state. However, the errors and flaws in the design of the accountability system and the failure of the Texas Education Agency to release test-equating items make the actual level of progress virtually impossible to determine. We endorse the importance of accountability, with its potential to improve schooling, but the system of accountability must itself be held accountable for its unintended outcomes. Our criticisms rest with the lack of quality use of available data and the reluctance of testing proponents to carefully examine the consequential validity of the system. Our obligation is to remedy the deficits rather than to minimize, deny, or disregard the evidence.

In addition, we are particularly concerned because of other issues that threaten the validity of the test from the perspective of those of us who are content experts (Confrey & Carrejo, 2002). Besides questions of validity, we are concerned about the tendency to assume that a test is, indeed, an accurate measure of student proficiency, when performance on tests may be influenced by other factors such as achievement motivation, opportunity to learn, and quality of instruction. Attention must be devoted to developing the means by which the issues of distribution and variation can become more accessible to practitioners, policymakers, and community members. In the final two sections of this chapter, we report on current efforts to effect such changes.

Teachers as Inquirers

Our work with data has led us to consider the importance of providing teachers with a deeper understanding of assessment, equity, and use of data to inform instructional decision making, without expecting major investments in learning complex statistics. In this chapter, we have not discussed issues surrounding the use of classroom-embedded or formative data, but these can be considered as an extension of the ideas addressed in our work with high-stakes data.

Examining the distribution of scores provides great insight into the performance of students and subgroups of students, but this insight comes only after considerable and repeated experience with looking at distributions of data. We find that teachers who are novices at performing data analysis tend to focus on individual students and on mean scores and pass rates, ignoring the distribution of student performances (Confrey and Makar, 2002). For this reason, teachers need instruction in the concepts of variation, distribution, sampling, and difference, and they need experience in handling and interpreting student data.

In addition, we are currently extending previous work in teaching teachers to examine their own data for patterns and trends. We report on previous studies with a small group of middle school teachers who undertook investigations of their own after a set of professional development workshops (Confrey and Makar, 2002). Our design for teachers-as-investigators was modeled after the National Writing Project; based on that example, we developed the philosophy that the best way to teach mathematics teachers to include data, statistical concepts, and technology in their instruction was to provide them with an authentic experience in acting as inquirers themselves. At the end of the pilot project, teachers posed, investigated, and documented statistical evidence related to statements such as the following:

- Practice TAAS tests are not taken as seriously as the real TAAS test and are of limited value, even for the students who need them most (remedial students).

- The schools in our district remediate students at a much higher rate than those in other districts of similar size.

- Test objectives that are problematic at the exit-level (tenth-grade) TAAS are also problematic at lower grades. Furthermore, if students do well on the problem-solving objectives, they are highly likely to pass the overall test.

- For "typical" (middle 50 percent) students, there is a strong relationship between the reading and math portions of the TAAS exam.

- The relationship between student performance on the TAAS and performance on the Iowa Test of Basic Skills (ITBS) is rather weak; in addition, the passing level for TAAS is well below grade level on the ITBS. Furthermore, students who do well on ITBS will almost certainly pass TAAS, but the converse is not true.

Makar (2004) further extended this research to investigate the use of similar approaches to assessment, data, and inquiry with a set of preservice secondary-level teachers of science and mathematics. In her research, these preservice teachers undertook investigations similar to ones given as examples in this chapter. Immersing prospective teachers in inquiry into student assessment data will provide them with a deeper understanding of students' thinking skills and help them learn more effective ways to evaluate the learning of students at various levels of performance; learn how to consider making changes in a classroom as a function of student gains over time, differences among subgroups, distributions, and variation; and become more fluent with the concepts and technologies of statistical reasoning and inquiry. Our research suggests that scaling up must include focused efforts to build professional capacity to analyze data provided by the state and to carry out investigations of student performance in local settings in relation to theories of assessment and equity.

Toward a Theory of Distributed Equity and Steady Improvement

Even careful use of data and application of concepts of distribution, variation, and sampling by themselves will not remedy the inequities in the system, nor will they prescribe appropriate actions. As we saw with the case study involving African American test performances, when data are translated into actions, racism and systematic bias may creep into the system. We see here in Texas, as well as in other places, a failure to employ adequate and robust theories or frameworks of fairness; this hampers intentions to use accountability as a lever for equity. We do not dispute the fact that disaggregation of data can be useful in shining light on pockets of extremely unfair practices or failures to educate, but we assert that current portrayals of comparative performance are too narrowly defined and too thin on analysis.

The literature on equity documents a movement to advocate for the use of multiple measures in all high-stakes decisions, in accordance with the recommendations of the National Research Council (Heubert and Hauser, 1999). Under such an approach, one set of measures can be used to compensate for performance on another measure, so that overall performance does not rely on any single measure (McNeil and Valenzuela, 2001; Valenzuela, 2002). In mathematics, there can be little doubt that practices such as timed tests, the use of multiple-choice items, or heavy reliance on language can disadvantage some students and benefit others. More specifically, in mathematics, we see significant differences among children in their likelihood of using visual representations as opposed to symbolic or numerical ones, being able to reflect verbally on their learning, or recalling long and complex strings of formulas. The use of multiple measures clearly contributes to equitable education, because it reduces tendencies to unduly privilege certain forms of canonical knowledge in ways that are of limited or varied relevance to successful pursuit of a field of inquiry or career.

Besides the proactive arguments for multiple measures in assessment, we find that literature on equity is dominated by identification and ways to eliminate negative practices. Thus, the research on deficit thinking (Valencia, 1997) and subtractive schooling (Valenzuela, 1999) all demonstrate convincingly and profoundly how teachers' actions in schools can systematically depress children's performance by making negative assumptions about their potential to succeed or by denying them the use of their own culturally rich heritage and resources as positive contributors and facilitators of learning.

What we are proposing differs markedly and may add strength to those efforts to eliminate bias. We believe that it is essential to provide teachers with an explicit framework for engaging with diversity of performance in classrooms, particularly in mathematics, where assumptions about variations in abilities often undermine reform efforts. Teachers must be guided in how to act on trends in students' performance without reifying them into stereotypes. They must be advised on how to handle the increasing diversity in their classrooms without simply targeting instruction to a modest and possibly nonexistent middle group, which may not represent real students. Teachers must enact approaches that permit recovery and reentry by students rather than promote high levels of attrition by at-risk performers. And teachers must know how to continually challenge high performers without leaving their peers frustrated or lost. We claim that teachers must not only be versed in the fundamental concepts of distribution, variation, and difference but also receive explicit guidance in varied but mutually supportive instructional approaches that meet the needs of a diverse student population.

To explore these ideas, we created a prototype of a simulation tool called distributed equity and steady improvement (DESI). This tool created a means of gauging progress in student learning as a function of its distributed impact on students: (1) across topics, (2) across subgroups, (3) across time, and (4) across units of analysis (student, class, school or school type, district, region, or state). DESI was designed to permit inquiry on how to differentiate systematic progress from random variation or standard error. This tool enables theory building and empirical monitoring. As a theory-building tool, it permits entry of data for sets of students with different levels of prior knowledge and different speeds of learning. These differences could be assigned randomly or according to predetermined characteristics of groups of students. If further developed, DESI could permit consideration of how different instructional treatments might affect those students in terms of knowledge and rate of learning and could project the resulting impact on the performance of students in terms of distribution and difference. As an empirical monitoring tool, it could also permit examination of the actual distributions over time and provide feedback on their implications for individual student learning in terms of distribution and difference.

A simulation tool like DESI would have the potential to do the following:

- Track students' progress in educational settings as a product of what they know and at what rate they learn new material
- Monitor changes in overall progress and by subconstruct and by subgroup over time as indicated by (1) changes in the quartile performance of subgroups and (2) changes in the distribution of scores as a whole group
- Monitor the accountability system to see how students perform over time on individual core concepts
- Provide comparisons among groups on factors such as race and gender in terms of distribution, means, and tests for significance of difference; if differences occur, track the changes in differences over time
- Provide comparisons between performance groups by quartile over time
- Track losses in population due to failure or dropout by adjusting the measures of success to reflect the losses

Once the monitoring system is constructed, instructional treatments could be interpreted in terms of their potential impact on student learning in regard to coverage and rate of learning; instructional treatments could also be examined in relation to performance by all levels of students. A trajectory of distributed progress could be projected and compared with data on student performance as predicted through simulations.

We are seeking to describe a means of appraising a kind of distributed justice in a recursive way across classrooms, schools, districts, and states to provide policymakers, practitioners, and community members with a more complete and fair portrayal of the progress of the educational system. We seek to investigate how to use the educational system as a means of meeting the needs of all children fairly over time and distributing classroom resources, including teacher time, effectively in order to ensure reasonable progress for all children. In mathematics, we must create frameworks that support the development of talent; in this subject area, talent is fragile and needs considerable attention and nurture. Indeed, approaches to equity in the classroom must ensure that talent, not privilege or competitive advantage, is fostered. Gaining competitive advantage refers to implementing practices that propel certain subgroups of students forward while ignoring the needs of others or making them a lower priority. Our mathematics and science classrooms are loaded with competitive advantage for some children, but not for others. This concern for only some students is evidenced by how certain groups are permitted to migrate out of mathematics classes and how atypical it is for them to recover and successfully reenter college-bound course sequences.

The concepts outlined in this chapter—distribution, changes in performance over time, differences in performance across subareas of content, and differences in preparation—all illuminate issues that make the teaching of mathematics challenging, even in the absence of forces that suppress and distort performance. A theory of equity would have to provide guidance to teachers on how to manage the range of preparation at both tails of the distribution, the differences in rates of learning, and the differences in students' individual preferences. Our proposed solution to the problem is to monitor all instructional treatments in terms of their effects on the overall data set, as represented by their central measures, distributions, and measures of difference, taking into account sources of variation.

In summary, we argue for a framework for distributed equity and steady improvement (DESI) composed of a system of monitoring for overall progress and the distributions of outcomes across student groups and content objectives over time. We suggest that the model may be useful in evaluating the effectiveness of different instructional systems, especially if fundamental instructional components can be translated into their proposed impact on students' level of knowledge and rate of learning. Through the visual display characteristics of the new information technologies, a wider range of practitioners can gain insight into features of distribution, variation, and difference. We further suggest that the use of such capability will lead to revised theories on how to effectively achieve both progress and fairness.

REFERENCES

Confrey, J., & Carrejo, D. (2002). *Can high-stakes testing in Texas inform instructional decision making?* Paper presented at the twenty-fourth annual meeting of the North American Chapter of the International Group for the Psychology of Mathematics Education (PME-NA), Athens, GA.

Confrey, J., & Makar, K. (2002). *Developing secondary teachers' statistical inquiry through immersion in high-stakes accountability data.* Paper presented at the twenty-fourth annual meeting of the North American Chapter of the International Group for the Psychology of Mathematics Education (PME-NA), Athens, GA.

Eisenhower National Clearinghouse. (2003). Data-driven decision making [entire issue]. *ENC Focus, 10*(1).

Finzer, W., & Swenson, K. (2001). *Fathom!* (Version 1.12) [Computer Software]. Emeryville, CA: KCP Technologies.

Heubert, J., & Hauser, R. (Eds.). (1999). *High stakes: Testing for tracking, promotion, and graduation.* Washington, DC: National Academy Press.

Love, N. (2003). Uses and abuses of data. *ENC Focus, 10*(1), 14-17.

Makar, K. (2004). *Developing statistical inquiry: Prospective secondary mathematics and science teachers' investigations of equity and fairness through analysis of accountability data.* Unpublished doctoral dissertation, University of Texas, Austin.

Makar, K., & Confrey, J. (2002). *Comparing two groups: Examining secondary teachers' statistical thinking.* Paper presented at the sixth International Conference on Teaching Statistics (ICOTS6), Cape Town, South Africa.

Makar, K., & Confrey, J. (2004). Secondary teachers' reasoning about comparing two groups. In D. Ben-Zvi & J. Garfield (Eds.), *The challenges of developing statistical literacy, reasoning, and thinking* (pp. 353–374). Dordrecht, Netherlands: Kluwer.

McNeil, L., & Valenzuela, A. (2001). The harmful impact of the TAAS system of testing in Texas: Beneath the accountability rhetoric. In G. Orfield & M. L. Kornhaber (Eds.), *Raising standards or raising barriers?: Inequality and high-stakes testing in public education* (pp. 127–150). New York: Century Foundation Press.

Messick, S. (1995). Validity of psychological assessment: Validation of inferences from persons' responses and performances as scientific inquiry into score meaning. *American Psychologist, 50*(9), 741–749.

Supik, J. D., & Johnson, R. L. (1999). *Missing: Texas youth—Dropout and attrition rates in Texas public high schools.* San Antonio, TX: Intercultural Development Research Association.

Texas Education Agency. (2000a). *Academic Excellence Indicator System: Campus, district, and state reports, 1996-2000.* Austin, TX: Author. Retrieved September 2000 from www.tea.state.tx.us

Texas Education Agency. (2000b). *Academic Excellence Indicator System: Campus report, 1999-2000.* Austin, TX: Author. Retrieved September 2004 from www.tea.state.tx.us/perfreport/aeis/2000/

Texas Education Agency. (2002a). *TAAS data set of 10,000 students in Texas.* Austin, TX: Student Assessment Division, Texas Education Agency.

Texas Education Agency. (2002b). *Texas student assessment program: Technical digests for the years 1996-2002.* Austin, TX: Author.

Valencia, R. (1997). Conceptualizing the notion of deficit thinking. In R. R. Valencia (Ed.), *The evolution of deficit thinking: Educational thought and practice* (pp. 1–12). London: Falmer Press.

Valenzuela, A. (1999). *Subtractive schooling: U.S. Mexican youth and the politics of caring.* New York: State University of New York.

Valenzuela, A. (2002). High-stakes testing and U.S.-Mexican youth in Texas: The case for multiple compensatory criteria in assessment. *Harvard Journal of Hispanic Policy, 14,* 97–116.

SCALING UP SUCCESS

A SYNTHESIS OF THEMES AND INSIGHTS

Chris Dede, James P. Honan

*This chapter highlights and synthesizes key concepts and findings
from the conference papers and discussions.*

A NUMBER OF COMMON THEMES AND INSIGHTS regarding the scaling up
of successful educational innovations emerge from the chapters in this volume and from the subsequent conference discussions about these studies.
Four key themes underlie many of them:

- *Coping with change:* context, leadership, and funding
- *Promoting ownership:* building constituent support; institutionalizing innovations
- *Building human capacity:* working with collaborators and partners; providing professional development
- *Effective decision making:* interpreting data; creating and applying
  usable knowledge

Each theme is summarized briefly in this chapter, as are insights that
emerged from the conference and key topics and questions for future
research.

Coping with Change

A fundamental theme that resonates through many studies about scaling up success is how a given innovation can be successfully implemented in different contexts, including those with differences in leadership structure and availability of funding. Only innovations with strong mechanisms that foster resilience and evolution can survive the complex process of change involved in moving to scale.

Adapting to Changing Contexts

Educational innovations must be adapted to the contexts within which they will occur. Similarly, schools and educational organizations must adapt to the innovations themselves. The overall context within which school leaders, teachers, and other education professionals work is constantly in flux. For innovators, it is essential to acknowledge these many levels of simultaneous adaptation and learn to work effectively under such conditions. Susan Moore Johnson from the Harvard Graduate School of Education (HGSE) noted during our conference discussions, "We know that we do not have stability and every day can count on having less stability and continuity. We have some ideas of how to scale up in a rational or predictable world. Nevertheless, since there is so much instability, it is interesting to think about how scale could be achieved without stability."

Political considerations are a particularly important part of the ever-changing context and play a crucial role in scaling up educational innovations. Policymakers and practitioners need to understand one another's perspectives and respective roles in a scaling-up effort. Susan R. Goldman observes in Chapter Four, "Education is as much about politics as it is about learning, assessment, and instruction."

The political climate in most contexts is constantly evolving; as a result, the time line for developing and implementing educational innovations with strong political sponsorship may be brief. For example, as the states become more powerful in shaping what districts can and cannot do, the current instability of state politics forces short timetables for innovation, since long-term planning is nearly impossible. In conference discussions of the paper by Fred Carrigg, Margaret Honey, and Ron Thorpe (Chapter One), Carrigg indicated that he plans a three-year timetable for scaling up innovations, recognizing that over the course of longer time frames, the political climate may well dramatically shift.

In the case of Union City, quick results helped sustain the momentum of innovation, but plans were simultaneously developed for long-term evolution. Carrigg's sustained leadership over ten years was essential to this strategy. As a result of this evolutionary progression, innovation is part of the culture of elementary and middle schools in the district, but the success of reform still seems fragile at the high school level. This is consistent with research by Michael Casserly and Jason Snipes on successful urban school districts, which concluded that progress is always greatest at the elementary school level. This may be due to the fact that there is somewhat more freedom from tests at the elementary school level.

In terms of sustained political will, Carrigg, Honey, and Thorpe remind us how important it is for various constituencies to work together to scale up fruitful educational innovations. They note, "A dynamic relationship should exist between practitioners and policymakers in an environment that encourages and supports local innovation so that it might become a model for best practice that then gets fed back into the larger system" (Chapter One).

Coping with Changes in Leadership

Stable leadership at multiple levels of school districts and schools is an essential ingredient in scaling up successful educational innovations. Leadership continuity issues played a key role in the Milwaukee reforms described by Chris Dede and Robert Nelson in Chapter Six. They observe, "The biggest challenge to sustaining and scaling up technology-reliant educational innovations in Milwaukee Public Schools concerns changes in school board members and superintendents. . . . The transition periods cause a loss of momentum; they are followed by a need to reframe work to match the new superintendent's preferred agenda."

With regard to leadership instability and its impact on scaling up educational innovations, Barry J. Fishman underscores the need for those enacting reforms to be proactive. He notes, "A champion who can maintain continuity through such changes is key to helping the innovation survive evolving capability, policy and management, and cultural changes" (Chapter Three). Successful innovators must not only learn to cope with changes in leadership at their local site but also should build capacity for leaders elsewhere to carry out adaptations of the innovation in multiple settings. Leadership and consensus in Union City stemmed in part from the localized, inclusive nature of the initiatives; the community felt a sense of ownership. Adapting innovations to other districts requires creating a similar sense of buy-in, which may be difficult to do for top-down mandates from the state or the federal government unless policies and resources are directed to fostering local ownership of externally designed reforms.

Addressing Fluctuations in Funding

Sustained and predictable funding for promising educational innovations not only facilitates the innovations themselves but also helps address the reality of changing political contexts and shifts in leadership. As noted by Fishman, "Funding cycles are . . . problematic, because many grants extend over relatively short periods of time (one to three years)" (Chapter Three). With regard to funding innovations that involve multiorganizational collaborations, Fishman adds, "Short funding cycles may catalyze partnerships, but longer-term funding is needed to sustain them."

In our view, it is essential for practitioners and policymakers alike to acknowledge and attempt to meet the need for funding streams that provide longer-term support for educational innovations. Without such support, it is likely that promising educational innovations will neither be sustained nor replicated at multiple sites. For example, state cutbacks in Michigan coupled with nearing the end of federal grant support forced the Detroit Public Schools to take creative measures in order to continue offering staff development opportunities and expanding them to other schools within the district. Altering teachers' pedagogy takes a lot of time because it involves new instructional strategies, the integration of technology, and alternative assessments. Detroit is cultivating communities of practice so that teachers will continue to have the opportunity to receive help and guidance beyond the end of external funding.

Promoting Ownership

Beyond coping with change as a crucial factor in scaling up, the original innovators must promote a transfer of ownership to those who would adapt the innovation to their own contexts. Such a transfer involves both building constituent support and institutionalizing innovations.

Building Constituent Support

In order to scale up educational innovations, school district leaders must gain the support of multiple constituencies toward a common vision. Carrigg, Honey, and Thorpe underscore the importance of this in their analysis of the Union City, New Jersey, reforms, noting: "Coherence and support across state, district, and school levels are essential to an effective scaling-up process" (Chapter One). In conference discussions, Deborah Peek-Brown described a close partnership and collaboration between the University of Michigan and the Detroit Public Schools. This collaboration was a key factor in reducing usability gaps in externally produced curriculum. However, differing schedules and time horizons, out-of-sync funding cycles, and alternative ways of measuring success posed challenges to collaboration. These two institutions were able to move forward based on mutual respect, communication, and a shared notion of ownership.

Goldman offers a similar affirmation regarding the importance of a broad base of support for the effective scaling up of innovations, noting, "Educational improvement is complex; it requires bringing together individuals from different disciplinary and professional backgrounds, each with its own norms and language. Coming together as a group focused on a specific educational improvement requires that time be spent negotiating shared meanings" (Chapter Four). As an example, Peek-Brown indicated that the Detroit Public Schools and the University of Michigan initially viewed success in different ways. The district asked, "How are kids doing on the high-stakes tests?" while the university used broader measures of success that included its own pretests and posttests, surveys, and interviews of students and teachers. As a result, the university privileged high- stakes test scores in its definition of quality, while the district used measures of success beyond test scores in its internal evaluations of the project.

Teachers' ownership of new instructional strategies is important, so inclusion of teachers in the process of defining common measures of quality is vital. One illustration of such teacher ownership is that a critical mass of teachers in the Detroit schools now can model successful instruction for their peers as well as provide data indicating improved student learning. Some of these teachers are creating their own new units. Goldman described this as one type of usable knowledge—when people using externally produced innovations can apply what they have learned in new ways.

In conference discussions, Fishman suggested that scale, or diffusion of innovations, is all about "tipping points" and "crossing chasms." Detroit started with building ownership of an innovation and has now reached a tipping point, working with enough teachers and producing enough student achievement data to validate success and encourage buy-in by others. The teachers are the carriers of the innovation in Detroit; in contrast, in Union City, innovation started with common teacher beliefs, and the students in grades K–3 became the carriers. The two cities began from different places; Union City took a comprehensive approach, whereas LeTUS began in a single subject area. Fishman suggested that the real test will be when Union City attempts to implement externally developed curricula and can examine its abilities to cross the chasm.

Institutionalizing Innovations

If particular innovations or reforms are to persist, they must be translated into common practice in multiple locations. Beyond the process of innovation itself, practitioners and policymakers should identify and support strategies that will leave a legacy of human and institutional innovation even if the reform should later be suppressed or abandoned. Because political shifts pose such a threat to sustained innovation, David Perkins coined the term "roller coaster principle" to suggest that any innovation may have a realistic lifetime of four years. Successful educational innovations should leave a legacy of lingering capacity to implement innovation and persistent practices that will serve as the foundation for future innovation. Gains in student achievement from each short-term initiative can fuel support for further innovation.

In addition to fostering an institution's capacity to sustain innovations, it is also important to clearly define the very concepts of scaling up and success. Goldman reminds us, "Differences in definitions of scaling up have implications for definitions of success. For some, success and its evidence are to be found only in gains on standardized test scores or in the number of teachers, students, schools, or districts involved in the effort, regardless of the quality of enactment. Other stakeholders may have in mind different indicators of success, such as changes in the way teachers relate to one another or to their students. These different meanings may lead stakeholders to posit different and, in some cases, conflicting goals, which in turn compete for limited resources. Failure to negotiate common goals can undermine educational improvement efforts" (Chapter Four).

In conference discussions, Goldman also indicated that innovators should have a clear sense of student outcomes, including benchmarks for success. She provided the example of being able to define what a literate student looks like: What is your example of a literate student by the end of sixth grade? Then innovators can ask how each grade level contributes to this goal and, within each grade level, how each classroom contributes.

Building Human Capacity

Beyond coping with change and promoting ownership, building human capacity in all the stakeholders necessary to implement an innovation is essential to scaling up. This involves educators not only in familiar activities of professional development but also in less common situations of working in consort with external collaborators and partners.

Working with Collaborators and Partners

Based on findings presented in several of the conference papers, it appears that multisector collaboration among organizational partners such as schools, universities, state agencies, funders, and so on, is an essential ingredient to scaling up. The paper by Chris Dede and Robert Nelson (Chapter Six), describing reforms in Milwaukee, underscores the need for active participation of collaborators and partners. When considering how to scale up an educational innovation, this key question arises: What combination of collaborating organizations constitutes the optimal configuration for sustaining the innovation over time?

When multiple parties are involved in the implementation of reforms and innovations, these partners must understand one another's ways of working. For example, Fishman cites the importance of understanding differences related to the dimension of time: "Schedules are a major challenge to collaboration, in that the calendar and pace for work in schools tend to be very different from those of universities or research groups" (Chapter Three).

In conference discussions, participants attempted to identify what types of organizations and partnerships could form the best mechanism for the scaling up of innovation in education. John Willett of HGSE observed that certain characteristics of scaling up, such as needing a client-centered perspective, products of genuine value, and customer support, appeared to resemble characteristics of a business. Allan Grossman of Harvard Business School (HBS) responded that business does not necessarily have all of the answers to questions involved in scaling up but does extensive research on this issue in the corporate world. However, there are limits to how much this research can be applied to other contexts (for example, the franchise business model does not work for multisite nonprofits).

In a later discussion, Dorothy Leonard from HBS indicated that many professions are not very good at adopting innovations and changes. Defining one's principles sometimes limits one's ability to innovate. For example, if one thinks of oneself as case teacher at HBS, then it is hard to understand how technology might aid instruction. One of the challenges of scaling up is that we define our capabilities by what we are most comfortable with; this can create resistance to change and innovation in professions from the construction industry to the business sector.

Participants also discussed organizational development issues. Glenn Kleiman from the Educational Development Center (EDC) discussed the role of external institutions in the scaling-up process, indicating that EDC views its job as being a technical assistance provider as well as serving as a liaison between universities, schools, and businesses. Casserly discussed the possibility of schools becoming technical assistance providers for other schools. Honey suggested that, in addition to the right institutions, the right partnerships for scaling up innovation also need to be identified. Dede added that the questions regarding the right institutions are similar to the question of why there should be schools of education. Schools of education bring together multiple perspectives (including those of business, policy, and other fields), and the whole ends up being greater than the sum of the parts.

In commenting on Michael Casserly and Jason C. Snipes's paper (Chapter Eight), Dede observed that neither using a research-based innovation strategy nor having higher education partners emerged as key ingredients for success. Conference participants discussed whether this was further evidence of the weak link between research and practice. Robert Peterkin of HGSE offered a possible reason for the lack of connection: "Superintendents work in isolation because they own the problem, and researchers want to solve a different problem." Subsequent discussion indicated that researchers are more concerned about the evolution of theory than the improvement of practice. Casserly expressed agreement with this point and spoke about the need for more pragmatic future research; he suggested that more research be devoted to change and reforms in systems and districts rather than individual programs or parts of school systems.

Providing Professional Development

Several papers noted the importance of building human capacity at all levels to ensure that educational innovations will be implemented and will persist. The key role that professional development played in the Union City, New Jersey, reforms is affirmed as follows: "Of all the components of the reform effort in Union City, none is more important than the way the district imagined, designed, and delivered professional development for teachers and aligned it with specific strategy and goals" (Chapter One). The paper by Martha Stone Wiske and David Perkins (Chapter Two) illustrates the potential uses of technology as an effective professional development tool and examines the importance and challenges of going to scale with such an approach. Laurence Peters describes the universality of professional development challenges across a range of countries and educational settings (Chapter Five).

Effective Decision Making

Making effective decisions based on research, data, and analysis is a fourth crucial dimension of scaling up. Considerable time at the conference was spent in discussing these issues. Researchers, practitioners, and policymakers all play important roles in this aspect of scaling up.

Accurate Interpretation of Data

The paper by Sam Stringfield, Jeffrey C. Wayman, and Mary E. Yaki-mowski-Srebnick (Chapter Seven) underscores some of the challenges concerning the use of data in schools and school districts. They observe: "Formal research and our own observations indicate that being data-driven is a phenomenon more often observed in the breach than in the basic structure of the typical school. We believe that the absence of data-informed decision making is not due to educators' aversion to being informed. Rather, the wealth of data potentially available in schools is often stored in ways that make it virtually inaccessible to teachers and principals and generally far from analysis-friendly."

In conference discussions, Honey indicated that we often think of data as transparent, when that is not, in fact, the case. Researchers understand their role as assigning meaning to data and have been trained to do so. As mentioned previously, this is a powerful role, one that many people represented at the conference felt requires training. Much anxiety was expressed about practitioners who are put in the role of interpreters of data, without having any training to understand its meaning; many felt that they are likely to do more harm than good. For example, conference participants noted that data-based decision-making tools are often designed to create standard data representations, which form the first step in the process of interpretation; they can have powerful effects on the way practitioners interpret data. Whereas in the past, schools received data only after the initial analytical work had been done by researchers, now, with these tools, practitioners can potentially choose to display the data (a task that also requires interpretation) in any way they like. Since particular representations featured by the software might lead practitioners to inappropriate conclusions, research should certainly provide guidance in choosing appropriate types of representations.

Another issue raised in this discussion centered on appropriate strategies for schools to employ in response to assessment data. Practitioners may focus on "bubble kids" whose scores are close to passing, thereby neglecting other students. Such ineffective strategies may be suggested by certain representations of data or seem attractive in the context of meeting accountability mandates to improve aggregated performance in the short term, based on the structure of the accountability policy. To avoid this and similar problems, conference participants generally felt that researchers need to inform the selection of data interpretation strategies used in schools.

In her opening remarks at the conference, Ellen Condliffe Lagemann, dean of HGSE, stated that the goal for the education field is the creation of schools as professional organizations. The relationship of other professional organizations to the data that they generate is characterized by access and ownership. Stringfield noted that if we are to treat school practitioners as professionals, then we must recognize their ownership and facilitate their access to data as well as their ability to make decisions based on the information it conveys.

If the effective use of data requires that practitioners become, as Stringfield noted, good diagnosticians, a real question remains regarding what types of training educators need to achieve that goal. There is currently a lack of standards concerning what types of data analysis and statistics practitioners should understand and use. Further, no guidance, found by research to be effective, is available concerning what types of strategies can be employed to directly target the weaknesses highlighted by assessment data. Jere Confrey and Katie Makar describe the types of problems that arise from this lack of guidance (Chapter Ten). The issue of whose job it is to convey this information to teachers is important.

Creating and Applying Usable Knowledge

In her foreword to this volume, Lagemann articulates the concept of usable knowledge (knowledge from research immediately applicable to practice), which results from principled collaboration among scholars, practitioners, and policymakers to link theory and research to sustainable, affordable, and scalable improvements. Nora Sabelli affirmed the concept that practitioners will play a key role in the increased use of scholarship, but she noted, "There needs to be a change in how practitioners view research so that they can embrace it." As discussed earlier, practitioners likely will need additional education on the use and value of research, analysis, and data in order to develop the desire and the capacity to participate in creating usable knowledge.

The link between research and practice is important, but not always effectively made. As Peterkin described earlier, there is a need to align the agenda and activities of researchers with those of practitioners and to better understand the perspectives and interests that both groups bring to the table. Scaling up is an ideal topic for promoting this alignment, because it combines a crucial need in practice and policy with very interesting questions and issues from the perspectives of research and theory. As Barbara Means and William R. Penuel (Chapter Nine) describe it, "The research base needed for scaling up goes beyond the question 'What works?' to include research that sheds light on a more complex question: 'What works when, and how?'" This alternative statement of the problem draws researchers' attention to the need to deal with issues of enactment and context in their designs in a way often neglected by studies focused on main effects. "Rather than an average effect size," state Means and Penuel, "local decision makers need research findings that shed light on the expected effects under different circumstances and on the contextual and implementation factors that are likely to influence success. An emphasis on average effects can be counterproductive if it results in inattention to these critical factors" in efforts to move interventions to new settings and to scale.

Means and Penuel identify the types of usable knowledge that might be needed to bring educational innovations to scale. They note, "The policymaker or practitioner needs not only knowledge that some intervention has been shown to be effective on average but also knowledge that can permit a reasonable judgment concerning (1) whether the intervention would prove effective with the students, teachers, and schools for which that person is responsible; (2) an understanding of the supporting conditions necessary for success in these settings; and (3) the range of adaptations that can occur under local conditions without compromising the intervention's essential principles or reducing its efficacy" (Chapter Nine). This type of research and analysis can play a key role in fostering innovation. In addition, the resultant ability to cite gains in student achievement also helps practitioners and policymakers make the case for further innovation.

In conference discussions, Means and Penuel indicated that they did not have to invent new methodologies to capture the relationships between outcomes and contexts. Instead, they combined data from different sources, assembling disparate pieces of evidence through a wide variety of data collection instruments. Penuel stated that we do not begin evaluation programs early enough and that preplanning—thinking deeply about all parts of implementation and evaluation—is important. Means suggested that scholars should start with the research questions, then match methodologies to the questions. These types of insights, which flow from studies of scaling up, can also inform larger issues of creating usable knowledge.

Key Questions and Topics for Further Research

As happens with many undertakings that deal with complex problems, we acknowledge that many unanswered questions remain concerning the scaling up of successful educational innovations. In identifying some of these, we hope that researchers, practitioners, and policymakers will continue to pursue data collection and analysis that provide insights into the subtleties and complexities associated with educational innovations that can move to scale.

The chapters in this volume suggest many questions that deserve further consideration and investigation, among them the following:

- Across a variety of situations, what does the concept of scaling up success mean to different constituents (such as practitioners, policymakers, and researchers), and how can we measure success on the many dimensions of this construct?

- In fostering and expanding educational innovations, what level of investment should be apportioned among the four themes of coping with change, promoting ownership, building human capacity, and making effective decisions based on research, data, and analysis?

- How does the organizational unit of innovation (for example, individual teacher or classroom, school, district, or state) empower or constrain processes of innovation and scaling up?

- What conditions for success are essential in enabling technology-reliant innovations to go to scale in educational environments?

- How can the innovation process be constructed to reduce instability and turnover among the leadership structure (for example, principals, superintendents, school boards, and politicians) required to sustain scaling-up efforts as they evolve?

- What side effects and second-order impacts (positive and negative) does the scaling up of innovations typically have on the larger educational systems within which it occurs?

This list of questions is illustrative, not complete, but it indicates the types of themes and issues that deserve and require extended, principled study.

How can we create mechanisms to provide funding and build capacity in research, practice, and policy for studying these and other questions that speak to larger agendas of scaling up and usable knowledge? In an era in which federal resources are focused on the creation of "scientifically based knowledge" through clinical intervention studies involving random assignment, the challenge of funding the types of scholarship this chapter discusses is substantial. This volume provides powerful ideas and case studies that exemplify the value of defining research more broadly to encompass large-scale issues central to policy and practice, as well as the creation and application of usable knowledge. Hopefully, this and similar work will inspire the field of education to tackle these difficult, important issues with the broad range of tools and methodologies validated by the studies in this volume and with support from public and private sources who realize the crucial nature of such research.

THE CONTRIBUTORS

Fred Carrigg
Special Assistant to the Commissioner for Urban Literacy
New Jersey Department of Education

Michael Casserly
Executive Director
Council of the Great City Schools

Jere Confrey
Professor of Mathematics Education
Washington University in St. Louis

Chris Dede
Timothy E. Wirth Professor in Learning Technologies
Harvard Graduate School of Education

Barry J. Fishman
Assistant Professor of Learning Technologies
University of Michigan

Susan R. Goldman
Distinguished Professor of Psychology and Education
Co-Director, Center for the Study of Learning, Instruction, and Teacher
      Development
University of Illinois at Chicago

James P. Honan
Lecturer on Education
Harvard Graduate School of Education

Margaret Honey
Vice President, Education Development Center
Director, Center for Children and Technology

Katie M. Makar
Doctoral candidate
University of Queensland

Barbara Means
Director, Center for Technology in Learning
SRI International

Robert Nelson
Director of Technology (retired)
Milwaukee Public Schools

William R. Penuel
Senior Researcher
SRI International

David Perkins
Professor
Harvard Graduate School of Education

Laurence C. Peters
Director, Mid-Atlantic Regional Technology in Education Consortium
Center for Research in Human Development and Education
Temple University

Jason C. Snipes
Senior Research Associate
MDRC

Sam Stringfield
Distinguished University Professor
Co-Director of the Nystrand Center for Excellence in Education
University of Louisville

Ron Thorpe
Vice President and Director, Educational Resources Center
Thirteen/WNET

Jeffrey C. Wayman
Associate Research Scientist
Center for Social Organization of Schools
Johns Hopkins University

Martha Stone Wiske
Lecturer, Harvard Graduate School of Education
Co–Principal Investigator, WIDE World

Mary E. Yakimowski-Srebnick
Chief, Division of Research, Evaluation, Assessment, and Accountability
Baltimore City Public Schools

ACKNOWLEDGMENTS

THE EDITORS would like to thank the following people whose efforts were vital in the success of the conference. Faculty at Harvard Graduate School of Education (HGSE) who generously gave of their time to serve as facilitators, interviewers, discussants, and participants include Katerine Bielaczyc, Allan Collins, Richard Elmore, Thomas Hehir, Ilona Holland, Susan Moore Johnson, Glenn Kleiman, Katherine Merseth, Richard Murnane, Robert Peterkin, Paul Reville, David Rose, Robert Schwartz, and John Willett. HGSE staff who worked for months in advance to ensure that all the logistics for the event were outstanding include Linda Chisom, John Collins, Dottie Engler, Linda Greyser, Margaret Hass, David Langlois, Shelley Lawson, Carla Lillvik, Kati Livingston, Melissa Lynch, Dave Nuscher, Siovhan O'Connor, Christine Sanni, and Suzanne Teuteberg.

In addition, we would like to acknowledge the contributions of the Mid-Atlantic Regional Technology in Education Consortium (MAR*TEC), part of the Center for Research in Human Development and Education at Temple University, particularly the leadership of acting dean Trevor Sewell, the focused insights of Patricia Hendricks, the support of Judith Stull, and the diligent efforts of Bonnie Hartman, who organized a great many of the conference details from the MAR*TEC end.

The editors are grateful for the aid of Susanna Brougham, whose editing skills were invaluable in preparing the final version of the volume.

Finally, we would like to thank Ellen Condliffe Lagemann and Katharine E. and Albert W. Merck for the generous financial support that made many aspects of this conference and volume possible.

Chapter 2 Acknowledgments

The ideas expressed here are based in large part on our experience with Internet-based projects developed at the Harvard Graduate School of Education with the support of many collaborators. We would like to acknowledge and thank Al and Kate Merck for their valuable counsel and generous funding of ALPS (http://learnweb.harvard.edu/alps), ENT (http://learnweb.harvard.edu/ent), and WIDE World (www.wideworld.pz.harvard.edu). These projects also benefited from encouragement and assistance from the dean's office over several years, including advice and support from dean Jerry Murphy, co-deans John Willett and Judy Singer, and current dean Ellen Lagemann. The Harvard provost's office and Harvard's Provost's Fund have also contributed important backing. Finally, we want to acknowledge the expertise and dedication of our many colleagues on these projects, especially Nathan Finch, who has been the project manager and a key designer of WIDE World since its inception.

Chapter 3 Acknowledgments

The author is indebted to Phyllis Blumenfeld, Joe Krajcik, Ron Marx, and Elliot Soloway, with whom the ideas in this chapter were developed, and Deborah Peek-Brown, who was instrumental in our shared work in Detroit. I also thank the administration and teachers of the Detroit Public Schools, and the staff of the hi-ce. This research was funded with support from the National Science Foundation under the following programs: REPP (REC-9720383, REC-9725927, REC-9876150) and USI (ESR-9453665). Additional funding was provided by the W. K. Kellogg Foundation, the Joyce Foundation, and the Spencer Foundation. The views contained in this work do not necessarily represent the views of either its funders or the University of Michigan.

Chapter 4 Acknowledgments

The design principles presented in this chapter were influenced by discussions with many Chicago colleagues, although they should not be held responsible for the views expressed herein. They include Connie Bridge, Anthony Bryk, Vicki Chou, Barbara Eason-Watkins, John Easton, Danny Edelson, Joe Fratarolli, Marty Gartzman, Louis Gomez, Andy Isaacs, Cathy Kelso, Tom Moher, Christine Pappas, James Pellegrino, Taffy Raphael, Sharon Ransom, Brian Reiser, Mary Jo Tavoramina-Porn, William Teale, Phil Wagreich, and Donald Wink. Colleagues in the Schools for Thought effort at Vanderbilt University included Helen Bateman, Kadira Belynn, John Bransford, Melinda Bray, Kay Burgess, Nathalie Coté, Carolyn Cottom, Cynthia Gause-Vega, Ted Hasselbring, Cynthia Mayfield, Linda Miller, James Pellegrino, Anthony Petrosino, Teresa Secules, Diana Sharp, Jeff Swink, Nancy Vye, Susan Williams, and Linda Zech. A distributed center funded by the Mellon Foundation from 1994 to 1997 catalyzed the integration of the organizational perspective in the Nashville Schools for Thought implementation. Along with me, senior personnel involved were John Bransford, Ann Brown, Joe Campione, Nancy Conitt Casey, Ed Haertel, Ted Hasselbring, Milbrey McLaughlin, James Pellegrino, Judy Shulman, Lee Shulman, and Joan Talbert.

Chapter 7 Acknowledgments

The work reported herein was supported under the Center for Research on the Education of Students Placed At Risk (CRESPAR), PR/Award No. OERI-R-117-D40005, as administered by the Institute of Education Sciences (IES), U.S. Department of Education (USDOE). The contents, findings, and opinions expressed here are those of the authors and do not necessarily represent the positions or policies of the National Institute for the Education of At-Risk Students; IES; or the USDOE.

Chapter 9 Acknowledgments

The material described in this chapter was supported in part by grant numbers ESI-9509718 and ESI-9802033 from the National Science Foundation. We would like to express our gratitude to our colleagues Geneva Haertel and Nora Sabelli, who provided feedback on an earlier draft of this chapter.

Name Index

SUBJECT INDEX

A

Abbott Implementation Regulations for Improving Standards-Driven Instruction and Literacy (Intensive Early Literacy), 16–23

Academic achievement, in urban school districts, 155–159, 160

Access, technology, 119, 127, 186

Accessibility, of student data analysis software, 139

Account software, 142–143

Accountability systems and pressures: data-driven decision making and, 137, 141, 151; equity and fairness issues in, 198–224; GLOBE science education program and, 187; high-stakes test data in, 198–224; of No Child Left Behind, 106–107, 181–182, 199, 209; professional development in technology and, 98, 106–107; in Texas, 199, 203–221; in United Kingdom, 98; in urban school districts, 163, 167. *See also* No Child Left Behind

Achievement gaps: data analysis of, 199–224; in urban school districts, 158, 172; variety of, 200

Active learning, teacher, 30

Adobe Acrobat, 140

Advanced placement courses, 170

African American student performance, in Texas, 200–201, 202–208, 213, 218, 221

Aggregate data, 200

ALPS (Active Learning Practices for Schools), 35; Web site of, 35

Artemis, 51, 57–60

Asian and Pacific Islander student performance, in Texas, 202

Assessment: alignment of, 71; equity and fairness issues in, 198–224, 235–236; of GLOBE science education program, 189–192; high-stakes test data and, 198–224; multiple measures in, 221–222; in scaling up urban school districts, 155; technology-enabled, 127; in Union City's literacy programs, 13, 21; in WIDE World professional development program, 38, 39

Asynchronous communication: in student learning, 119–120; in WIDE World professional development program, 40

Atmosphere-investigation program, 191–192. *See also* GLOBE

Average effect size, 237

Awareness building, in Union City professional development, 13–14

B

Balanced literacy, 13–14

Basal readers, 9

Beliefs: changing, 73; about technology roles and functions, 97–108, 111, 117

Big Books, 20

Bilingual and English as a second language (ESL) education, in Union City, New Jersey, 8, 9–15, 20, 22

Bloom's taxonomy, 12

"Bookends" approach to reform, 199

Brio, 123

British Education Communications and Technology Agency (Becta), 100

Brookings Institute, 7

"Bubble kids," 209, 216, 217, 235–236

The Teaching for Understanding Guide

Tina Blythe & Associates

Paper / 144 pages
ISBN: 0-7879-0993-9

"In exploring the process of teaching for understanding as teachers practice it, this monograph succeeds, as few do, in providing different ways of entering a teachers world. Building on teachers' 'inside knowledge,' the authors engage, provoke and coach—in just the right ways—so that I, as a teacher, excited by these new ideas, want the semester to begin tomorrow!"

—Ann Lieberman, Teachers College, Columbia University

What does it mean to understand something? How do students develop understanding? How can teachers know how well they understand and support the development of understanding?

Teaching for Understanding: Linking Research with Practice describes an approach to teaching that requires students to think, analyze, problem solve, and make meaning of what they've learned. introduced the approach and the research that supports it. Now this companion workbook shows teachers how to use the four critical components of the Teaching for Understanding Framework.

Based on extensive research conducted by Project Zero and the Harvard Graduate School of Education, *The Teaching for Understanding Guide* offers teachers a practical way to apply the concepts of the Teaching for Understanding framework—both in the classroom and in curriculum planning.

Using classroom examples from science, mathematics, language arts and social sciences, and reflecting the input of practicing teachers, the workbook shows how teachers can

- Choose topics that engage student interest and connect readily to other subjects
- Set coherent unit and course goals
- Create activities that develop and demonstrate students' understanding
- Improve student performance by providing continual feedback

Brief case studies of teachers using this approach illustrate the process in action. Simple planning sheets and teaching units make this guide a useful resource for developing curriculum. Reflection sections at the end of each chapter suggest related activities, issues, and questions to facilitate further exploration of the chapter's ideas. The challenging process of rethinking classroom practice can lead to a new level of student understanding and learning. This how-to guide gives teachers the practical tools for making understanding more achievable in the classroom.

Tina Blythe is a project coordinator for Project Zero at Harvard University's Graduate School of Education. She lives in Cambridge, Massachusetts. Contributions were also made by the teachers and researchers of Harvard's Teaching for Understanding Project.

Teaching for Understanding with Technology

Martha Stone Wiske with Kristi Rennebohm Franz and Lisa Breit

Paper / 192 pages
ISBN: 0-7879-7230-4

This book will extend the popular "Teaching for Understanding" model by focusing on using new technologies to enhance the learning experience. Teachers will learn how they can use resources like the online curricular resources, web information, and professional networks to research topics to teach, set short- and long-term learning goals, create assignments, and assess student understanding.

Teaching for Understanding with Technology is:

- Based on solid research from Harvard's Project Zero
- Offers step-by-step advice for innovative lesson-planning
- Presents technology-integration tips for daily teaching practice

Martha Stone Wiske is director of the Educational Technology Center and a lecturer at the Harvard Graduate School of Education. Her research is concerned with the integration of new technologies and the incorporation of learner-centered teaching for understanding. She is co-editor of *Teaching for Understanding: Linking Research with Practice*.

Kristi Rennebohm Franz is an award-winning teacher who is known for her innovative use of new technologies in the classroom.

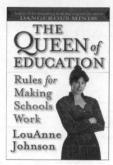

The Queen of Education: Rules for Making Schools Work

LouAnne Johnson

Cloth / 240 pages
ISBN: 0-7879-7470-6

"LouAnne Johnson's book is a blend of common sense, humor, and practical, down-to-earth ideas of how each one of us, as a parent or a concerned citizen, can make a contribution toward improving America's public schools. I highly recommend it."

—Michele Borba, Ed.D., author, *No More Misbehavin'*

Though we have "education presidents" who give lip service to fixing schools—what we really need is a Queen of Education who will get the job done. Anyone searching for such a candidate would put LouAnne Johnson's resume on the top of the stack of likely applicants. LouAnne Johnson is the gutsy ex-marine turned teacher who has wrestled with tough kids and even tougher adults. Her life inspired the movie, *Dangerous Minds*—which was based on her book, *My Posse Don't Do Homework*. Johnson's knack for finding original solutions to intractable problems has not only made her an exemplary teacher but a popular speaker on the lecture circuit.

In this engaging book, "Queen" LouAnne offers her down-to-earth advice about fixing schools. Johnson makes no secret about the fact that she is fed up with an educational system that is too quick to label and write off children who don't fit the mold. Among her royal rules for fixing the system: no class shall have more than twenty students, all elected representatives must teach in a public school classroom for two weeks, and the testing frenzy must stop this very second! LouAnne is a passionate advocate for schools that are smaller, healthier, more humane, and more attuned to different learning styles. With humor and good sense, she shows how a compassionate teacher or parent can cut through the red tape and make a crucial difference in the life of a child.

Her edicts address all aspects of the schooling enterprise—bad behavior, reading problems, junk food, detention, overcrowding, sub-par facilities, class size, and more. Everyone from parents to presidential candidates should take note of Johnson's "rules for schools" concepts.

LouAnne Johnson is a former U.S. Navy journalist, Marine Corps officer, and high school teacher. She is the author of several books, including the bestseller, *Dangerous Minds*. Johnson is an ESL teacher, author, student advocate, and educational consultant.

Edutopia:
Success Stories for Learning
in the Digital Age

The George Lucas Educational Foundation

Paper / 320 pages
ISBN: 0-7879-6082-9

"This book provides educators and parents alike with an unprecedented opportunity to see the future. We must support the efforts of these national heroes—teachers and students from primary and secondary education, foundation and community leaders—as they use technology to make our students and our nation more competitive."

—Bob Kerrey, president, New School University and former
United States Senator and chair of the Congressional
Web-Based Education Commission

Edutopia offers a tantalizing glimpse into the classrooms of innovative educators who are using technology to connect with students, colleagues, the local community, and the world beyond. In doing so, it provides a blueprint of teaching examples for the "Digital Age." *Edutopia* offers a unique perspective on education in which technology is employed to make schools more exciting and dynamic for everyone involved—students work on real-world projects and consult with the best outside experts; teachers learn by tapping into the best people and practices in their field; and classrooms regularly connect with the rich resources of their communities and the world beyond. A lively resource that teachers and parents will want to refer to again and again, *Edutopia* is filled with more than forty full-color photos, has a useful resource section, and comes with a unique CD-ROM that contains more than seventy minutes of video footage of these classrooms in action.

This landmark book lays out the vision of the George Lucas Educational Foundation and explores the enormous potential that technology has to transfer the learning experience.

The George Lucas Educational Foundation (GLEF) is a nonprofit foundation in Northern California that gathers and disseminates the most innovative models of K–12 teaching and learning in the digital age. The foundation serves its mission through the creation of media—from films, books, and newsletters to CD-ROMs and a Web-based multimedia resource center.